Janos Starker

"KING
OF
CELLISTS"

1-26-11
Linda !
All good wishes !
Joyce Geeting

THE MAKING OF AN ARTIST
by Joyce Geeting

CHAMBER MUSIC PLUS PUBLISHING • LOS ANGELES, CALIFORNIA

Janos Starker, "King of Cellists"
Joyce Geeting

Copyright ©2008 by Joyce Geeting

Published by Chamber Music Plus Publishing
1409 Kuehner Dr., #4
Simi Valley, CA 93063-4478

(805) 341-1249
(818) 712-0587 fax

e-mail: joyce@joycegeeting.com

www.joycegeeting.com

Cover, book design and layout by Randy Tobin at Theta Data
Cover photograph by George Lang
Edited by Carol Worthey
Proofread by Cyndie Tobin and Carol Worthey

ISBN: 0-9754734-0-4

First printing: 2008

Printed and bound in the United States of America

CONTENTS

ACKNOWLEDGMENTS

Many thanks to those who have encouraged me in this adventure of book writing, especially my husband, Dan. Randy Tobin, computer and graphics wizard, has my undying thanks. Thanks to: 1. Professor Marsha Markman and to Zoltan and Piri Bodnar for their insights regarding aspects of Hungarian history. 2. Cyndie Tobin, Randy Tobin, Diane Pearce, Carol Worthey and Garth Weber for proofing the manuscript at various stages. 3. Pat Eagle and Joann Tomlinson for transcribing Mr. Starker's stories. 4. Mary Johnson of the Kennedy Center in Washington for the news clippings about Janos Starker. 5. George Lang for the cover photo and calligraphy for the title page. 6. Seymour Rubinstein, for the photographs of the Franz Liszt Academy in Budapest. 7. Janos Starker and Jorge Sicre for permission to use cartoons from *The Roll Call of the Blessed Ones.*

Thanks to each person interviewed for this book: Victor Aitay, George Lang, György Sebök, Aldo Parisot, Joseph Gingold, Maria Kliegel, Gary Hoffman, Rafael Figueroa, David Shamban, Rowena Hammill, Sebastian Toettcher, Shigeo Neriki, Danny Rothmuller and Tsuyoshi Tsutsumi. Each has shared his or her interesting experiences with Starker. I believe these stories help to give the reader direct insights into his relationship with his close friends and students, making the man and the book more personable.

Last but foremost, thanks to Janos Starker for the many hours of telling me (and my tape recorder) many life experiences, sharing knowledge and insights, musical or otherwise. Thanks for the photos, for letting me eavesdrop in lessons, and for sharing with me many lessons on various pieces of the cello repertoire. Thanks for insightful teaching in master classes with my students and for encouraging me with my career as a cellist.

FOREWORD

In 1976, I attended a weeklong cello seminar led by Janos Starker as part of my doctoral dissertation research on the teaching techniques of five prominent American cellists. This was a fascinating time in my life as I travelled across the country to spend time with some of the greats in cello playing, observing and absorbing their wisdom. It was a time of tremendous growth and inspiration for me, truly an eye opener. While each cellist was an "artist-teacher," it was Starker who made the most lasting impression on me. His sharp analytical sense focused on one or two key aspects of each student's performance. Rarely complimentary, his comments were clear and concise, and his analyses were articulate and incisive. His performance-demonstrations, meant to clarify remarks directed toward the students, became rare and wonderful musical treats for all. Because he knew the listeners were cellists familiar with his work, he knew he was admired and appreciated. Perhaps this knowledge enhanced his playing and brought out his best. Although his performances were never encumbered with extraneous sentimentality, he played with warmth, finesse, clarity and the inner fire that comes from a true balance of intellect and emotion.

Following my first seminar performance, Starker's comments to me were, "This is a very high level of cello playing." Not only was I relieved by his words, but through the years his instruction and example have rekindled my love for the cello and its repertoire. His influence on me has been the most powerful, positive influence in my musical life. Starker has given generously to me and to thousands of cellists around the world. Each one of his students knows that teaching is of utmost importance to him. This is why he shares his wealth of knowledge and experience without hesitation. He hopes that all of his students excel both as performers and teachers.

I have met numerous times with Starker since that seminar and always feel inspired and energized. At one of these sessions, in 1994, I inquired if anyone was writing about him. He replied, no. I was curious to know the events in his life that shaped his thinking, what influences made him the unique person he is. As a longtime student of psychology, it was my opinion that his reminiscences would be of interest not only to cellists but to all music lovers. This has become a reality and is my way of showing gratitude for Starker's generosity toward me and the "cello world." It has been a fascinating process and rewarding from the moment it began.

INTRODUCTION

Not long ago a leading American music critic said of the Hungarian-born virtuoso, Janos Starker: "He is the king of cellists, and having said that, what more is there to say?" The same critic wrote more recently: "He has the edge of authority that comes with international touring and worldwide acclaim." His performance experience has covered the gamut of cello playing. As an eight-year-old he was already teaching, and by age twelve he had five students. At age eleven he was playing the string quartets of Bartók, Debussy, Beethoven and others. As a youth, he played jazz, played in coffee houses and later played in over one thousand opera performances, played in about a thousand symphony concerts, plus over a thousand of his own recitals and concertos with orchestras all over the world. There is no one else who has done all of that. Now age 85, with a long and unparalleled career, Janos Starker is acknowledged as one of the greatest musicians of the twentieth century (as well as a gifted writer of fiction stories, some of which are included in this book).

Audiences everywhere from college campuses to the great concert halls of the world have cheered Starker's peerless performances of virtually the entire repertoire for his instrument. He has recorded nearly all of the standard repertoire and premiered many new works including music by Miklos Rozsa, David Baker, Antal Dorati, Bernard Heiden, and Jean Martinon, to name a few.

A teacher as long as he has been a cellist, Starker discovered in his youth that his own understanding of music and the possibilities of the instrument grew as he helped others, a philosophy that has remained the touchstone of his career. Musicians of all descriptions packed his seminars, which became an expected bonus of his concert tours. Emerging professionals eagerly played for him and cherished his comments. A much-honored Distinguished Professor, he served on the faculty at Indiana University since 1958.

James Smart and Joyce Geeting

JANOS STARKER

Part I

The Cellist in the Making

Kodály *Solo Sonata* Performed by a Boy in Knee Pants

The year was 1939, and fifteen-year-old Janos Starker was about to perform Zoltán Kodály's *Solo Sonata for Cello*. Back stage he waited for his turn to play in the student recital. He fidgeted a bit with his bow from excitement, noting that the hall was packed with many of his fellow students. From behind the curtain he spotted Kodály in the balcony sitting with Schiffer, his cello teacher. Just six weeks earlier, Starker had played the piece for Schiffer and Kodály.

JANOS
STARKER

He reflected a bit over the past couple of months since the day he stopped by Gabriel Magyar's house to pick up some music. Magyar was a fellow student at the Franz Liszt Academy of Music, eight years older than Starker. At the front door he heard Magyar practicing his cello. Standing at the door, Starker listened intently. The sounds were very interesting to him. He waited until the music stopped to knock. "What is that you are playing?" he asked Magyar. "The *Sonata for Solo Cello* by Kodály," came the answer.

Starker's thoughts moved to the Hungarian composer, Zoltán Kodály, professor of composition at the Franz

ZOLTÁN KODÁLY

Liszt Academy of Music in Budapest. Everyone knew he was a man who developed a style of never uttering an unnecessary word. The boy had heard that he would look over a composition student's piece and say only, "Bad. Rewrite it," or "Okay." There were books about his teaching, very small books because he said very little.

After the event at Magyar's house, Starker returned home. Over dinner that night he mentioned to his mother that he had heard a piece which sounded intriguing. She knew he wanted a copy of the piece. Although it was Easter holiday and most stores were closed, she did some searching and was able to find a used copy of the sonata in an antiquary shop. While he was away at school, she placed the music on his music stand at home.

The next morning Starker discovered the sonata. After dinner he sat down with his instrument to look through it. After several minutes of experimenting with the first few phrases, his brother asked, "What is this mess you are playing?" Starker took a closer look and realized that the piece was written scordatura. The two lower strings are to be tuned down a half step to B and F sharp in order to achieve the key of B Minor. Now with the cello retuned, the sounds began to make sense.

One week of working on the first movement and Starker wanted to play it for his teacher. At this prospect Schiffer was delighted. He hadn't heard it since 1925 when Paul Hermann played it. When Starker reached the end of the first movement, Schiffer instructed the boy to wait there while he went to fetch the composer. Kodály was just down the hall in his office. In Schiffer's studio the composer listened intently to his creation. He asked the boy, "When do you intend to perform this?" to which his teacher promptly replied, "June the first." That was only six weeks later. To this Kodály made no comment, not even a word about how Starker played it. He only said, "Good night."

Starker had six weeks to learn this thirty-minute work of monumental scope, a piece which has actually expanded the technical repertoire of the cello, asking the performer to do things on the instrument which had been previously unknown, unheard of, even considered impossible.

Now, six weeks later, after investing many hours carefully cultivating each phrase, each chord, every scale passage and harmonic for their brilliant effect, this was the night for the performance. The violinist performing before him took his bows and came off stage. Janos walked on stage, took his chair and then quietly and unobtrusively rechecked his open strings. He never liked tuning in front of an audience. Focusing his mind fully into the task at hand, he took a deep breath and began the resonant B minor chords at the beginning of the first movement. The sounds filled the recital hall with rich resonance. The performance went as planned. It was flawless.

After the last note, Starker acknowledged the tumultuous applause. In a few minutes the composer appeared back stage. He looked the lad in the eye and said only, "The first movement....too fast. The second is in good order. The third, don't separate the variations so much. Good night." That was all. To himself, Starker shrugged, thinking, "I didn't know the last movement was a set of variations."

A legend was born that night, one that shook the music world, the story of this Hungarian boy in knee pants performing Kodály's *Sonata for Solo Violoncello*. That was in 1939. The reviews were sensational! Even *Musical America* was talking about it, calling this performance in Budapest "a miracle." This was the night that launched Starker's reputation and his career.

Although Kodály wrote the piece in 1915, it was not until 1921 that it was finally published. Kodály sent it to the world's foremost cellist of the day, Pablo Casals. Casals sent it back saying, "It looks interesting, but, alas, I am too old to learn it." Casals was at the time thirty-nine years old. Because of that rejection, no publishers wanted to touch it.

However, in 1921 Kodály said to Schiffer, "In twenty-five years no cellist will be accepted into the world of cellists who does not play my piece." Kodály did not calculate into his figuring the years of World War II. It so happened that thirty-five years later, in 1956, the piece was required for the first time in the Casals Competition in Mexico City.

Kodály wrote the piece for Eugene Kerpely who at the time was teaching at the Franz Liszt Academy. But Kerpely reportedly never performed it. No one dared to even approach the piece because of its level of difficulty...except a few courageous young students, namely Starker, Magyar, and another Schiffer student, Paul Hermann, who played it in Salzburg and Maurice Franck in Holland. George Neikrug was the first cellist to perform the piece in the United States. Starker became identified with the piece, performing it many times.

Later in his life, after hundreds of performances of the Kodály *Sonata for Solo Violoncello* on the concert stage and a long and brilliant career, Starker received as a gift a plaque which hangs on the wall in his indoor pool in Bloomington, Indiana. In that room where he swims daily for the purpose of physical conditioning, hangs the plaque which says, "The pool that Kodály built." Perhaps there should be another plaque over the front door of his house reading, "The house that Dvorák built," due to the many times he has performed the Dvorák *Concerto*.

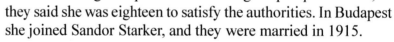

Janos Starker's origins were not extraordinary. His parents were both Russian, born just before the turn of the century. His father, Sandor Starker (1890-1976) was born in a little village and became a tailor. When Sandor was a teenager, he moved to Warsaw, Poland. In 1912 Sandor and several of his friends became involved in the young socialist movement against the czars. When many of them were arrested for political reasons, he left for Budapest to join friends.

His mother, Margit Chaikin (1896-1978) was born in the Ukraine. She had a brother who had escaped the Russian-Japanese War of 1905 by going to Hungary. Shortly after, she went to Budapest to join him. Because she was underage her parents could not get a passport for her, so they said she was eighteen to satisfy the authorities. In Budapest she joined Sandor Starker, and they were married in 1915.

JANOS AND HIS BROTHERS

Because Starker's parents were both foreign-born, immigrants in Hungary, they and their three sons were denied Hungarian citizenship. They were neither Polish, nor Russian, nor Hungarian, simply a family without a homeland. They had no documents, such as passports, to prove their identity. There was the Nansen Passport for such people who were "stateless," which the Starkers did not have. Each year they had to obtain permission from the government in order to live in Hungary. Some years they were able to hire for a small fee the services of a lawyer who filled out their forms for government permission to stay in Hungary.

Margit and Sandor had three sons, born in 1916, 1920, and 1924. Tibor was the oldest, then Ede, then Janos. Janos birthdate was July 5th, which in America was really July 4th. So perhaps one could say he was born on America's Day of Independence.

JANOS AND HIS BROTHERS

The Starkers were a traditional family. Father took the responsibility for putting food on the table, and Margit took care of home and children. Theirs was a lower middle class existence with primitive housing by today's standards. But they never suffered from hunger or lack of clothing. Since father was a tailor, they were always adequately dressed.

Margit Starker was very simple and uneducated, a perfect example of an "earth mother." She thought nothing of herself. Everything was for the children, but not just her own children, any children, all children. Whenever friends of the Starker boys came over after school, they were treated just like family. There was always some food to eat, sandwiches for all. They would all eat, eat, eat. She took care of everyone.

Margit was very practical. If she had a dollar to spend on household items and food, she spent only ninety cents so as to have money to pay for the children's music lessons. She loved music and wanted her sons to have music lessons. Both of Janos' older brothers played the violin, and, of course, Janos played the cello.

Those were very happy days in the Starker home. Usually when business was good, Father would be home by around seven o'clock. His workplace in the city was about a five minute walk from home.

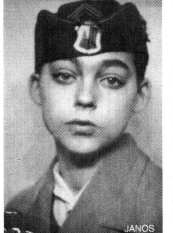

JANOS

One day in May when the children were young, Margit decided to take the train to the outskirts of the city to the village of Gyömrö. There she found a peasant house which they rented for the summer months. The peasants moved into the stable, giving over their two-room hut to the city folk. Father joined them after work and on the weekends as he was able.

There was no running water, only a well nearby where they pulled up the water with a bucket. On one side of the hut was an outhouse. A garden with fruit trees was on the other. Sometimes for

THE STARKER HOME IN BUDAPEST

some moments of solitude Janos would climb one of the fruit trees and read by himself.

The best part of their summer place was the pond, originally a rock quarry with underground springs where water bubbled up to form a pool. In the heat of summer the children spent endless hours in and out of the water where sometimes the Starker boys and their friends ran around like Indians with painted faces. In a small building nearby, there were a couple of dressing rooms for the children to change into their swimsuits, a room for the boys and a room for the girls. On the walls were nails where the children hung their clothes. One area of the pond was separated for water polo, a favorite of the Starker brothers. On the other side of the pond was a sandy beach where many children played.

One day the owner of the lake bought two dozen turtles and threw them into the lake. He expected that soon the lake would have a nice population of turtles. But by evening they had all disappeared. Everyone took one home for a pet.

Periodically Janos had cello lessons in the summer with a Hungarian woman who was a graduate student at the Franz Liszt Academy, a very fine cellist. She travelled to Gyömrö for his lessons. Because of his cello playing, Janos developed very strong arms and upper body muscles. As a boy with long hair, he was sometimes teased by other children. But they quickly learned to treat this lad with respect. He easily wrestled the offender to the ground, then asked if he wanted more.

Very early on Janos played in a string quartet together with Arthur Garami, Robert Gerle and his brother Ede.[1] All three played the violin. Since no one played the viola, they arranged quartet music for three violins and cello. They played quartets by Mozart, Beethoven and Debussy. This usually took place after the day's swimming was done. They sat in the garden while their friends gathered around to listen. They considered the measure of the success of their performance by whether or not someone started to cry during the slow movement of the Debussy *Quartet*.

One summer during their sojourn at the lake, the boys tried to play the *First Quartet* by Bartók. Starker took the music and, throwing it to the ground said, "I am not going to play that junk!" Time and experience changed his attitude and level of understanding.

In the summers, Sandor would take the 17-mile train ride to join his family at their country village. Together they would enjoy the swimming, the fresh garden fruits and vegetables, the water polo games, and summer freedoms. With the end of the hot summer, they reluctantly packed up their goods and headed for their home in Budapest. This was the first of several summers spent by the Starker family in the countryside, some of the happiest times of their lives.

Starker began cello lessons at age six with Frigyes Teller who ran a private music school for young children with weekly performances. Margit noticed after a few months that her son was making no progress, and the two little pieces he did know were getting worse. Then his brother's violin teacher took Janos to Adolph Schiffer, cello teacher at the Franz Liszt Academy of Music. Starker was assigned by Schiffer to study with Hochstrasser, one of Schiffer's graduate students. Then Schiffer heard the boy every two weeks or so. Thus he was accepted into Adolph Schiffer's cello class, learning at the practice class level. For about two years he studied with one of Schiffer's graduate students.

Schiffer was a natural player and a good musician, although a late recruit to the cello. He was actually a bookkeeper with a love for the cello. When he met Casals in 1895 and heard him perform, his life was transformed. At twenty-two years of age, he moved to Budapest to study the cello with David Popper. Before that Schiffer was largely self-taught. Because of his late start on the cello, Schiffer stopped performing rather early on. But when he played, it was always beautifully in tune with lovely phrasing, very natural. He was just uncomfortable with public performance.

∿∿

In 1900, Schiffer became David Popper's assistant. After Popper's death in 1913, he was appointed professor, remaining in that position until 1935. Putting off retirement, he continued an additional four years so that he could establish the pedagogy class. There were several levels of instruction: the practice class, the preparatory class, and then full admittance to the Franz Liszt Music Academy.

When Starker began cello lessons in 1930, he quickly progressed to the preparatory class and, at the age of seven, became Schiffer's prize pupil. He was such a brilliant student that Schiffer never charged for his cello lessons! In his once or twice weekly cello lessons, Starker was given assignments by Schiffer. After a few days of practice he would return for another lesson. Then Schiffer made corrections, perhaps different fingerings and bowings, pointing out phrasings. Schiffer was a very fine teacher for Starker in that he never gave him any obviously incorrect instruction. He never attempted to explain anything either. But then, at the age of six or seven, one does not need much explanation. Generally, Starker played things through, and Schiffer made some corrections and suggestions, demonstrating certain passages.

At the Franz Liszt Academy there was a general piano proficiency requirement, so Starker played to a small extent. Since they did not have a piano at home, he never practiced and therefore did not become very proficient. It was a useful tool through the years, however, in studying a score or sorting out the mechanics of a new piece before applying it to the cello.

ADOLPH SCHIFFER AND JANOS

ADOLPH SCHIFFER

Schiffer put a lot of importance on the playing of etudes. When Starker started the cello he went through Schiffer's own cello method for several weeks, doing exercises in various positions with different bowings, etc. Then he studied all of the Dotzauer *Etudes*. Starker played all fifty of Popper's etudes by the age of eleven. At the age of twelve he took the exam at the Academy, performing Piattis *Etude #6*. With Schiffer, Starker learned to play octaves, thirds, sixths, and arpeggios. Schiffer just said, "Learn this," and he demonstrated how to do it. He did not use any books. Starker also played a great number of pieces by Popper which were fashionable at the time such as two *Gavottes, Village Song, Elfentanz, Papillion, Little Russian Fantasy*, and others. Sixty years later he recorded twenty of Popper's pieces, some of which he had played as a child.[2]

At the grand old age of nine, Starker decided that he was going to play the cello as long as he lived and would try to play it as well as possible! He practiced the *Etude #40* by Popper, a piece with many harmonics. Later in his life he would often warm up with that piece to see that he "had his left hand in order." Playing it, says Starker, "always brought back memories of summers when he heard the old horse-drawn carriages squeaking in the village street." Starker has always felt that the playing of Popper's etudes is as vital to efficient cello playing as anything he has ever encountered. He was a gifted composer and innovative especially in his use of harmony. Together with his wife on the piano, he created many lovely salon pieces for the instrument. However, he frequently borrowed musical ideas from other composers. Having lived in Austria, he was exposed to many Western European styles. Popper could write in the style of Spanish, German, Italian, Russian music, even cello music sounding like Chopin.

David Popper used to spend a great deal of time in coffee houses. Whenever he would run up a tab for his meals, he would go home and write a small piece. The next day he went with his new piece to the publisher who then gave him some money for it. With that he would pay for his charges at the coffee houses. He eventually played the pieces, but in recital, not at the coffee houses. Clearly, Popper was a major influence on Starker's cello playing.

When Starker was a boy, his family had a large coal or wood-burning ceramic tile stove. It was as tall as the ceiling and radiated heat for the entire apartment. When bedtime came, there was still warmth coming from the stove. As a boy, Starker took three chairs, making a semicircle around the stove, and curled up there with his blankets and his crystal radio. The crystal radio had two buttons, one for the volume and the other for the station. Says Starker, "If you turned the dials side to side you would hear wailing, whistling sounds between stations, until the station was found and tuned in. I entertained myself by composing little tunes with these between-stations whistling sounds. Once I found the pitch, I could do double stops," a two-voice tune. From ages six to sixteen he tuned in to radio stations in Moscow, Leningrad, London, and cities all over Europe. When he was sixteen the family bought a Victrola. Then at home he played recordings by Heifetz and Feuermann and others. But most of the music he heard in his youth was on the crystal radio.

Among the first concerts he ever heard was a performance by the violinist Bronislaw Hubermann and a concert by the legendary cellist, Pablo Casals, who performed in Budapest each year for many years. Following the cello concert Schiffer introduced the six-and-a-half-year-old prodigy to the great cellist. Casals leaned down and gave this long-haired boy a kiss on his forehead. Starker was so thrilled that, as the story goes, his forehead went unwashed for a week!

Margit helped her young cellist develop good practice habits. During the summers at ages eight, nine, and ten, he was expected to practice from eight in the morning until eleven. Without so doing, he was not allowed to go swimming or to the movies. This was also the rule during weekends and vacations. Once school began, practice came later in the day. Margit ensured that he would not have reason to leave his practicing in order to eat and provided him with bite-sized pieces of sandwich and a drink placed on a nearby table. Time was limited, and he was expected to make the most of it. "Three hours of practice in a day at that age," said Starker many years later, "would be the equivalent of perhaps six hours of what an adult could absorb." Years later Starker's former colleagues gathered in the Starker home just to hear the family parakeet repeating Mother's instructions, "Practice, Jancsi."

One time during a cello lesson, Schiffer asked him to demonstrate something for a new student, Eva Janzer. Thereafter he was asked to work with Eva a couple of times each week. Thus, at the age of eight he was already teaching the cello. Since he had to explain how to do things, he was analyzing cello playing and music making at an early age. Eva Janzer was one of his first students, Mihaly Virizlay another.[3] As a ten-year-old, Starker was invited to play

EVA JANZER
STARKER'S FIRST STUDENT

principal cello in the orchestra of another school. At that school they did not have cellists who were very capable. At ages twelve, thirteen, and fourteen he was teaching a handful of students. At the same time he was making money by playing recitals and chamber music around town. So at an early age he earned some money as a professional. Sometimes his brothers and friends would play concerts together, all sitting around the piano, each reading from the piano score and picking out their own parts to play, performing as an ensemble.

As a young boy, Starker woke to the sound of the school bell at 7:50 a.m. At that time the Starker family lived on the fourth floor of an apartment building, just a stone's throw from the school. In just ten minutes time, he threw on his clothes, grabbed a bite to eat, and dashed to school just in time for the eight o'clock bell. Until two o'clock in the afternoon he studied language, history, arithmetic and other subjects. Then in the afternoon he went to the Franz Liszt Academy for music study.

By that time, his musical experience was primarily in quartet or trio rehearsals and performances with a handful of friends his age, and several of these have been lifelong friends. At one time Starker played in a quartet with Victor Aitay who later became the concertmaster of the Chicago Symphony, and with Francis Akos who became the assistant concertmaster of the same orchestra. Other chamber music companions, as has been mentioned, included Arthur Garami, Robert Gerle and György Sebök. All of their lives these friends, others as well, got together to play chamber music. Coming from a common experience in Leo Weiner's chamber music class at the Franz Liszt Academy, they all had a similar way of looking at and performing music.

For a while during his childhood years, Starker got together once each week with several doctors to play chamber music. With them he played nearly the entire chamber music literature, every Mozart quartet ever written, even very early works which were in print. Although the doctors were not very good players, and at times the sounds they made were miserable, they knew the repertoire intimately. This was valuable experience for Starker, acquainting him with the string quartet repertoire. The doctors admired the young cellist and were pleased to make music with such a fine player.

Starker was on the stage at the Academy as an eleven-year-old performing the Boccherini *Concerto in B flat Major* with piano accompaniment and at age twelve the Locatelli *Sonata*. Within a few years he played all of the concertos that he knew existed at the time, including the Saint Saëns *Concerto in A Minor*, Lalo *Concerto*, Schumann *Concerto*, Dvorák *Concerto*, *D Major Concerto* by Haydn, (*The C Major Concerto* was not yet discovered.), Vivaldi *D Major Concerto*, and even the *Adelaide Concerto*. (This was a piece ascribed to Mozart and supposedly discovered by the violinist Yehudi Menuhin, but only after the pianist Henri Casadesus died did Menuhin admit that Casadesus had written the piece for violin.) This piece, like many others, was transcribed for cello by the young cellist. Many cellists over the years have found it amusing to make transcriptions of violin pieces and play them on the cello.

The works for cello and piano that Starker and pianist György Sebök played together as youths include the Couperin *Suite*, the Beethoven *Sonatas*, the Brahms *Sonatas*, the Debussy *Sonata*, and Mendelssohn *Sonatas*. They also played at times from manuscripts, works of different composers some of whom have since been forgotten.

In 1936, when he was twelve-years old, Starker was invited to spend the summer with his teacher in Italy at the elegant resort, Cortina d'Ampezzo, one of the world's finest ski areas and later the home of the winter Olympics. But paying for Starker's hotel stay in Italy as well as his travel was beyond the means of Mr. and Mrs. Starker, so Schiffer personally raised some money to cover the boy's expenses. Once all the plans were made, it was apparent that since he did not have legal citizenship, Starker would not be able to get a Hungarian passport. He was considered by the Hungarian government to be a foreigner even though he was born in Hungary. Only the Polish embassy was willing to give him a passport. So for two months, with a differently spelled name, he was a Polish citizen! After that summer Starker could speak passable Italian and was very proud of it. Over the years his command of the language faded but came back whenever he was in Italy again, although maybe not as well as when he was twelve.

As legend has it, Starker was fourteen when he played his first solo with orchestra. At noon one day Schiffer called to ask if he would like to play the Dvorák *Concerto* that evening with the student orchestra. He was to take the place of Gabriel Magyar who had been rehearsing the piece with the orchestra but called in sick.[4] So at the last moment Starker stepped into the limelight and performed the piece.

In 1938 Starker often played chamber music with a wealthy lady, an amateur pianist by the last name of Toszeghi. Her son, Anton, was a medical student and studied cello with Starker. They had a Piatellini cello, a very fine one. But they thought that it was too good an instrument for their son, who was not a serious student, and loaned it to Starker to use. He played this instrument until 1946 when he returned it.

Starker attended regular school while attending the Franz Liszt Academy but never finished either one. By the age of fourteen he was teaching seven private students in addition to all of his other work in school and at the Liszt Academy. That did not leave much time for practice. So he and Schiffer agreed that he should stop going to regular school and focus on his music education at the Liszt Academy. But graduation from the Academy was contingent upon the student completing the requirements of general school as well. When Schiffer completed preparation of the pedagogical cello course at the Academy, he retired. Starker, however, did not know that Schiffer was about to retire, and he did not want to study with anyone else. So at the age of fifteen he quit the Academy. Contrary to popular opinion, it was not because of the war that he quit but rather because of Schiffer's retirement. So at age fifteen Starker started working as a full time professional, teaching and playing, leaving his general education as well as his music education at the Academy incomplete.

Starker's concert experiences as a youth were unlike anything that is expected of child prodigies. He was not concertizing at a young age as one would expect but rather went to school, studied, learned the repertoire at an early age, and played chamber music with his friends. From early on he taught students, and he played concerts at the Academy and in town. He did not tour as a concert artist.

While he was still a student at the Franz Liszt Academy, Starker heard the famous cellist Emmanuel Feuermann in a concert with Bela Bartók. When the Nazis came to power, Feuermann, who was Jewish, was forced to leave Germany. He had been professor at the Musik Hochschule in Köln. After that he embarked on a world concert tour in 1934-35 during which time he came through Budapest. He made a great impact on the young cellist and showed Starker that the cello could be played better than most cellists had imagined and with more variety than Casals had ever played.

From time to time Schiffer asked Starker to go with him to perform in people's homes. One time at such an event he met a widowed Hungarian countess. She suggested that she adopt Starker (age seventeen) and take him to England where some of her extended family lived. Had that happened, his life would have undoubtedly unfolded in different ways. Starker and the countess met again twenty-five years later at a concert he was playing in Switzerland and enjoyed a warm reunion.

Equally impressive to the young cellist were his experiences in hearing the famous Russian violinist, Jacha Heifetz. Starker heard him first in a performance in Budapest, and he became immediately taken with the "Heifetz sound." Heifetz impressed the young cellist with his tonal perfection and equilibrium of phrasing, never imposing extraneous elements on the music. From 1941 to 1946 people in the Communist countries were completely cut off from the West by radio or otherwise. Starker was living in Paris after the war when he first saw the movie, *Carnegie Hall*. It was his first opportunity coming from Eastern Europe to see the great musicians he admired as he was growing up: Heifetz, Reiner, Rise Stevens, Rubinstein and Piatigorsky.

What drove him "sleepless for a week" was he could not see anything that Heifetz was physically doing to achieve such excellent musical results. Starker could not figure out how Heifetz could travel such distances with the left hand, how he could play so unbelievably fast, with repeated motions, and nothing was visibly happening. Starker came to the conclusion that the secret to such fine sound production with so little visible effort was all in the preparation, the anticipation process. Each movement needs to be prepared, usually from the back and shoulder muscles, with the minimum amount of effort for the desired result. He concluded that if the motion is prepared in such a way that it is exactly the same as what follows, then one does not see anything happening. One should avoid any abrupt or interrupted motions which are contrary to legato playing unless using them for musical reasons. Starker became totally attached to the purity of sound that Heifetz produced and throughout his life sought to capture with his cello the purity of the "Heifetz sound."

During the 1948 - 1949 concert season, when Starker was playing as principal cellist with the Dallas Symphony, Heifetz performed with the orchestra. Another time when Starker was principal cellist with the Chicago Symphony, Heifetz recorded his famous Brahms *Violin Concerto* performance. Perhaps they exchanged no more than four or five sentences together over the years, but Heifetz made a lasting impact.

There were several giants in twentieth century music history who lived in Hungary and influenced the young cellist, providing a rich and stimulating learning environment. Among these greats were the composers Ernst von Dohnanyi (1877-1960), Bela Bartók (1881-1945), Zoltán Kodály (1882-1967), Leo Weiner (1883-1960), in string playing, the violinist Jeno Hubay (1858-1937) and the cellist David Popper (1843-1913). This group significantly influenced the musical life in Hungary and made a great impact on the world of music in general.

Chamber music sessions with Leo Weiner at the Franz Liszt Academy were important for Starker and all of the other string players of that era. Weiner was a composer and a mediocre but functional pianist. However, he had a powerful mind and incredibly disciplined ears. According to Starker, he was one of the greatest music pedagogues who ever lived. He taught his students the many aspects of hearing. For example hearing the lengths of notes, whether a note starts with a vowel or consonant and if it is a hard or soft consonant. He taught them to apply piano pedal principles to string playing. He taught them to hear when a crescendo starts. With ritardandos the units change. When something slows down, there are more units (subdivision of beats). When something speeds up, there are fewer units. He also talked about interval differentiation: for example, it takes longer to get from one note to a fifth away than from the same note to a third away. Weiner's students learned how to make it so that the shift is not obvious to the listener; that is a matter of the player's ability as well as aesthetics. Decoration, such as an ornament, is not supposed to take precedence over the main line. When drawing an up-bow, one is not supposed to make a crescendo unless the music calls for it. He also discussed the value of the dot after a note. Weiner's chamber music classes met twice weekly, during which time students performed sonatas, trios, quartets, whatever they had prepared.

Leo Weiner remains a legendary figure in Hungarian music. At one time he won a composition competition over Dohnanyi, Kodály and Bartók. They all sent in their works, but Weiner won the first prize. Although not a trailblazer as a composer, according to Starker, he was nonetheless one of the greatest musicians who ever lived. His effectiveness was mainly as a teacher. That fact is evidenced by the many Hungarian conductors and performers who have held major positions in the world of music in every civilized country. In addition to teaching, he was also responsible for the start of the original Budapest String Quartet. At one time there were several famous string quartets which dominated the world music scene including the Budapest Quartet, the Lehner Quartet and the Roth Quartet. All of the players were Weiner students. Weiner's influence is an important part of every Hungarian musician's life and recollections.

Budapest at the time had a number of scientist-teachers of music, men who spent their lives studying all of the motions and psychological aspects of playing a musical instrument. Starker was under the influence of two of them. One was Imre Waldbauer (1892-1953), string quartet coach at the Franz Liszt Academy. At that time he had a well-known string quartet with Eugene Kerpely, the cellist for whom the Kodály *Sonata for Solo Cello* was written. This was called the Waldbauer-Kerpely Quartet, the group for whom Bartók wrote some of his string quartets. Waldbauer was one of the first persons to immerse himself with the technique of body movement involved in instrumental playing. He was himself a fine quartet player, a highly respected violinist of his renowned string quartet although not a virtuoso violinist.

The second was a violin teacher at the Fodor School of Music, Dezsö Rados, an eccentric person who, according to Starker, was a "total maniac" on the science of instrumental playing. His ideas were based on the Riemann-Steinhausen books of the nineteenth century which became the Bible of instrumental playing. He was, however, not a particularly good player. Starker's brother and another friend, George Lang, studied with him for a time. But those who studied with him always went later to another teacher to learn how to make music, not just body movements.

The two men read all of the available biological and neurological literature in the music field in addition to experimenting with body motion and balance studies. They were called scientists because it sometimes seemed that the priority was to adhere to these physical principles almost to the exclusion of the beauty of the phrase. However, Starker learned that if someone makes the right motions with the desire to create a beautiful phrase, then the visual and aural aspects coincide. These two men gave Starker the first tools that enabled him to justify and explain this principle.

One time Starker and Rados got together for a chamber music session. Because Rados was such a poor violinist, it was for Starker an excruciating experience. But he lectured Starker, talking nonstop for three hours about certain physical aspects of instrumental playing. From all of this, Starker remembered two or three sentences, largely about circles and circular motions in the physical processes of making music.

At that time these ideas did not make any sense to Starker. But while he was walking home, the idea of circles became almost obsessive in him. Just what did he mean by circles? Starker's lifetime then was spent discovering that practically everything Rados said applies, in that every motion that we make is part of a circle. Musical sounds are circular, waves of tension and non-tension. Every musical phrase is part of a circle, just not a finished circle. All changes whether instrumentally, physically, and musically are based on this concept of circular motions and are the basis of legato playing. This is an issue of physical motion that has a quasi-philosophical basis, that is, uninterrupted lines, a circle of lines as a part of the universe. Starker's whole approach in his *Organized Method of String Playing*[5] is based on this idea. This concept later became the basis for all that he did in terms of his own body movement and in helping students to analyze the effectiveness of their own body use.

According to Starker, these are not principles which dictate only one way of doing things. They are overriding principles which allow for varieties in playing but based on sound and logical use of the body to produce musical sounds. These non-alterable physical and philosophical principles are true for all instrumentalists. Their application is limitless in variables according to each individual player. These principles are expanded upon by Gerhard Mantel in his book about cello technique.[6]

∧∧∧

After WWII Starker was playing recitals in Rumania when he pondered more the relationship of body movement to instrumental playing. He thought, "What if I started having physical problems caused by playing the cello?" He set out to learn how to solve them. He saw child prodigies disappearing from music performance because of their lack of understanding or their teachers' failure to explain to them what it physically means to play their instrument. Thus began an in-depth process of thinking which began years before in Budapest with his experiences with the scientist-teacher.

Weiner

a story by Janos Starker

The young man looked up at a picture hanging on the wall of my studio. "Who is that?" he asked. "Leo Weiner," I answered. He stared in disbelief, "You mean The Leo Weiner, the great teacher?" "Yes," I said. "I would never have believed it," he muttered. "What do you mean?" I countered. "Well," he said, "I envisioned someone powerful like Franz Liszt. Ever since I was born my parents, then later my teachers, were always telling me that he was the greatest teacher of music that they had ever known."

A vision of Weiner came to mind and I couldn't help smiling. I saw the downward turn of his nose, almost touching his lower lip and covering his mouth, the sloping shoulders, the pigeon-toed walk of a man who spent his life sitting or lurching over his instrumentalist students, and pointing at the music.

"You see," I told the young man, "it wasn't his size or his features that were responsible for his greatness as a teacher. I remember the day when I sat down to play a Beethoven *Sonata* with a Hungarian pianist in Switzerland. She was my senior by about 15 years, so our paths hadn't crossed in the Franz Liszt Academy." After five minutes of playing I stopped. "You must have been in Weiner's class for two years," I said. "Two and a half years," she responded, surprised. "How did you know?" "Obvious," I said.

There was another day, when, due to an emergency, four musicians were thrown together to perform four evenings of string quartets at the most prestigious musical centers. One day of rehearsal was all that was available. After ten minutes, four Hungarian musicians were smiling contentedly. They were, of course, all Weiner students.

There are hundreds of evenings when musicians or music lovers ask the inevitable question: How come so many famous musicians came and still come from such a small country as yours? The answer, after some elaboration on ethnic and sociological backgrounds, will always be, we had one thing in common: We were all in the class of Leo Weiner. Invariably the long list of conductors, pianists, violinists, violists, cellists, and a few others follow, and the questioners' faces grow incredulous. Was he a great instrumentalist? they ask. No, is the answer. He could manage to play a lovely phrase on the piano, to demonstrate his point, but usually on the third try. Violin? Cello? No way, but he could figure out and advise better bowings and fingerings than our instrumental teachers. Was he a conductor? No. Was he a composer? Yes, He wrote some lovely music and even won some prizes with his works in his youth. But compared with his contemporaries, his output was less than memorable. He was a real professional who could dictate a Webern string quartet or write anything. But emotionally (and stylistically) he stopped at the end of the 19th century, and so his creative output found little response after World War I.

"Well, then what in heaven's name are you speaking of?" the young man asked. "No instrumentalist, no conductor, and a composer of minor significance. Was he a charismatic person?"

When this question is asked, I said, "All Hungarian musicians from his class start to grin. We recall many stories. For one, his encounter with the ladies of the night. 'Where are you going, Sweetheart?' asks the lady thinking she has a potential customer. Weiner earnestly replies, 'To a musicale in the house of Mr. X. Where are you going?'"

Then there was the time when he dropped a bit of mashed potato from the baronial table onto the rarest Astrakhan carpet. He then rubbed it into the rug with his shoes so no one would see it. There was the time when he travelled for the first time to the Mediterranean in Italy. He looked at the waves, turned green, spun around, and headed home. His eating habits were limited to eggs and fried chicken, which resulted in his refusing chicken paprikasch the day after the starvation of the Budapest ghetto ended.

There are many other stories, but my personal recollection goes back to my first encounter with the Master. At the age of twelve I was told that I was admitted into his class. There were sessions twice a week for piano chamber music coaching. After weeks of listening to senior colleagues, who perspired under his scrutiny, I was called to play Beethoven's *Sonata No. 2*. At that age, artistic responsibility had yet to manifest in nervousness, and my status as a child prodigy was firmly established. Leo Weiner listened. Then, five minutes into my display of greatness, he stopped us. He told several things to the pianist, such as use of the pedal, legato phrasings, etc. Then he asked me to play the theme on the D string instead of the A string. I blurted out that that was difficult. I was then told to go home and practice it, and we were dismissed. My ego was shattered, and for the rest of my life I never again chose an instrumental solution for its ease against musical necessity. I did learn to play the theme on the D string, and the frequency in which I was called to play increased. Years went by, and the string quartet, of which I was a member, went to his home many times to be instructed.

About this time a much admired and wealthy friend invited us often for a superb dinner, after which we young musicians played a wide variety of repertoire for ourselves as well as for a few selected music lovers. As we invariably related our Weiner stories, our host suggested we invite Weiner to his legendary table. To our surprise, the Master agreed. Course after course of the Lucullian feast was served. Weiner waved off all the exotic offerings. Then he asked for an omelet and inquired as to when the playing would begin. Our quartet sat down and launched into Mozart. After a maximum of two minutes of fidgeting he interrupted us with, "No, you cannot do that." What ensued afterward was three hours of the most detailed coaching session I or my colleagues ever had. The music lovers were mesmerized and learned more about music in those three hours than in a lifetime. So in this sense he may have been charismatic.

But what did he really do? Leo Weiner taught us to hear and helped us to gain the tools with which to make music. He taught us that in music every note matters. He taught us discipline which first demands the observation of the composer's intentions, and only then can we enhance it with individual recreative ideas. He made us aware of the direction of beats, rhythmic consistencies, breathing, rubato, agogic, unit changes, and pulse. He increased our inner needs for the ideal legato for lines ascending and descending. He helped us to understand the necessity of building climaxes and anticlimaxes. He demanded purity of sound, simplicity of expression, and balanced structure. When a musician was first stopped by Weiner he was perplexed as to what the Master wanted. Weiner spoke of bowings, fingerings, the pedal, dynamics, staccato, spiccato, length of notes, accents, upbeats, downbeats, vibrato, decorations, emotions, tensions, and releases. But six months later the musician knew that Weiner's demand will be one of three possibilities. Two years later he knew that his suggestion will be one of two possibilities. Three years later and on when he stopped us we said, "Yes, Sir, we will watch it." Then he smiled as he knew his job was done.

Yes, his job was done. He taught hundreds of musicians the essentials of music making, music making that is not measured in sold-out halls, but as the truth is measured in eternity. The hundreds he taught have then taught thousands whose effect has been and will be upon millions. Leo Weiner may not be the most famous musician the centuries produced, but when Bach, Haydn, Mozart, Beethoven, Brahms, Schubert, Schumann, Mendelssohn, and others meet in the Elysian fields, they all know how much they owe to our beloved Uncle Leo.

Thanks, Professor Weiner.

"Thank you, Professor," said the young man.

J.S., Bloomington, Indiana, 1984

When Starker was seventeen he encountered the strongest intellectual influence of his life, a woman named Macko. She was originally a professor at the University in Budapest, a highly respected, well-educated and cultured person. Although one of the most homely persons he had ever known, she had a brilliant mind. She sent a message to Starker at a concert. In her concern for him she wondered what would become of this young cellist, playing the instrument as he did, having dropped out of both the regular school and the music academy. She wanted to know about his educational background and his plans.

They began working together, a four-hour session each week studying art, history, English, and related subjects. She was instrumental in helping him develop a keen mind. It was, in a sense, a more Classical Greek kind of education. Between weekly sessions he would read and prepare as he was able. Perhaps this is an ideal education.

After about a year and a half she asked him if he shouldn't take some exams in order to get a degree and finish high school. For two months he prepared to pass the equivalent of ninth or tenth grade. When he failed the arithmetic section, he had to prepare for another month or two and retake the exam. Ironically, at a very young age he was, among his friends, a prodigy in arithmetic. As early as the age of five he found that he was easily able to multiply figures in his head, actually better than on paper. Once he retook the exam, he completed the tenth grade level of education. He prepared for the matura, the last two years of school, but the war then prevented him from going further and completing the high school equivalency.

During their four-hour sessions, he and Macko drank brandy and smoked like chimneys, a habit that Starker maintained throughout his life. Seldom was he ever seen without a cigarette in hand, except in performance.

Perhaps there were some holes in his education. At least he did not waste time sitting in tedious classes. His sessions with Macko resulted in the development of a keen, analytical mind, always searching for answers, a mind that memorizes readily, one that is quick to grasp. Starker is a man who chooses his words carefully and means what he says. He does not exaggerate. He tells concisely what he thinks. His education, unorthodox though it was, has served him well.

〜〜〜

As a seventeen-year-old Starker was out one evening in the park until about one o'clock in the morning with a young lady, Maria Rozsa, a gorgeous actress, according to his description. As predicted, his mother was very worried. He was to play a performance of Haydn's *D Major Concerto* the next day, which apparently went as planned. Not long after, he and Maria Rozsa did some mutual concerts together, he playing cello-piano music and she reciting poetry. Another time he performed mutual concerts with the young lady's sister, who was a fine singer. This type of collaboration was fashionable then.

Starker was a devoted card player. He had a group of former classmates, some who were still in school, some who were trade apprentices, all of them avid card players. On weekends they would often play until late at night. One time his father showed up at four o'clock in the morning. The card players finished the hand. As Starker and his dad were walking home, his father said, "I do not think you should stay out so late. Your mother is very worried, and it is not very good for your health." To this he replied, "I am sure you are right, but I have to find out for myself."

Only one time in his life did his father interfere with anything Starker wanted. His parents reminded him that he was Jewish. However, he was exposed to Judaism only on rare family occasions, such as holiday dinners with distant relatives. At age thirteen boys were to be inducted into the Jewish religion with the traditional Bar Mitzvah. Once each week a distant relative, a very knowledgeable man, came to their house to teach him about Jewish traditions. Although Starker was reluctant, he went along with it, that is, until his father told him how to pronounce a certain "h" sound according to the Jewish language. It struck him funny, and young Starker made a joke of it. At this his father slapped him, the only time in his life. He decided that he was not going to be put through the rite if he was slapped for not pronouncing the "h" correctly. So according to some Jewish beliefs he is not actually a Jew.

In most people's minds one is born Jewish. There is a strong kind of feeling about it all of one's life. Whether proud or not, one is born into this kind of religion. But then there are some like Starker who have not had any kind of adherence or association with Jewish religious practices and the theology/philosophy of Judaism. In fact, in his life he has had some extremely bad experiences with Jews, particularly during the war. "There is a certain segment of Jewish society which is just as resentable to me as the Ku Klux Klan, those who designate a certain group as the enemies of society," says Starker "On the other hand, I have experienced fabulous and fascinating things that the Jewish Israeli State has done. This issue of discrimination is a very far reaching, complex issue of which my life is a part."

"In history there has been discrimination against the Christians, then another time against the Jews, then the Catholics against the Anglicans in Ireland, the Turks against the Greeks, the Serbs against the Moslems, Islam against the rest of the world," says Starker. "It goes on and on. It has nothing to do actually with religion. People just need a group to look down upon because it makes them feel better. Seeing the injustice, the dirt, and the stupidity of discrimination requires a response. If anyone says something against a Jew, then obviously I become emotionally a Jew. More important to me is the human being. Belonging to a certain country, color, class or religion has no reference to the human qualities of an individual."

FRANZ LISZT ACADEMY OF MUSIC IN BUDAPEST

Based on his war experiences, encounters with numerous morons with guns and murderous inclinations, and experiences with prejudice of one sort or another, Starker concluded that only about ten percent of the human race deserves the title of being human. The rest are *two-legged animals*. When working among musicians, one meets many of the select ten percent. Musicians are among the most disciplined, devoted, diligent, and cooperative people on the earth. They will function together effectively regardless of differences. Although this is an elitist statement, it is part of his philosophy.

Many times while in Israel he has been asked if he were a Jew. To this he replies. "Yes." If they say, "You are not Jewish, are you?" his reply is, "No." To him it really makes no difference.

1. Robert Gerle taught at Catholic University in Washington, D.C. and the University of Maryland. He wrote about violin playing, made a number of recordings, and toured with von Karajan. Arthur Garami became the concertmaster of the Montreal Symphony. He was intensely afraid of the cold and always wore coats, hats, and shawls. Whenever he opened the door, he would put on a coat. Ironically, his life ended when he froze to death.

2. *Romantic Cello Favorites*, Janos Starker, cello, Shigeo Neriki, piano, Delos 3065

3. Years later Eva Janzer joined Starker on the faculty at Indiana University. Mihaly Virizlay followed Starker as principal cellist in the Chicago Symphony and later joined the Baltimore Symphony, teaching at Peabody Conservatory.

4. Magyar later became the cellist with the Hungarian String Quartet. When the quartet disbanded, he became a professor at the University of Illinois in Urbana.

5. Starker, Janos, assisted by George Bekefi, *An Organized Method of String Playing*, Violoncello Exercises for the Left Hand, Peerless, Int., New York, Hamburg

6. Mantel, Gerhard, *Cello Technique, Principles and Forms of Movement*, Indiana University Press, 1975

Part II

Emerging from Youth

Early in this century European cities and towns were largely self-contained. Commerce, communication, and travel were rudimentary. About 80% of the shopkeepers in European communities were Jewish with their goods on display in the store windows. The haberdasheries displayed men's ties and suits made by the tailors. Another store displayed linen goods hand-woven from hemp fibers. The cobbler displayed shoes and boots. The stores were very small, perhaps 400 square feet, but goods were always on display for the passersby to admire.

Life for the Hungarian people was very hard, and they were for the most part very poor. A person worked from sunup to sundown for about $.20 per day. It was common to work for any amount of money, just to have something to eat. Human labor was cheap, and goods were expensive. It took about a month's wages, around $6.00, to buy a pair of boots or a piece of clothing. This led people to be very jealous of Jewish shop owners. Gentiles thought that Jews were wealthy, controlling all of the money. In the capital of Hungary as well as in the small towns, bankers, doctors, journalists, and lawyers were very often Jews. In a country with a landed aristocracy and a large peasantry, the Jews were distinctively middle class. To the barely literate peasants, Jews meant commerce and capital. They were conspicuously successful compared to the uneducated artisan and peasant. Of gainfully employed Jews, thirty-eight percent were self-employed businessmen in industry (including small craftsmen), commerce, banking, and professional occupations, twenty-eight percent were salaried, and thirty-three percent were wage earners. With the Depression and chaotic economic conditions, the price of goods skyrocketed. Merchants were forced to inflate prices just to stay afloat.[7]

The "first Jewish question" came about in 1920 when the Hungarian government established hiring quotas for business employees. Out of five workers, four had to be Gentiles, and only one could be Jewish. Less than two years later came the "second Jewish question," further establishing quotas. Then came the "third Jewish question" where Jewish store ownership was forbidden. The policy called "numerus clausus" was adopted, meaning that only a small percentage of Jews were allowed do certain things, such as opening shops, performing concerts, attending universities, or holding a government or military post.[8]

As early as the middle of the nineteenth century anti-Semitism was the official policy of the Hungarian government. The feeling was that the activities of the Jews must be restricted. Jews were bad because "they killed Christ," they amassed fortunes, they exploited other people. If one hated them other than for these reasons, then one is anti-Semitic. But a certain level of anti-Semitism was generally acceptable. A prominent man of Hungarian history once said, "anti-Semitism is hating the Jews more than necessary." Until the mid-forties, Hungarian anti-Semitism retained an almost polite quality.[9]

In Hungarian cities and towns the population was largely Catholic, with a sizable minority Protestant, and a very small percentage Jewish (about 445,000 people or about five percent, around 1930). Half lived in Budapest where they made up about twenty percent of the population. The rest were dispersed. There were twenty-four communities with about one thousand Jews each and one hundred eighty with fewer than a thousand Jews. Intermarriage and baptism rates were quite high. In 1938 there were 35,000 baptized Jews. That fact coupled with a continuing emigration as a result of Hungary's anti-Semitic policies reduced the size of the Jewish population in Hungary to about 350,000 in 1949.

People were generally cooperative and friendly toward each other with no particular hatred, that is until the Hungarian government officially adopted anti-Semitism. This was highly encouraged by neighboring Germany. During the war there were many Hungarians who sympathized with Nazism although there were others who were against the regime. With a loss of territory in World War I and an abortive Communist dictatorship of Bela Kun, resentments on the part of non-Jews spread.[10] Miklos Horthy came to power and with him pogroms raged in Hungary, especially in the provinces. Anti-Semitism spread quickly especially among youths, many of them turning against their Jewish classmates. Later these youths joined the Hungarian Arrow Cross, and in many cases killed their former friends for the cause of Nazism.[11]

In 1939, shortly after the Nazi Anschluss, there was little cultural activity allowed for Jews in German and Austrian cities. Many of the Viennese musicians were Jewish. Some of them, as well as those who were against the Nazi regime, had escaped to other Western as well as East European countries. Some were fortunate enough to go to America via England.

From 1939-1942 there were no visible signs of the German Nazi regime in Hungary. As a result there was an influx of Jewish musicians into Budapest. The musical and cultural life of Hungary was very much alive in the 1920's and 1930's. The city on the Danube had fashioned itself into a sophisticated urban center. The two banks of the Danube, Buda and Pest, had merged fifty years earlier and for some time had already given Vienna a cultural rival. In fact, Budapest was often called the Paris of the Balkans or Paris of the East. In spite of simmering anti-Semitic feelings, the Starker family lived for a long time in relative security.[12]

For several years, Starker and his friends had a concert series in private homes, five or six concerts each year. In many of these concerts, Starker performed with pianist György Sebök. They performed most of the cello-piano repertoire together. But the time came when Starker found that he was cut off from performing in the community because of his being a "foreigner" and a Jew. The Hungarian Nazi government passed a ruling that only one person in a concert of eight musicians could be Jewish. That prevented many concerts from happening since so many musicians were Jewish. So Starker devised a plan. He invited his colleagues to come and play the Mendelssohn *Octet*. Starker then played the rest of the concert. Another time the musicians played the Beethoven *Septet*. Then a blind Jewish pianist played the rest of the concert. They also performed with piano the Brahms *Double Concerto*, Beethoven *Triple Concerto*, and Hindemith *Cello Concerto*, and other pieces.[13] Each time, the place was filled with people who wanted to hear the concert. Finally the police discovered their trick and put a stop to it.

Those were the years when the Germans were not yet controlling everything. In 1941 Hungary was still a rather safe haven. But from then on, the Hungarian Nazi party dominated the political scene more and more. They increasingly passed laws bringing about restrictions, "tightening the screws," with regard to foreigners and Jews. In 1941 the Hungarian Nazis made a move to get rid of all foreigners, most of whom happened to be Jews. Friends of the Starker family learned of this expatriation policy toward those who came from other lands. Because of their help, the Starker family was spared. But the Starkers were among the few. These friends sent a car for the Starker family to take them to the mountains. There in a mountain hut they hid for about six weeks.

By that time, thousands of people had been taken out of their homes and shot. Any kind of resistance received swift retribution. If a Nazi official learned that a family was either Jewish or foreign or even heard rumor of someone resisting their authority, several Nazi soldiers came to the person's house before dawn, banging on the front door with the butts of their rifles, giving the entire family ten minutes to pack their belongings. They were summarily dispatched to the woods where they were forced to dig their own grave and then shot. If someone was found possessing a gun, he was shot on the spot.[14] An entire part of the extended Starker family was butchered at this time. An aunt of Starker's in Ukraine was shot and left for dead, but somehow she survived. She walked from there to Budapest, a considerable distance, and lived with the Starker family until the end of the war.

The friends who interfered on behalf of the Starkers were members of a prominent Jewish family. The woman, Amalka Baracs, was a schoolteacher and amateur pianist with whom Starker used to play chamber music.[15] Her mother was the president of the Jewish Women's Organization, and her grandfather was one of the few Jewish members in the Hungarian Parliament.

Once the Starker family learned that the killings had ceased, they returned to their home in Budapest. But they were required to get permission each month from the police to continue living there. Before that, they were required to get permission from the government only once each year. There were many years until 1941 when, for a small fee, they hired a lawyer to register with the police on their behalf. But when Starker was seventeen, his parents selected him to go to the police to register for the family. They thought that since he was only a boy, the police would do him no harm. At the police station the police captain said they had searched everywhere for the Starker family. The captain was so furious, he slapped the boy across the face. This was in 1941, and word was spreading to other countries about the Nazi repression and killings in Hungary. By then thousands of people had been shot. As word spread to other countries, there was pressure from the international community to stop the killing. So the Hungarian government clamped down on this repressive expatriation policy. At the time the government was not entirely Nazi. There were still a few humane people left in the government, and so the killing ceased for a time. Because the atrocities were aimed mainly at foreigners, many of the Hungarian Jews were not so concerned about all of these happenings. From then on, however, the Hungarian Nazis consolidated their power.

Then Hitler decided that the Hungarian government could not be trusted to handle their own Jewish problem, and by April of 1944, the Germans marched into Hungary and took over. Then the real horror stories started. It was ordered that all Jews had to wear the yellow star on an armband. In response, Hungary's Roman Catholic Primate, Cardinal Seredi, requested of the Hungarian government that consideration be given to Jews who had been baptized into the Christian faith. They were given the right to wear a cross next to their yellow star.[16]

In 1943 the Nazis started the labor camps. Jewish males between the ages of fourteen and sixty-five were drafted into labor camps. They had to build roads and bridges and dig trenches at the fighting lines, supervised by the Hungarian soldiers.[17] The laborers were equipped with neither uniforms, boots or helmets or any protective clothing or arms, only a yellow arm band. Many of them were sent to Yugoslavia and the Ukraine including Starker's two older brothers. For some years the Starkers hoped that they had somehow escaped. No one knew for sure. Eventually they had enough data to reconstruct the ugliness. They were very likely forced to dig a mass grave, and then they were gunned down with machine guns. Although it was in Yugoslavia, they were probably killed by Hungarian soldiers. Many Hungarians ended their lives in the concentration camp, Mauthausen. The only worse place was Auschwitz in Poland. Only a few of Starker's schoolmates survived that period of time.

Starker was supposed to go to a labor camp with his friends. Instead he was sent to a detention camp at Csepel-Sziget, an island in the Danube River. He was held there for four months, April through July in 1944. This was a place where not only Jews but Catholics and Protestants as well were held, anyone who was against the Nazi state. As a "foreigner," he was considered an enemy.

On this island there was a Messerschmidt plant where Nazi warplanes were produced. Months before there had been a bombing in part of the camp by American planes. Starker and others were assigned the duty of picking up the unexploded bombs and restoring some of the buildings. The Hungarian Nazis tried to get him out of the detention camp to join the work brigade. Every day the Nazis lined up the men and collected people for work brigades. But each time, the police officer told Starker to step out of the group and sent the other men away. The third or fourth day this happened, Starker said, "I want to go." The officer said, "Are you sure you want to go?" That was not the usual way they spoke to the prisoners. Strong pressure was put on the police company commander because of Starker's musical connections. There was some communication stating that he was protected. Apparently, this officer knew that through the Swedish diplomat there was a move afoot to get Starker a contract to play principal cello with the Göteborg Symphony in Sweden. By then, he had been issued a genuine Swedish passport and was granted Swedish citizenship. He was thereby protected. Besides, the military commander where Starker was detained said, "He is working here at the Messerschmidt plant, so let him stay."

The Messerschmidt plant had been producing planes for the Nazi war effort. After the first American bombing, they could produce only one a day. At the time American soldiers were doing strategic bombing all over Europe. By bombing the Hungarian oil fields, the Americans were trying to inhibit the war efforts of the Germans and Hungarians. On July 31, 1944 the American planes came overhead, carpet bombing the industrial part of Budapest, the oil fields, and the Messerschmidt plant as well as the adobe houses on the island. Starker was on the island when the American bombs hit. There were no basements in the adobe houses on the island, so the prisoners went to the V-shaped trenches outdoors. These trenches were well known during the war. They were used in order to prevent people from being inside a building which might collapse, killing everyone.[18]

Twenty-two people were killed in the bombing. During the explosions in the trenches, people on either side of Starker in the trenches died. From the intense noise of the explosions, one man had a brain injury, and another was permanently deaf. The planes returned, first one, then another, and another. More bombs exploded. Miraculously, Starker survived this episode without even so much as a scratch. His immaculate hearing was fully intact.

A few hours later a car came to the island to pick up Starker. The police were looking for him. Nobody knew why they were looking for Starker. The next day he was set free because he was declared a Swedish citizen. Someone had convinced the police that if anything happened to Starker, there would be a big diplomatic mess with Sweden. That was really an ironic joke because if anyone recognized him, they would know who he really was and arrest him. But at that point Starker was given a Swedish passport and his freedom.

Years later Starker learned a story from a friend about an eighteen-year-old whom Starker referred to as "the great impostor." He went to his uncle who was the head of the Hungarian railroads and asked, "What are you doing, Uncle?" The reply was, "I am making a report of how many trains were destroyed by the American bombs." The boy asked, "Do they have to be bombed in order to be written off?" The uncle looked at him and asked, "What do you mean?" He repeated, "Do they really have to be hit by the American bombs to be written off?" This young punk, according to Starker, suggested to his uncle that he write off a train which was not hit. It happened to be an oil train. They sold it to Switzerland and cleared a huge sum of money. His share was something like $20,000, the equivalent of half a million dollars in modern terms. It reportedly took the young man six months of "reveling with friends and budding actresses" to use up his gain.

In the early days of 1944, the Nazis completely took over the Hungarian government, thereby eliminating one of the last safe havens for Jews in Europe. Already, Jewish communities in neighboring France, Belgium, Holland, and Norway had been systematically wiped out. On the first day of Passover, Hungarian gendarmes had begun their house-by-house rounding up of Jews in Eastern Hungary, moving the people into ghettos. Then from the ghettos all across Hungary, Nazi soldiers systematically moved the Jews by train to Auschwitz.[19]

Raoul Wallenberg, a courageous young Swedish diplomat, arrived in Hungary in July, 1944, to help save the Jews who were destined to die. He was one of only a few heroes to emerge from this squalid chapter of history. Although his epic lasted only about six months, he saved an estimated 100,000 Jews from extermination. He took over the Swedish Red Cross in Budapest and went with Red Cross trucks to rescue people from the "death marches." Captive Jews were forced by Nazi soldiers to walk one hundred and twenty-five miles, sometimes twenty miles a day in severe winter weather, with no protection from the elements. Some died along the way. Others of their fellow prisoners would stop and pick up their bodies from the road, putting them in wagons pulled by their comrades. The "death marches" were instituted by Adolph Eichmann when the trains could no longer be spared to transport the Jews to their deaths.

Wallenberg created Jewish "safe houses" under Swedish protection. These buildings were decorated with the blue and yellow flag of Sweden and were regarded as diplomatic property. He gave them phony, protective Swedish passports, baptismal papers, and personal identification. All of his activities were financed by the Swedes. The eventual intention was that these "Swedish citizens" would eventually be "repatriated" to Sweden. Sweden was a neutral country, and the Hungarians did not want trouble in the international community. Hungary's indecisive leader, Miklos Horthy, bent to the pressure from the King of Sweden and world opinion.[20]

Starker became acquainted with Waldemar Langlet, a man who worked with the Swedish Red Cross in Hungary. He was a professor at the university. His wife was a pianist with whom Starker played Franz Joseph Haydn's *D Major Concerto*. It was with his help that Starker was offered the job as principal cellist with the Göteborg Symphony in Sweden. He told Starker about a train that was supposed to leave for Sweden. Starker and his fiancée, Eva, had their names put on the list of people who were to be on this train. It was his hope to take Eva out of this terribly dangerous situation. They anticipated the arrival of the train for Sweden. But to their great disappointment, the train never left Hungary. Their hopes faded, and they were stuck in Budapest, living through a fearful and dangerous time.

In December of 1944 with the Siege of Budapest, the Russians started to pound away at the city from the distance. Soon the entire city became a battleground while the Russians sought to push the Germans back. This was one of the bloodiest battles, the six-week struggle for control of the capitol. Gradually they closed in on the battered remnants of the Reich. The sky was a fireworks display of long-range artillery fire from the Russian Katyusha rockets. Soviet planes bombed Buda, German Messerschmidts planes bombed the outskirts of Pest, and the American Air Force liberators bombed industrial sites and railway lines. There were daily air raids. The fighting went on for over a month until the Russians were able to push back the Germans. By January of 1945, the city was cut off from the rest of the world.

During this time, Jews no longer dared to venture out. Many were confined to dark, airless, underground holes or cellars. They were rounded up at random, even those wearing the yellow armband. Those not wearing the yellow star, a crime punishable by death, were easily spotted. Their clothes were in rags. Like the others, Starker and his parents wore the same clothing for months. During that time most Jews lived like prisoners, twenty or thirty to a room. Washing either themselves or their clothes was a luxury. Starker's parents survived that difficult period of time in an apartment with false identification papers.

Because of their persecution as Jews and foreigners, a Lutheran pastor, who was a client of Starker's father, suggested that Starker's parents should be baptized into the Lutheran church. They requested that Starker also be baptized. As the situation in Hungary worsened, the pastor thought that by having papers saying that they are Lutherans, they might have a chance at survival in a very dangerous world. Not only that but they might be able to get papers, government documentation, perhaps even passports, perhaps even freedom, a remote, wished-for possibility. The pastor said, "If that would increase your chances at survival, why not?"[21]

The next day Starker went to the home of his fiancée, Eva Uranyi, to ask her parents' permission to marry her. Because she helped Starker and his family and did many fine things for other people, he told her parents, "When this war is over, if I can make my way in life, I should like to marry your daughter." They asked, "How do we know that you mean it?" To this he replied, "Because I am saying it." They required that first of all he should be baptized. So Starker was sprinkled with some holy water and, like his parents, became a Lutheran.

The pastor arranged for special permission so that a Lutheran might marry a Catholic according to a papal encyclical about what to do in such a situation.[22] They did not have to go to the Pope for permission, just fill out some papers. Therefore since Starker was now a Lutheran, he could marry Eva who was a Catholic. In a very brief and simple ceremony in the back of the church with one person as a witness, Starker and Eva were married.

The Secret Police and the Nazi officials were becoming increasingly suspicious of Eva. Daily she was saving the lives of many people. She cared for and fed people in the ghetto, smuggled many of them out, and helped to fabricate documents so that many could get out of the labor camps. She did many heroic deeds. Because the Hungarian Secret Police and the Nazis were after her, she evaded them by going into hiding. Starker was eager for the two of them to escape from this awful mess and leave for Sweden. Some years later, when Starker was concertizing in Israel, he learned that there were those who wanted to name a street after Eva or do something noteworthy to honor her. They knew about her heroic deeds during the war.

During the Siege of Budapest,[23] some went to the school for their district where there was an air raid shelter. There they had water, also some food. Eva's father was a reserve officer in the Hungarian army. There were some men who were not fit to go into the military and were assigned to various districts to watch the air raid shelters. A few hours after the bombing of the Messerschmidt plant, Starker was taken into his unit and was appointed a member of the fourteenth district air protection brigade and the warden for an air raid shelter at one of the schools in Budapest. He was given a brigade armband and looked rather official. His job was to see that people went into the shelter at the school during the bombings. There were about fifteen people, including Starker, who were housed at the school. When the city center was occupied, Starker's father-in-law escaped from the fighting and went to be with his family. Starker was an air raid warden for about a month before the area was overrun by the Russians.

One day a woman came in from across the street crying that her husband had been hit by shrapnel from one of the Katyusha weapons. The Katyusha had fallen into the yard. He was coming up from the shelter to fetch some food for his children when it exploded. Splinters of shrapnel covered half of his body. The Russians were shooting from one side of the street, the Germans on the other. The first aid man, whose job it was to deal with medical emergencies, had run home to his family. There was no one around to help the injured man, and no one wanted to go into the street because of the machine gun fire.

Responding to her state of panic, Starker agreed to help. He picked up the box that had been left by the first aid man and examined its contents. Then he agreed to follow the woman to where her husband lay. She said, "One, two, three, run!" and then dashed to the house across the street. This was followed by the inevitable machine gun fire. Starker followed with the medical kit in his hand. As predicted, his dash was also followed by machine gun fire. Fortunately, neither of them was hit.

"Please, please, doctor, save my husband," said the woman. Suddenly Starker was a doctor. Little did she know he was really a cellist and did not know the first thing about medicine. But he dutifully followed her into the basement where they found her husband all covered with blood. He saw that the man's vital organs had been hit.

"Get some hot water," he ordered imitating what he had seen in the movies. Searching the medical kit Starker found gauze, alcohol, scissors, and such. He washed his hands, and using the pair of scissors he removed the man's clothing. With the alcohol and other disinfectant he cleaned his wounds, then bandaged him to the best of his ability.

Later Starker read that whenever there is shrapnel in the body, one should leave it in to help stop the bleeding. He did this purely by accident, without knowing anything. The next day he ran into a young medical student from Yugoslavia, Harry Breuer. He had gotten some false papers for himself with medical credentials. Thus he was able to avoid being drafted into the military. He worked as a medic during the war instead. As a Yugoslav he spoke Serbian and could communicate with the Russians. Through this friend, Starker was able to learn to speak some Russian.

Late at night the two of them sneaked over to the house of the injured man and examined his wounds. His friend said that what Starker had done was medically correct. At that point he invited Starker to work with him. So after that night the two of them worked for about a month as medics.

Then the two medics, Starker and Breuer, broke into an abandoned pharmacy and stole all of the sulfamid as well as other pharmaceuticals. They took over an abandoned house and made it into a health station for the sick and injured. Breuer knew enough about doctoring to give medication and care for small injuries. For things that were more serious, they called the hospital to come and get the people.

Every day the Russians wanted to kill them. Starker often found a Russian gun at his stomach because he looked as though he could be really a German in disguise. They talked their way out of being killed by telling the soldiers, "Sulfa, sulfa." They had the cure for venereal disease, sulfa drugs. The sulfamid was in little tubes of twenty-four pills to be taken over five day's time. There was no penicillin yet. At that time the only known cure was sulfa drugs. Since many of the Russian soldiers had venereal disease, they were very eager to get the sulfa drugs. When they got the drugs, they offered Starker and Breuer bread, vodka, food, whatever they wanted. In addition, each day Starker and Breuer enjoyed a big meal with the Russian soldiers and got drunk with them on their Russian vodka.

This went well until the medics started running short of the sulfa drugs. Then they discovered that the equivalent of today's alka seltzer looked just the same as the sulfamid. So they started mixing them together. Instead of giving them the whole cure, the Russians were getting a diluted mixture. Whenever the medics gave them the drugs, they were happy and they left. Then they went out and got killed in the fighting or were moved on to another area. There was one really nasty Russian major who was being sent with his soldiers to another area. Starker and Breuer gave him twenty-four of the alka seltzer-like tablets!

As a result of their acquaintance with the Russian soldiers, the two medics received papers from the Russian commander stating that they helped the Russian army, saving lives and doing other heroic deeds. For many years Starker lost track of his fellow medic. Then in 1981 on a concert tour in South America, he and Breuer were reunited in Rio de Janeiro.

There were stories in Budapest similar to that which took place in Amsterdam in The *Diary of Anne Frank*.[24] When Starker was a young boy, he played in a string quartet with a violinist friend, Robert Gerle. This friend lived through the Siege of Budapest hiding in a secret space above the bathroom in a friend's apartment. At the entrance to the dining room, with a typical high ceiling, there was a fifth-century madonna above the doorway. Behind the madonna was the secret space. The only way to get there was by removing the madonna and crawling into the space with a ladder. The apartment owner, Leo Hochner, entertained the officers of the German Werhmacht in the dining room while just a few feet away were twenty-two Jews hiding above the bathroom! Hochner was a wealthy textile factory owner. Perhaps he paid the Germans to keep quiet. Or perhaps the Germans did not know. At any rate, these twenty-two, including Gerle, were spared.

Leo Hochner, a very wealthy man, owned one of the biggest textile factories in Hungary. He was part Jewish, but somehow he got by. Either the Germans did not know, or he paid them off. Sometimes people were implored or bribed to take in the persecuted.

Starker's war experiences, preceded by his being "stateless" in the country of his birth, led him to become very independent and self-sufficient. His attitudes toward music, musicians, critics, and those people around musical life evolved in large part from his wartime experiences. During his lengthy music career, he has been unafraid of anyone because he concluded that nothing worse could possibly happen to him. After all that he went through, his resolve was like steel. No one would ever tell him what to do. No one was ever allowed to help him, and if he believed in something, he could not be influenced otherwise. What he later achieved with his life, he has said, was "only the result of his head and his hands. He had no help, no gifts, no mentors," perhaps with the exception of Fritz Reiner.

Once he got out of that mess, he realized that there must be some reason for him to survive when so many others did not. To him that was the frightening aspect of this whole war experience. He felt there must be some reason for it. Thus he felt that he had a duty to help prevent such horrors from happening in the future. Although not politically active, he always refused to remain silent when seeing an injustice. For him it was almost obsessive. Unfortunately, because of this, he has sometimes alienated others.

His sense of mission was strengthened by war tragedies which decimated his family as well as the musical population in Hungary. "Those of us who stayed alive feel that this is more than just a way of living," says Starker. To him it seemed, most important of all, he had a duty to do something which would benefit others and not just himself. Because he had the good fortune of learning the principles of music from some of the "giants" in the world of music who had a straight line from great masters, he felt that it was his duty to see that this line of influence would continue.

His purpose was never to amass fame or fortune. Nor was he ever interested in having his students play the way he did. It was his aim that they would become aware of the principles that led Starker to what he attained musically.

With the end of the war, Starker had to come to terms with the loss of his two brothers. According to Starker, "The tragedy was that my brothers' lives were not only cut short but they did not lead anywhere. They were unfulfilled."

He was influenced after the war by a book about fatalism, *The Bridge of San Luis Rey* by Thornton Wilder.[25] The story takes place in a Latin American country in a community where there is a suspension bridge that connects two parts of the city over a deep gorge. One day as the people are going home from work crossing from one side to the other, the bridge breaks, and the people on the bridge fall into the gorge and are killed. The book tells about the people who would normally be on the bridge at that time and why they were there, then which people were actually on the bridge at the time of the fatal event. It seemed to Starker to be preordained. For Starker and others who survived the war, they accepted the message which Wilder's book offered: "You'll die when your mission on earth is completed, not before and not after."[26]

Eventually the Russians pushed the Germans back to Austria. Ironically, Hitler "chased" out of Germany a prominent physicist, Albert Einstein. Had Einstein developed his atom bomb in Germany instead of America, Germany might have won the war and changed the tide of history. With the Nazi defeat and the close of the war, Starker's goal was simply to get out of Hungary. Starker's job offer with the Göteborg Symphony was supposedly a bona fide offer. His plan was to go first to Rumania and from there to Sweden. What he did not know was that because of the destruction of the railroad lines, there was no possible way of getting there.

In the cold of winter in January of 1945, the Russians occupied Budapest. The city was destroyed, rubble everywhere, electric power lines down. In contrast to Hungarians, Rumanians were spared much of the destruction as a result of their policy of nonresistance. The Americans did not do much bombing in Rumania because of the oil fields. So Rumanians experienced peace sooner than their Hungarian counterparts.

Shortly after the Nazi defeat, Starker and Eva, with a couple of suitcases in hand and the Piatellini cello in a soft bag, got on one of the first freight trains heading for Rumania. The border crossing in those days was quite difficult, particularly since they had no Hungarian passports, only Starker's Swedish passport. They depended on the goodwill of the Russian, Hungarian, and Rumanian soldiers to let them through. To win them over, he played Viennese waltzes and Hungarian dances for the soldiers. This went on all night.

They were going to an area of Rumania that before World War I was part of Hungary where many people spoke Hungarian. Glad to leave behind them the turmoil in Hungary, they boarded a freight car with about fifty people crowded together. That particular freight car had no top since the train had been bombed. So to protect themselves from the bitter February cold, they built a fire on the train. They gleaned warmth from the fire as best they could.

In one area of the countryside when the train was going very slowly, Russian soldiers with machine guns jumped onto the train. The soldiers attacked the passengers and stole everything from them. They had no interest in the cello but took everything else. Somehow they missed a little fourteen karat gold chain, about fifteen grams that Starker had hidden away in the seam of his pocket. He also had a rather large piece of Hungarian currency printed by the Hungarian Nazi government. Once the Russians took over Hungary, it was worth nothing. In Rumania, however, no one knew that, and Starker was able to sell his worthless Hungarian money. That money allowed them a trip to Temesvar, Rumania, and a few days of survival. When he sold the gold chain, they were able to survive a few weeks. Then he started earning some money playing concerts, first in private homes. That was the beginning of his new career after the war.

Getting off the train, they went up to a house asking for directions. Starker wanted to locate a friend, Gabriel Banat, a violinist who had been a fellow student with Starker at the Franz Liszt Academy. As chance would have it, Banat and his parents just happened to be renting an apartment from the owners of this building. Unfortunately the Banats were temporarily in Bucharest. Starker, however, met the owners of the building, Andrew and Csupi Naschitz, and they immediately became fast friends. Just ten minutes after they met, Starker found himself in the bathtub in the Naschitz home, relishing a hot bath the likes of which he had not had in months and months! With these newfound friends, Eva and Starker ate heartily and enjoyed rest and recuperation. They were able to use the Banats' apartment for a few months. Andrew and Csupi Naschitz arranged for Starker to meet people and to play several house concerts. They were instrumental in "launching Starker's life" after the war. This was the start of a lifelong friendship.[27]

In July of 1945, Starker returned to Budapest for a hernia operation. Besides, he wanted to see his parents. Conditions immediately after the war were not ideal, to say the least. By modern standards, the hospital was rudimentary at best. Food was still rather scarce. During his stay in the hospital, he became seriously ill with pneumonia and nearly died. Lacking good nourishment for so many months, his health was precarious.

While he was in the hospital he received a message inviting him to visit the new directors of the Budapest Opera House. A group of people got together after the war for the purpose of rebuilding the partially destroyed opera house and once again opening a season of opera performances in Budapest. Once he left the hospital, Starker visited the opera house. He was told by the directors that he must help to restore Hungarian musical life and become principal cellist of the Budapest Opera. Although he did not tell them, he had no intention of doing so. In fact he was looking for the first opportunity to get out of Hungary!

He remembered that as a twelve-year-old boy, he had been told that he was "stateless," a foreigner in the country of his birth. At the age of seventeen he had to flee from home in order to escape deportation from the country of his birth. After four years of relentless persecution as a Jew, as a foreigner, as an enemy of the state where for years he had been blacklisted, he was then told that it was his duty to help restore the culture to the country of his birth! In spite of it all, Starker accepted the position and signed the contract, and at the age of twenty-one became the principal cellist of the Budapest Opera House as well as the Budapest Philharmonic. These were one and the same orchestra. The agreement was reached after he was promised the highest salary, the same as that of the principal conductor.

But Starker informed the opera director that he must have a passport in order to go back to Rumania and get his cello. This he was granted. Within three days he received one of the very first new passports issued after the war. With that passport he became officially Hungarian for the first time in his life! Because he could speak a little Russian, he was able to go with the Russian soldiers by truck to Rumania.[28] And so for half a year from September of 1945 until the end of February of 1946, he played principal cello with the Budapest Opera House and the Budapest Philharmonic.

In the fall of 1945, when Starker returned to Rumania for concerts, he met Georges Enescu (1881-1955). Because of his experiences with Enescu, Starker came to respect him highly and considered him the greatest musician of the twentieth century. Enescu was, in Starker's words, "an incredible violinist, a superb pianist, a very effective conductor, and an excellent composer." He is commonly regarded in his country as Rumania's greatest and most versatile musician.

Says Starker, "I was introduced to him, and he invited me to come to his house. We played the Brahms *E Minor Sonata*. He told me how he remembered hearing Brahms play the work. After playing it, Enescu started playing the *F Major Sonata*, and I joined him. Later he said to me, 'The last time I played that was twenty years ago with Casals.' Enescu played it entirely from memory. He had a legendary memory, a memory like Mozart's." Two days later Enescu performed on piano the Brahms *A Major Sonata* with violinist Gabriel Banat. Then he played a Beethoven sonata himself on the violin as well as one of his own works on the piano. Later he performed cello-piano music with Starker. When Enescu started the Brahms *E Minor Sonata*, it was to Starker "one of the most glorious and unforgettable musical experiences of my life... unbelievable sound, such phrasing, the most beautiful piano playing such as one dreams about a whole lifetime."

Enescu invited Starker to come to his house in Bucharest the next day. He was rehearsing three Beethoven violin sonatas that he and a pianist were to perform the following day. He invited a few friends to come and listen. In the audience of about sixteen people were several elegantly dressed ladies. They spoke only French that evening since they considered Rumanian not elegant enough. There was a throne chair reserved for Enescu's wife, the princess, who made her entrance once the music was playing. The concert started with Beethoven's *Spring Sonata*.

Since Enescu never had time to practice the violin, the first few minutes were excruciatingly painful for the listeners. His fingers were not yet working, and he played out of tune, scratchy sounds, and such. But then within a few minutes it was "the most beautiful violin playing Starker had ever heard." It was one of the rare occasions that brought tears to Starker's eyes. The evening was unforgettable for Starker in another way. During the concert there commenced a great snowstorm accentuated by an earthquake. The entire city of Bucharest was immobilized.

Then shortly thereafter, Enescu conducted a concert with the Bucharest Symphony featuring a guest pianist performing Mozart's *D Minor Piano Concerto*. Because of the snowstorm the pianist was not able to get to Bucharest. György Sebök just happened to be in town and performed the concerto with the orchestra instead. The concerto was followed by the Brahms *First Symphony*. Because of the war, the orchestra was basically a low class ensemble. But with Enescu's direction, according to Starker, they sounded like this was the world's greatest orchestra. It was wonderful music making on the part of everyone involved. All of these things, playing violin and piano, as well as conducting, Enescu did at the highest possible level.

In 1947 the director of the Conservatory of Music in Limoges, France, told Starker a story about Enescu. Once during World War I, a friend of the Conservatory director met Enescu and showed him a piano sonata which he had written. Enescu looked through the entire sonata and said to the young composer, "Very nice, very nice. Just keep on working." A year later he learned that this young composer was injured during the war and was in the hospital. Enescu arranged to bring a piano into the hospital room and played for him the sonata that he had merely looked at the year before. He played the entire piece without music.

From September of 1945 until February of 1946 Starker and Victor Aitay were performing together with the Budapest Opera Orchestra and Philharmonic as concertmaster and principal cellist. At that time, a doctor friend went to Vienna on business and got a contract for the Aitay Quartet and Starker to play concerts for the soldiers of the American Special Forces in Vienna. The doctor's wife was one of those who survived the Siege of Budapest hidden in the secret space in Leo Hochner's apartment. Victor Aitay was eager to go to Vienna. Through relatives in America, he had connections to immigrate from Austria to the United States. Starker just wanted to get out of Hungary.

With his Hungarian passport, Starker expected that it would take about six weeks to get a visa. If he did not get his passport renewed, there was no way to travel, no way to cross borders. Without being able to travel, he could not concertize and therefore could not make a living. For several years after the war's end, getting official documents was of utmost importance to him.

The border between Hungary and Austria was Russian occupied, and it was impossible to get permission to cross the border. But with some quick talking, Starker and the Aitay Quartet members managed to slip through the border by train. At the time Vienna was under occupation by four powers: French, Russian, British and American.

Once they got to Vienna, they went to the American Special Forces. The officer who looked at Starker's documents said, "You had better forget about it. It would be better if you would just disappear. The American woman major in charge of the Special Forces Entertainment Section who signed the paper had an affair with a Nazi official and was dishonorably discharged. They may accuse you of being somehow involved." From that moment on, they were "out in the cold," so to say.

They stayed at the Hungarian Institute in Vienna for six months, from March until September of 1946, with little or no money in their pockets. Fortunately, they did not have to pay to stay there. At that time there was hardly anything to eat in Vienna. The Viennese people were receiving government coupons for basic necessities. Every month one of the Allied powers supplied the city with food. But what they did supply was sometimes only enough for about three days. At one time the food supplied the city was Russian salt herring. All of the biggest restaurants in town were offering only salt herring on their menus. Another month salad greens were supplied. Everywhere people were eating salads. They were even cooking their salad greens. When it came time for the Americans to supply the city with food, they gave the people Canadian bacon. It was so unusual, actually unheard of, and so tasty that the whole supply which should have lasted a month was used up in only a few days.

The string quartet members were sometimes able to receive food from their parents in Hungary via the Russians. Sometimes the food they sent was stolen en route. One time a friend brought a whole suitcase full of food from home. They needed to survive only one day at a time.

At the time Starker's cello was not sounding right. This instrument was the Piatellini cello that he had borrowed from wealthy friends in Budapest about ten years earlier. He did not know about adjusting the sound post, so he sent the cello back to the family. With about $80 worth of flour, sugar and fat smuggled out of Hungary, he bought a cello made in 1816 by a Viennese maker, Stoss.

One occasion in Vienna, Starker, together with a clarinetist, French composer Olivier Messiaen and Victor Aitay, gave a performance of Messiaen's *Quartet for the End of Time*. This was the first performance of this piece outside of France after the war. It is a stunning work, written while Messiaen was a prisoner in a French concentration camp, envisioning the end of life on this earth as we know it. It must have been an apt reflection of how those who experienced the Second World War perceived their era.

Eventually they gave several performances. Universal Publishers gave them sponsorship for recitals. Also Starker gave a recital sponsored by the Bösendorfer family, makers of the Bösendorfer pianos. He was accompanied in that recital by a pianist named Walfisch, an

American army major. For the reception following the concert, people ate Russian salt herring on little sandwiches. Eventually they performed for the soldiers of the American Special Services. Through the Bösendorfers, they made contacts for other concerts.

Conversations with Victor Aitay

Victor Aitay, concertmaster of the Chicago Symphony since 1955, and great friend of Janos Starker says, "I have known Janos since age six. We were students together at the Franz Liszt Academy in Budapest. Our parents used to wait for us in the lobby of the school during our lessons, rehearsals and concerts. Because they spent so much time together, they became very good friends. Janos was considered by everyone, as a seven, eight, and nine-year-old, a wunderkind who played magnificent cello and with the most natural equipment, mentally and physically. Everyone knew his name from childhood on. As we know now, he is considered by many to be the world's greatest cellist.

"We spent many years studying and playing chamber music together. One time, as very young children, we were performing a string quartet concert, and we got irretrievably lost. It was potentially very embarrassing. One of us figured that the only possible way out of this predicament was to knock the music over. He kicked the stand so that it fell onto the ground. Music was scattered all over the floor. We proceeded to pick up the music, and with that we started the piece all over again. This time things went well. The audience was happy, and so were we!"

Aitay was in the audience when Janos, as a fifteen-year-old, played the Kodály *Solo Sonata* at the Franz Liszt Academy. "It was absolutely unbelievable! Everyone's eyes were just popping! They could not believe it! His performance of this fantastic piece was astounding! I have one of the original recordings of him playing this piece. At the time he was moving fairly often, and he said, 'Here, you keep this. If I give it to you, then I will know where it is, and it will not get lost.'"

"Another time he played the Dvorák *Concerto*, and it was fantastic! He had only a few hours' notice to fill in for another student playing the concerto. Obviously he was well prepared.

"We were blessed in Budapest by having as faculty members at the Franz Liszt Academy several great composers including Bartók, Kodály, Dohnányi, and Weiner, a rare combination of talents. Leo Weiner was the mentor of musical knowledge for all of us. We all loved him and spent many an afternoon with him. We learned practically everything from him. All of the musicians who came out of this environment in Budapest were successful, mainly because they all went through Leo Weiner classes. In each class there were at least ten to fifteen listeners. A few people performed sonatas, trios, and quartets for the class. Listening to his corrections and to his piano demonstrations, the few bars that he showed were absolutely heavenly, the most wonderful music making.

"At that time Kodály and Bartók were considered very modern composers. People then could not understand Bartók's music. I remember hearing Szigeti play a Bartók piece, and half the audience walked out. The sounds were so new and unusual. Today Bartók's name is a household word, but then his music was far ahead of his time. During his life he was practically starving. If it were not for Reiner, Szigeti, and a few other colleagues who tried to get money from the Kousevitsky Foundation for commissions, he would probably never have written his *Concerto for Orchestra.* It was not until after his death that he was fully recognized."

Starker once said that when he was a little boy playing quartets with Aitay and his brothers, the group decided to play a Bartók quartet. After a while, he threw the music on the ground and said, "I am not going to play that junk!" Later Starker came to recognize Bartók as a composer of great merit and went on to commission him to write new works for the cello. Kodály's music was more moderate and more understandable at that time. Unlike Bartók, who was fifty years ahead of his time, Kodály was perhaps only twenty years ahead, according to Starker. That made him more accessible.

"After the war," says Aitay, "Janos was the youngest principal cellist in the history of the Budapest Opera Company. At the same time I was the concertmaster. But neither of us was very proud of our achievement. At that time I had a string quartet, the Aitay Quartet, and we received an invitation to play quartet concerts as well as recitals for the Vienna Radio. Getting permission to leave the country then was very difficult, but with that invitation we managed to get visas for Austria. We were looking for any opportunity to leave Hungary. Janos and I both asked for a leave of absence from the Budapest Opera, knowing that we would probably never return. We were on the very first train from Budapest to Vienna, six of us including our wives.

"We went through great difficulties in getting to Vienna. The conditions in the city were really horrible. We were practically starving. Sometimes in Vienna we had an afternoon concert, then an evening concert. In between there was absolutely nothing to eat. So our wives went to the lady who was scrubbing the floors, asking for some bread which would tide us over until the next concert.

"Those were terribly difficult times in Vienna! No one had food, and, in fact, food tickets were rationed. Across the street from where we lived was a restaurant, really an awful place. They offered us gemüse, vegetables, the only food available. The concerts we played were for the American soldiers who helped to tide us over. For our performances we received not money but either food or cigarettes. Housing at the Hungarian Institute was free, just a couple of rooms. We were fortunate to not have to pay for a place to live. In spite of the severe hardships, somehow we always felt that things would get better, so we had the greatest of times together!

"In Vienna we performed the *Quartet for the End of Time* with the composer Oliver Messiaen playing the piano. That was the first time the piece had been performed outside of France. The man who was the head of the publishing company, Universal Editions, organized these concerts. We also played piano quartets with an American pianist who had a Hungarian background. Not knowing that he understood Hungarian, we said among ourselves, I hope he will give us some cigarettes. We were just starving for a cigarette at that time. Naturally he understood, but we did not know that. To our great pleasure, he shared his cigarettes with us.

"After Vienna, we went to Badgastein where we met my wife's cousin and fellow Hungarian, George Lang. We found a little hotel, Hotel Hindenburg, a very old hotel, just the right place for us. In Badgastein we had endless hours to get to know each other and had a wonderful time together.

"From there we went to Salzburg and performed a number of concerts in and around Salzburg as well as Vienna. In Salzburg we admired the Österreichische Hof, a grand hotel where at the time we could not afford even a cup of coffee. I promised myself then that someday we would stay there. Since then, I have been in Salzburg many times, and I always stay in that wonderful hotel.

"Altogether we spent several months in Austria. It was a time of joy and anticipation since my wife and I had applied for visas for the United States. George Lang and my wife and I came to the United States together. In New York George became a highly successful restaurateur. With him and his family we have formed a lifelong and wonderful friendship. When we left for the United States, Janos and Eva went to France. From there he received an invitation from Dorati to play with the Dallas Symphony in Texas. My wife had relatives in the United States. Because of them we were able to get to the United States sooner than Janos.

VICTOR AITAY, LONGTIME CONCERTMASTER OF THE CHICAGO SYMPHONY, AND STARKER'S FRIEND AND COLLEAGUE SINCE CHILDHOOD DAYS IN BUDAPEST. THEY SPENT MANY YEARS PERFORMING TOGETHER.

"As a point of interest," says Aitay, "Dorati had a most unusual talent. He could draw simultaneously two completely different pictures with his two hands independent of each other.

"Janos came about a year and a half later. That was the only time out of many years that we were not together playing in the same orchestra. We were waiting for Janos in New York when he arrived in this country, saying that we were already natives here. The first things that caught his eye were the beautiful cars on Broadway, and, of course, he wanted one. There was nothing like it in Hungary. Hungary was such a poor country, and after the war it was in a shambles.

"After a year we both managed to get positions with the Metropolitan Opera Company as concertmaster and principal cellist. We spent some wonderful years there together, Janos four years and myself five. Then Reiner invited Janos to come with him to the Chicago Symphony where he stayed for five years. After a year I joined him in the Chicago Symphony as concertmaster. Janos then started his solo career, accepted the position at Indiana University, and was doing more and more recording.

"Just recently we had a reunion celebrating our forty years in the United States. For the event, we rented a yacht in New York City, invited about forty guests, and went round and round the Statue of Liberty all night. What a celebration that was!"

∿∿∿

Following Starker's recital in April, 1946 in Vienna, a reviewer wrote that Starker played like a sleepwalker, completely detached. He played immaculately, never a mistake, never faltering, never out of tune, but the music just did not make any sense. He could not sleep for days after that. There had been an eighteen-month stretch of time when he did not play the cello. Terrible things had happened during the war. He faced death many times. Emotional traumas too horrible to speak about had left their impact.

Then he realized that he had to take some time off. For about seven months, during which time he was in Vienna, also Paris, he went through a very bad stretch of time when he just could not play. He did not trust himself to perform and did not know what he was doing. Besides recovering from the traumas of the war, he had to make the transition from being a child prodigy to being a professional. No longer did he have family to help and support him. Now he was on his own with a wife to care for. In dealing with his inner turmoil, he did not go to a psychiatrist or start using drugs. But he smoked a great deal as he had before, and he struggled to work through his problems on his own. Then the healing process from the war's effects began.

Through all of this he hearkened back to one of his most important experiences as a boy in Hungary, an evening that he spent playing chamber music with a violin teacher, Dezsö Rados. Now Starker pondered his comments about circles and their relationship with body movements. This information began to come home to him as he developed his own theories. With this began his lifelong search for answers as to how and why one moves physically in order to effectively play an instrument. This, he feels, is of vital importance to anyone who wants to become a professional. Developing consistency and a logical, economical use of the body has become essential to his cello playing.

With Starker there is a great deal of difference between dilettantism and professionalism. Dilettantes are inconsistent although they are able at times to produce greater music than professionals, other times not. As a professional, Starker knew that he had a responsibility to produce on a consistently high level regardless of how he felt or what the circumstance might be. If a player does not know what he is doing, then he will be affected by the prevailing conditions. A professional must rise above these. His goal is to present music in a context of simplicity, purity and balance unencumbered by gyrations or effects which detract from the music. He knows that the focus belongs on the music, not on the performer.

He started developing his concepts and testing his ideas on his close friend and colleague, George Bekefi, who also had great difficulty in playing after the war. Bekefi was also a Hungarian and former student at the Franz Liszt Academy although several years later than Starker. When Bekefi came to the Academy in 1941, his studies were interrupted. He was drafted into the service with the outbreak of the war. Because of a late start on the cello, coupled with a two-year interruption by the war, he had to start over as a beginner. After the war Bekefi left Hungary and spent some time in Paris where he and Starker met again. He was literally crying from nervousness and lack of confidence, and thus was unable to play. Starker began teaching his friend how to play again from the very beginning stages, working with him a couple of times each week. Because of their work together, Starker devised a set of exercises that eventually became the *Organized Method of String Playing*, (*OMSP*), a method which, technically speaking, covers the geography of the cello fingerboard.

After about six months Bekefi played a recital, and with tears in his eyes he said to Starker, "Finally I can play." Shortly after that he left for Brazil and became the principal cellist with the Sao Paolo Orchestra. In Brazil he wrote out the exercises in detail that Starker had given him in Paris. Later he returned to the United Stated to teach at the Cleveland Summer Institute. He spent one summer in Bloomington and then joined the Chicago Symphony where Starker was principal cellist. Later he built himself a house in Colorado but died very suddenly from hepatitis.

Since then, Starker has treated Bekefi's daughter and grandchildren like his own with the proceeds from the book going to his daughter. For months, even years thereafter, Starker verbalized his analyses of how one does things on the instrument and why. He would tell amateurs and music-lovers his analyses. If they looked at him "with foggy eyes," then he knew he must find other ways of explaining things. If they understood, then he knew it could be understood by professionals or aspiring professionals.

Starker was eight years old when he heard fourteen-year-old Yehudi Menuhin in a violin recital in Budapest, and he played brilliantly! But several years later this famous former violin prodigy and foremost instrumental star was experiencing serious performance problems. Then in 1946 when he was in Vienna he heard Menuhin in a recital. His vibrato was indiscriminate, he barely managed to arrive at the necessary destinations with his left hand, and a loud, irregular breathing penetrated the entire concert hall. Starker left at the intermission on the verge of nausea. He was well aware of the pressures of international concertizing, reluctantly accepting the fact of human frailty, justifying an "off night." Then

GEORGE BEKEFI, THE CELLIST FOR WHOM STARKER DEVELOPED HIS ORGANIZED METHOD OF STRING PLAYING. AFTER THE WAR YEARS, BEKEFI STARTED LEARNING THE CELLO AS THOUGH A BEGINNER. FOR HIM STARKER DEVISED A SERIES OF EXERCISES THAT BEKEFI LATER WROTE DOWN.

a series of sleepless nights forced on him the realization that this occurrence was more than just an "off night." He had nightmarish visions of the legendary peasant eye surgeon who, when told of the dangers involved in his activities, thereafter was never able to repeat his feats. Then he reflected on the historically low percentage of child prodigies who became mature concert artists. He was compelled to find out what governs the satisfactory mental and physical functioning of a performing artist when on stage.

Apparently, Menuhin dropped out of the concert circuit at age nineteen, taking two years off to study violin technique. Formerly a child prodigy who seemed able to play effortlessly, he had never focused on the essential mechanics of proper fingering and bowing. He found it difficult to progress beyond his youthful approach to playing. "At the risk of losing all the golden eggs of his future, he had to find out what made the goose lay those golden eggs." [29]

Around 1961 Starker heard Menuhin play the Bartók *Violin Concerto* in Berlin, and at that time he was playing very well. But before the concert, the conductor, Ferenc Fricsay, approached Starker and asked, "Couldn't you help him?" Starker replied, "If he should come to me and ask some questions, I would be happy to help him, and I could probably help him cure his playing problems."

For Starker, out of this grew questions about himself being a former child prodigy. He was trying to sort out the cause of his problem, that of playing like a sleepwalker. It occurred to him that child prodigies just get up one day and play, like a bird sings, not knowing how or why. Nature just gave them this extraordinary ability. But suppose one day they should start asking questions about the way they do things and what makes them successful at playing an instrument?

Through some horror-laden months of ineffective public experimentation followed by long stretches of self-imposed inactivity, he became aware that through conscious understanding of the elements of producing sounds on an instrument can one become a professional, reasonably independent of the constant hazards. Only through conscious understanding can one control the "skill" part of producing art, which distinguishes the gifted dilettante from the master professional. This realization induced Starker to search for the basic problems. These are problems that he discovered are identical for all musicians and inherent in all music making irrespective of subjective feelings and judgments. When his search reached the place where the problems were defined, solutions presented themselves in his mind, explaining and justifying different approaches. He says, "Invariably, advantages and disadvantages appeared that were humbling to those whose 'religious fervor' for a chosen approach deterred all contradictions, while for those with vastly different abilities, answers were provided." His emphasis was focused on professionalism.

Years later Starker and Menuhin performed together the Brahms *Double Concerto* with Antal Dorati in London. Menuhin was not comfortable using the frog half of the bow. When they rehearsed at Menuhin's house, Menuhin asked if they couldn't play the opening of the third movement in the tip half of the bow. "The Brahms *Double Concerto*," Starker replied, "lends itself to different views. So, you play it your way, and I'll play it mine. Maybe the mixture will be appreciated." Although Starker has always considered Menuhin an enormous talent, one of the giants in the history of music, that performance was one of the more painful evenings of his life.

After that performance Menuhin asked if he would record the piece with him and the Philadelphia Orchestra. Starker replied that he had recorded the piece recently, and the time limit was not yet up. (When recording a work under contract, one is not allowed to rerecord the same work in less than five years.)

In October of 1946 Starker managed to get a visa to go to Switzerland for the Geneva Cello Competition. Anyone paying the fee of ten Swiss francs could enroll in the competition and thereby get a Swiss visa. He thought that was the only way he could get out of the Soviet controlled territories in the East and move to more civilized countries further west. The problem was how to get through the American, French, and Russian zones! They needed permission from all of the occupying powers. Getting it was a harrowing experience! Somehow he and Eva got as far as Badgastein in Austria through the first zone and from there to Geneva.

In Geneva he competed in the cello division, getting into the finals and winning a bronze medal, the sixth prize, even though he did not feel like playing. Eva Janzer won third prize. The second prize went to Antonio Janigro, a terrific cellist, in Starker's opinion. The first prize, one thousand Swiss francs, went to an unknown cellist, Raimonde Verrandeau, a woman who played well but was never heard from again. One reward for the first prize winner was recording the Schumann *Cello Concerto* with orchestra. However, she was unable to do it. Apparently there were manipulators, as there often are in competitions, who decide in advance who the winners will be. Starker felt that Janigro should have been the first prize winner, not himself because just following the war he was not playing well.

Many years later, in the fall of 1997, Starker was in Geneva for a concert as well as a seminar for cello students. The day after the concert he was invited to go to the Geneva Radio Station for an interview. During the interview, the interviewer was telling him of things going on in the Swiss Romand area, telling him also about his favorite trio recording. Then he said he had a surprise for Starker and the radio audience. Suddenly Starker heard himself playing in the middle of the first movement of Haydn's *D Major Concerto* with piano accompaniment. He heard himself playing a stunning cadenza. Then it occurred to him. In 1946 when he played in the Geneva Competition, they recorded the various entries. The performances were recorded at that time on wax discs. Before the interview, they had found this old recording in the library and managed to clean up a five-minute segment of the performance for the radio broadcast. What a pleasant surprise!

Badgastein, Austria — Conversations with George Lang

"The very first time Janos and I met was after a concert in the Omike Concert Hall in Budapest where he performed the Dvorák *Concerto*. Omike Hall was a place where many Jewish artists performed during the war years when the authorities did not allow them to perform in the standard concert halls. At the time, I was a student of Professor Dezsö Rados, one of the foremost violin professors of Hungary.

"The intelligentsia of Hungary had all heard of Janos. They already considered him a musician and artist who was destined to become one of the great ones. Hungary is a small country, population perhaps ten million, surrounded by competitive nations and ethnic groups which are seriously handicapped by poverty and other disadvantages. Whenever someone in this small country achieved excellence in any field, be it music, mathematics, science, etc., he was and still is idolized by all. Hungarians want to tell the world, 'See, here is another Hungarian who is a trailblazer and better than you guys! You may have hundreds of millions of people, gold mines, etc. But we have Starker!' Everyone had known about him since his early teens.

"Of course, I was stunned by his playing, not only by his technical abilities. For someone who was studying a stringed instrument as I was, it was a revelation that the instrument could be played like that! It was generally known that the cello was a very difficult instrument to play in tune and with a good sound. For me Starker's cello playing was a miracle! I was truly mesmerized by his music making, way beyond mere technique.

"We were both nineteen when a mutual friend introduced me to Starker following his performance. Our meeting was casual at the time. We did not have any serious discussions or period of getting to know each other, but I was taken with him, aside and beyond his place as an extraordinary instrumentalist and musician. That was the only time I met him before the horrors of 1944.

"Once Hungary was liberated in 1945 by our so-called 'Russian friends,' I made my plans to escape to the West. I was hoping to join my cousin Eva, who had been liberated from Auschwitz, and her husband, Victor Aitay, who was invited to Vienna to play a concert. Eventually I was able to get through a minefield into Austria. Making my way to Badgastein, a small Austrian resort town, I contacted the Collegium Hungaricum in Vienna, where Victor and members of the Aitay Quartet were staying. A few days later, Victor called me back to say that not only were they going to join me, but that Janos Starker, the celebrated cellist (who had just given a command performance in Vienna) and his wife, Baba (Eva), were joining us as well. The Starkers turned out to be an important part of our Hungarian contingent in Austria. Baba was a young woman of wit and refreshing unpredictability, and Janos was already the pride of Hungary. At the time we were all 'trying to escape the cement shoes of reality.'

"There the two of us had an ideal time to get to know each other well, and within a very brief time we developed a deep and lasting friendship. Besides playing amusing but pointless games to stimulate our minds, such as who can come up with the most useless invention, we had a nonstop talkfest. Luxuriating in sunken marble tubs in the thermal baths, which had attracted kings and peasants to this small town since the Middle Ages, our conversations included many abstract yet important issues, such as spiritual aspects as they relate to sound perceptions. We even created new endings to well-known books. For about four months, we had very little to do in Badgastein. During that time, we threw around so many ideas that in the next half-century, reading learned essays whenever we met again, we would smugly say, 'Oh, we already solved that question in Badgastein!'

"It was an ideal state of limbo between worlds, old and new, between lives before and after. In the meantime, Eva, Victor, and I stayed in close contact with HIAS, a Jewish refugee organization. Eventually we left on the very first refugee ship from the German port of Bremerhaven and arrived in the United States on July 15, 1946. Janos and Baba joined us a year and a half later.

"These sixty years our friendship has grown and burgeoned. I recall reading of two Indians who looked into each other's souls for two weeks without saying a word while their relationship mysteriously deepened. Ours is not like that! Quite the opposite! It is very vocal, argumentative, and fun. Ever since our meeting in Austria, we still get together each year for a few days in some part of the world, such as a small remote island in the Caribbean, a spa in Florida, or a place in Cape Cod, to argue, laugh, grouch, banter, wisecrack, and just let our brains play hopscotch. It's just the two of us. Sometimes we meet at a place where Janos has a concert or someplace in the world where I have something to do. During that time we let go of all of our responsibilities, and the nonstop debate is on! We have philosophical discussions ranging from which books we definitely should not read, discussing someone whose life has crossed ours, and then sorting out how we see the next decade of our lives.

"We have the opposite of an unqualified friendship since we do not agree on many important issues. But ours is an extraordinary comradeship. I believe friendship requires almost as much talent as playing an instrument well, and Janos is as good at friendship as he is on the cello. In a way, I took the place of his brothers who died in the labor camp, and he became the brother I never had."

The A B Cs of Janos Starker According to George Lang:

Art — "To say that Janos Starker is a cellist is like saying that Michelangelo is a stonecutter. The Good Lord on occasion takes a few pounds of minerals, amino acids, and other exciting ingredients, and turns them into human beings of exceptional qualities. To me, the process of creating a great performer, such as Janos, is most mysterious."

Appropriate — "This is one of the key characteristics of Janos. This includes his reactions to things, the way he behaves, the way he dresses, the way he relates to people above him, below him, beside him, and around him, to his friends and his enemies, and above all—music making.

This is a tremendous natural gift, not something he thinks about. He is never gushing, never doing something just for effect. Forte is forte, not fortissimo. Allegro is allegro, not prestissimo. Nor will he succumb to the temptation of holding the bow and his breath at the end of the piece for forty-two seconds with eyes closed, holding his breath to create a pseudo-dramatic effect. This kind of drama is certain to get a reaction from the audience and critics as well, and has made many a performer successful, but it is anathema to Janos."

Bach — "To listen to his playing of one of the solo sonatas, one feels that the style and content of his interpretation combines yesterday and today and shows the road toward the future. Phrasing encodes the emotion and intellect of the artist, and Starker through his interpretation of the Bach *Six Cello Suites* offers a 'hologram' of himself to his listeners. As a listener in his performances of the *Suite in D Major*, I have had the impression that he was creating a 'geometric mirror of the universe.' In hearing his latest Bach recording, it seemed to me that he brought the score to life in such a way that it was as much his as the composer's music."

Battle — "He never seeks confrontation, but if it involves one of his basic tenets, regardless of the probability of winning or losing, you can be sure that the battle is going to be on! In the area of self-assurance, he is a phenomenon."

Belief — "If Janos believes in something, he will fight to the death for it. More than almost anything, however, he believes in loyalty. Throughout his life, his loyalty goes way beyond logic, reason, and common sense. There is no limit to what he will do for his friend. When he is a friend to someone, that person can do no wrong. He will rationalize almost anything, any action, any characteristic, any behavior as long as this person is his friend."

Breathing — "Technique has been Janos' basic concern since his student days. Once I heard him lecture brilliantly during one of his master classes on the importance and the method of taking a breath before the final note of a piece."

Cello — "It is spotlighting the obvious to state that the cello is a vital part of Janos' life. We call parts of the cello with names of the human body, such as the neck and the back. For him it goes way beyond this. To Janos, the cello is almost human. He approaches cello sounds as I would fine wines. He recognizes the voices of each of these 'creatures.' His whole life has been defined by the cello, even negative aspects, such as travelling with this bulky instrument, a very difficult task."

Concentration — "This is a characteristic of every person I know who has achieved something extraordinary. Janos' concentration is absolutely astonishing, even under the most untenable circumstances. He is quite a good chess player. One time he decided to play with a French chess champion. He wanted to test how he would fare though his skills were clearly on a much lower level, chess not being his main preoccupation. At this chess match his concentration was absolute. Every fiber of his brain was engaged in the process. The result? He actually had a draw with the French chess champion!"

Classicism — "Even something written just twenty years ago in Janos' refining hands comes out classical, in other words, *quite perfect*. In every sense of the word, he is a classical interpreter of music. In his world of music, things are in perfect order, well-balanced, symmetrical."

Debate — "When Janos believes in something, which, in my opinion, can be at times quite erroneous, politics for example, he'll do his utmost to change his opponent's mind if he respects this person."

Determination — "If Janos is anything, he is determined. Fortunately, his determination is directed toward estimable goals."

Education — "He considers forming the future generation of cellists his major function in life. This is more important to him than even concertizing. His teaching commitment is extraordinary. For most people teaching usually comes at the end of their lives, at the time when they barely can lift the bow. Janos started teaching at a very young age and has been teaching ever since, sharing what he received from his eminent teacher, Adolph Schiffer."

Fans and Fascination — "People's fascination with Janos Starker is most extraordinary. In various parts of the world I have attended his concerts, and over the years many have expressed to me that he is a cellist's cellist and a musician's musician. The people who come to pay homage to him are sincere and filled with admiration. Many understand either instinctively or from a professional viewpoint what he is doing and what he stands for."

"After concerts people often come up to me back stage and ask for my autograph, thinking that I am Janos. Something must be similar in our personalities. We do not look at all alike. So I sign, 'George Lang, would like to be Janos Starker.'"

ᴧᴧᴧ

While in Geneva for the Geneva Competition, Starker learned from his friend, Francis Akos, that there was the possibility of getting a Belgian visa. So he was able to get Belgian visas as well as train tickets for himself and his wife. On the visas was written, NO RIGHT TO STOP. But when the train stopped in Paris, they just got off, even with no means of support. With a sob story they first obtained a one-week permit to stay in France, then another week, then a three-month permit, and eventually a one-year permit. They could have stayed indefinitely, but without citizenship.

Once in France Starker was reunited with his lifelong friend, Francis Akos.[30] Akos told him that he had met an older man, Alfred Indig, who was once the second violinist with the Budapest String Quartet. Indig wanted to reestablish the quartet with himself playing first violin, Francis Akos on second violin, Istvan Deak on viola, and Starker on cello.

Indig had survived the winter in Cannes, France, during the war, living in a wonderful place called Hotel Meurice on the French Riviera. One could live there for a whole month on the equivalent of just ten dollars. They could join him there, practice the quartet repertoire together and become a world-travelling string quartet.

They discussed the possibilities and thought, "What have we to lose?" It was less money to live on the Riviera than in Paris. Besides, Starker had nothing to do in Paris that suited his goals, and at that time he did not feel comfortable performing as a soloist. So they went to Cannes.

In Cannes they lived very simply. It was always very difficult to get the money together to pay for their hotel room and food. For a while they lived on the third floor of a modest hotel with a group of other Hungarians. During that summer in 1947 there was a stretch of days when the temperature reached forty degrees Celsius. They were all melting in the heat! And they had no money to buy food. After the war their parents were working again, and they managed to smuggle some money for Starker and Eva so that they might survive.

One day Eva collapsed on the floor. They had not eaten for four or five days. Eva had become so weak that she could not get up. They had a few coins in their pockets. With their friends, the Deris, they pooled their meager monies and went together to the store to buy a baguette and the cheapest canned food item they could find. Not knowing much French, they did not know "what the hell they were buying." But with their few pennies they could afford a baguette and the canned food. They opened the can which contained some kind of fish, cut it into four pieces, and had a fabulous meal!

Later their friends, the Deaks, joined them. They spoke French and could read the label on the can of fish. They announced what it was the others had eaten, "one of those ugly sea creatures with all the legs, an octopus!" They had all been on the seashore when they lived in Cannes and seen the vendors selling raw octopus. Even then they found the sight of those creatures revolting! Knowing this the two wives ran to the bathroom and lost their food, threw up their whole meal! The men found this hilarious! And the story has been told and retold.

The quartet began rehearsing. They all knew immediately what to do. That was because they were all former students of Leo Weiner. It was almost like a secret society. They all knew the basic principles of music making. How well they individually played the instruments was another matter.

They got together and read the *Seventh String Quartet* by Darius Milhaud. They also played music by Beethoven, Mozart, Debussy, and others. But Alfred Indig "played awfully badly." It seemed as though he was mimicking playing, marking the gestures as though he was listening to the others. The others all assumed that the Budapest Quartet must have been a good quartet. They were puzzled by the way Indig played. Well, the rehearsal was over. They all had a good time. It was nice to read music, playing things they already knew, and in the company of fellow Hungarians.

Then over dinner Indig talked about how he survived during the war. In a nearby casino he had developed a system in which, given a modest investment, he always won half again as much as his original investment. That usually took about an hour. To Starker, an experienced card player and gambler, that sounded very interesting! So the two of them went together the next day to the casino. Instead of rehearsing at two o'clock, they went first to the casino and then joined the others for rehearsal at three o'clock.

At the casino the first day, Starker had increased his take from ten to twenty-one units. The point of the game was that one risks twenty in order to win ten units. When he and Indig told the others what had happened, they got excited. It all worked so well. But in the system, Starker soon learned, there was sometimes a hitch. One out of five times it just did not work. Then you had to just take your losses and go on, but with still thirty or forty units.

Then the other two said, "Why don't you play for us, too?" So they gave Starker the same amount of money that he invested. Instead of playing with one chip, he played with three. Then they would rehearse for three hours. The next day, the same routine. This time Starker won twelve units. Then they would rehearse. Suddenly with their original investment of twenty units, they had thirty, forty, fifty units. They had lots of money in their pockets, the equivalent of several months of rent.

On the fourth day they were discussing the possibility of hiring a manager. But they decided to manage their own concerts instead. Then on the fifth day the predicted catastrophe started! They started losing money. In just one hour on the fifth day they lost their original twenty units. They looked at each other and decided to try again the next day. So they came back the next, and the next, and the next. Pretty soon they had lost everything! They were back where they started. Not a great deal really was lost, but their dreams were shattered.

The unfortunate part was that the quartet continued to rehearse for another two weeks. Indig had arranged a concert in one of the churches in town. The only problem was that Indig was always playing as though he were absent, even during the concert. By then Starker and his two younger colleagues knew that they could not function as a quartet. They soon figured out that Indig did not have a hundred concerts for them in Germany. There were a hundred music societies in Germany, but there was no guarantee of any concerts at all! It was all just theoretical! Then came a breakup in the quartet with misunderstanding and animosity.

While living in France in 1946, Starker met the conductor Charles Bruch. He had studied conducting with Pierre Monteux and was for many years the director of music for French Radio. Later he became the director of the Monteux School of Music, a school for conductors in Maine. But at that time he was an underemployed, struggling conductor who had already had some successes.

One day he came to Starker and said that the next day he must leave for London to conduct the Schumann *Cello Concerto*. The cellist performing, Raimonde Verrandeau, incidentally, was the first prizewinner in the Geneva Competition.

A few days later he was back at Starker's door. "What happened?" Starker asked. "We started recording and tried several times to record the first page of the concerto." He said. "She just could not do it. So the recording was called off." Apparently this woman died years later in obscurity in Marseilles, France.

This caused Starker to wonder about competitions, but not for his own sake. He did not feel at that time that he was deserving of the big prize. Actually, by then Antonio Janigro already had an established reputation. He had won the Vienna Competition and was the only proven professional in the entire group of competitors.

Well, Starker and Bruch became great friends during that time. One day, Bruch came to Starker and said that he had had a job conducting the music for a film. But now the recording of the music was completed. Films then were made in such a way that the music was prerecorded. Then if the music called for singing or playing, it was mimicked.

A Hungarian composer had written a song called *Sad Sunday*. Around this song he created a love story in which the song itself caused an international uproar. Supposedly, when people heard this song, they committed suicide. The story involved scenes in a restaurant where a gypsy band was playing. Charles Bruch was a stand-in actor in the gypsy orchestra. So with a moustache and gypsy clothes, he imitated a cello player for the filming. Of course, the music was already prerecorded. Bruch got the job of playing the cello for the following day's filming.

Bruch said to Starker, "I have a very big favor to ask of you. Could I borrow your cello for the filming the next day?" So in the morning he came and picked up his cello and then returned it in the evening. That way he could make some extra money. Starker was not practicing a great deal at the time, so he did not mind.

A couple of days later he came to Starker and said, "Would you mind going in my place as the cellist tomorrow? I have a job conducting. If I do not show up to conduct, I will lose my job for the remaining days of the filming." So Starker took a job in the film for one day as a cellist. "Some of the scenes will take two or three weeks to complete, so will you stand in for me as the cellist tomorrow?" asked Bruch. "The only thing is that you do not really play the cello. It is just for the cameras."

So the next day Starker put on the gypsy clothes and the moustache and pretended to play the cello. At that time he even had a full head of hair! So for that day he earned a day's pay as an actor. Then the next day, Bruch was back on the job with Starker's cello.

By this time in January, 1947 Starker had established contact with Edith and Emile Tauszig. She was the sister of Csupi Naschitz from Temesvar, Rumania. Edith and Emile were living in Limoges, France. Meeting them was like a reunion of long lost brothers and sisters even though they were a generation older than Starker and Eva. For a long time they had not heard a word from their relatives in Rumania. Then a letter came telling about Starker and Eva, also Starker's friend György Sebök. Shortly thereafter Sebök joined them in France. Such a reunion! Starker and Sebök began anew playing much of the cello-piano repertoire together, just as they had as youths in Hungary.

It was in their home in Limoges that Starker took out his cello. He started playing as though a cloud had lifted. He was able to play as he had before the war. Perhaps it was due to the human warmth he experienced with his friends. From the time of his concert in Vienna in April of 1946 until January of 1947, it was like he was living in a nightmare. Suddenly the fog lifted, and he felt free again. Coming from playing like a sleepwalker, he was once again able to make sense out of the music. They stayed for a time in Limoges and performed recitals in private homes, such as the Havilland home owned by the maker of Havilland Porcelain. These concerts and others were organized by Emile Tauszig who was the president of the local chamber music society.

Starker and Eva needed to return to the Riviera to get their belongings. Upon their return to Limoges, the well-known cellist, Paul Tortelier, was to play a concert at the Jeunnesse Musicales of France, performing the Lalo *Cello Concerto* and the *Moto Perpetuo* of Paganini with orchestra. At this concert, the master of ceremonies introduced the solo cellist to the kids in the hall, saying, "Young people, you must realize that it takes an immense amount of energy to perform the pieces you are about to hear, the energy you would spend going twice up and down the Eiffel Tower!" According to Starker, Tortelier played extremely well.

The director of the orchestra that performed that day was also the director of the conservatory. Starker had met him a few days earlier. Following the concert he took Starker to meet Tortelier, introducing him as "a fantastic Hungarian cellist." At that meeting they agreed to have dinner together the following day. Their dinner was followed by a private performance by Starker performing the Kodály *Sonata, Op. 8* for Tortelier in the Tauszig home. Hearing this piece, Tortelier was nearly out of his mind with excitement! He had never before heard the piece or anything like it! Hardly anyone even knew the piece existed except a few Hungarians. Tortelier went back to Paris and arranged for Starker to play a recital there, his first public appearance in France outside of a few house concerts. That was the beginning of Starker's activities in Paris, which were, unfortunately, meager. Eventually he played several recitals.

During the summer of 1947 Eva and Starker returned to Hungary and spent a couple of months in Budapest. He was supposed to play several concerts in Hungary. The second day he was there he went for a pre-concert interview. During the interview he mentioned that he had heard a concert of Ernst von Dohnanyi, a great man of music in Hungary who had been the director of the Franz Liszt Academy when Starker was a student. After the war Dohnanyi was accused of being a German sympathizer. He had left Hungary with the Germans, and when the war was over, he was arrested and kept by the Americans under house arrest for a long time. As time went on, the officials learned that because of family conditions, Dohnanyi had to go along with certain things that he was against. In the meantime he saved many lives. Eventually the Americans allowed him to play some concerts. He came to Badgastein, Austria, in the summer of 1947 for a concert which Starker and Eva attended. Starker mentioned in the interview that he had heard Dohnanyi's concert, and that he played fabulously well. Because of this statement and Starker's connection with Dohnanyi, all of Starker's Budapest concerts were canceled. So, unfortunately, for three months while visiting his parents in Budapest, he was doing nothing.

1947 was the year when Hungary held its very first democratic election. The Communists won the election with only about 21% of the vote and became the majority party. Succeeding in beating all of the other parties, they took over. For the first time in his life with his Hungarian passport Starker was qualified to vote. The next day Starker and Eva left to go back to Paris, but before leaving, he went to the Musicians' Union where he saw one of his oldest colleagues. This friend advised him, "The next time you come to Hungary, be careful about whom you speak."

7. Marton, Kati, *Wallenberg: Missing Hero,* Arcade Publishing, New York, 1995, pp. 64-67

8. Vago, Bela, *Jewish Assimilation in Modern Times*, Westview Press, Inc., 1981, pp. 77-79

9. Marton, Kati, *Wallenberg: Missing Hero,* Arcade Publishing, New York, 1995, p. 67

10. Fenyo, Mario, *Hitler, Horthy, and Hungary*, Yale University Press, New Haven, 1972, p. 71

11. ibid, p. 139

12. op. cit., p. 175

13. The Hindemith *Cello Concerto* was written in 1942, and Starker had the first copy of the piece in Hungary.

14. Marton, Kati, *Wallenberg: Missing Hero,* Arcade Publishing, New York, 1995, p. 70

15. Amalka Baracs, an expert on Mozart's music, could play all of the Mozart operas on the piano. At the age of ninety-one, she was teaching English to Hungarian immigrants in England. The last time Starker played chamber music with her was in London when she was ninety-three years old.

16. Fenyo, Mario, *Hitler, Horthy, and Hungary*, Yale University Press, New Haven, 1972, p. 121

17. ibid, p. 77, 108

18. op. cit., pp. 83-84

19. Marton, Kati, *Wallenberg: Missing Hero,* Arcade Publishing, New York, 1995, p. 68

20. ibid

21. op. cit., p.75

22. op. cit., p.77

23. op. cit., p.92

24. Frank, Ann, *Diary of a Young Girl,* Doubleday & Co., 1952

25. Wilder, Thornton, *The Bridge of San Luis Rey,* Grosset & Dunlap, 1927

26. Lang, George, *Nobody Knows the Truffles I've Seen,* Alfred Knopf, New York, 1998, p. 135

27. Years later, whenever Starker performed in New York, their son, a lawyer, would always loudly yell from the audience, "Bravo!"

28. While he was away, he missed rehearsals for an opera. Upon his return to Budapest, he sightread the opera, no small task.

29. *Los Angeles Times*, "Violinist and Visionary Yehudi Menuhin Dies at 82," March 13, 1999, p. 1, 16

30. Francis Akos became the assistant concertmaster of the Chicago Symphony.

Part III

The Young Professional

While Starker was living in Paris, Andre Mertens from Columbia Artists heard him play in recital and invited him to come to the United States. Mehrtens said that he could not make any guarantees, but that he would do his best in getting concerts for Starker. Starker considered the offer but declined. He could not emigrate to the U.S. just on promises. He had to make a living. Besides he had a wife to support.

In 1947 while living in Paris Starker received a letter from Fritz Reiner. The letter said that if he should come to the United States that Reiner would like him to play principal cello with the Pittsburgh Symphony. He knew about Starker through Victor Aitay who was playing in Pittsburgh. Reiner wanted to replace his principal cellist, and Starker sounded interesting to him. Starker replied that he needed an American visa, but Reiner unfortunately did nothing about it.

However, Starker was performing in France and began to gain some recognition in the music world. He was then offered a recording contract with Pacific Records and recorded first the *Siete Canciones* by Manuel deFalla and the Hindemith *Sonata,* opus 11 for cello and piano. He had performed one movement of the Kodály *Solo Sonata* for the French Radio, so it was proposed that he record the whole piece. It was recorded on eight sides of a 78 rpm disc and required two cuts in order to fit it all in. He discovered that near the end of the last movement, there was an electronic disturbance in the sound, a humming noise. He proposed they re-record it. The extraneous sound was disturbing. But the recording people ignored his warning. Then in every review came the comment that the recording had an electronic disturbance. At that point the company recommended that they re-record it. However, by then Starker said that they should pay him extra to redo it. The extra session never happened.

This was the first record that reached the general public, making people aware of his existence. Then came the big surprise: for his Kodály *Solo Sonata* recording Starker was awarded the Grand Prix du Disque. The Recording Society printed a very nice diploma awarding Starker the coveted prize, but, ironically, he never received it. It was announced in all the newspapers, and the whole music world knew about it, but he never got it. Who knows where it got lost? It may still be at the Recording Society languishing on a library shelf, waiting for someone in the next millennium to discover it!

Shortly after the Grand Prix du Disque award announcement, Kodály was in Paris to receive an honor. Starker was invited to be there to perform. Kodály was on his way home from a trip to the United States. Together they went to the Hungarian Embassy and the Hungarian Institute. Everywhere they went, Starker played Kodály's *Solo Sonata.* He began to make more recordings and was concertizing more. Eventually he had an offer to play concerts in Switzerland, about a seven-hour train ride from Paris.

Emigrating to the United States through normal immigration channels meant "waiting until your number comes up." Some people waited for ten years. Because there was a shorter waiting period for visas to South America, many people went there instead. Some people bought passports or visas for Honduras for a very dear price. But Starker thought that he was better off going to the United States. If he could just get to the United States, he figured, he could eventually become a citizen, then get a passport and be able to travel and concertize.

In 1948 Antal Dorati, Music Director of the Dallas Symphony, came to Paris. He offered Starker a contract to play principal cello with the Dallas Symphony. Most importantly, he gave Starker the help necessary to get an American visa. The move to Dallas suited his goals.

Once he arrived in Dallas, Starker became a member of the Musicians' Union. He was the only cellist in the symphony who was a member of the local musicians' union. Because of this he had a call from the orchestra contractor. This man was a violinist and also the assistant conductor of the Dallas Symphony. Starker was offered a job playing a "gig." He had no idea what a "gig" was, but he said, "Sure, I'll do it."

The next day his ride came and picked him up and took him to a private home, the home of a wealthy Texan. The Texan and his Viennese wife had planned a celebration in honor of their tenth anniversary. They wanted some music for entertainment. Starker was one of five musicians. They reportedly played "all kinds of junk." Starker found himself playing a trombone part in one piece. As the party went on, the host asked the first violinist if the musicians would play some Viennese waltzes in honor of his wife. This they did, delighting all who were present. The music and dancing were elegant.

Vienna is located on the eastern edge of Austria but a short distance from Hungary. At one time Vienna was a part of the Hungarian Monarchy. With her Viennese background, the hostess of the party was familiar with the czardas, a Hungarian dance. The host asked if Starker would dance the czardas with her. There was much begging and pushing until he finally had to get up and do something. They danced the czardas over and over for at least fifteen minutes while his colleagues played the piece nonstop. People all around were caught up in the excitement, clapping to the beat. Starker was the hit of the party! This was his first "gig" in the United States.

Incidentally, a horn player in the Dallas Symphony, Lester Solomon, was one of the editors of the Musicians' Union newspaper. Later he played extra horn in the Met orchestra. One time he wrote an unpleasant column about Rudolph Bing's book, *Five Thousand Nights at the Opera*.[31] Solomon's experiences at the Met were rather unpleasant, perhaps because he was not one of the better musicians in the orchestra, so he vented his anger at Bing in print. Countermanding Solomon's writings, Starker later printed his own story of memories at the Metropolitan Opera which was printed in *Opera News*.[32]

For one of his first performances in Dallas he performed the Brahms *Double Concerto* with the symphony's concertmaster, Raphael Druian.[33] After six months with the Dallas Symphony, Starker was invited to go with Dorati to Minneapolis to be the principal cellist with the Minneapolis Symphony for the following concert season. Starker agreed to do this, and he and Dorati shook on it. But first he had to go to New York to join the Musicians' Union, the American Federation of Musicians. Between the Dallas Symphony concert season and the start of the concert season in Minneapolis, there was a period of about six months during which time Starker was in New York. He had no year-round employment and had six months free.

On the first of June, while he was in New York, he received a call from Victor Aitay saying that Fritz Reiner would like to meet him. Reiner was then the leading conductor of the Metropolitan Opera Company in New York. Starker showed up at the Met with his cello to meet Reiner. It turned out that this was an audition. No one had told him that there was to be an audition. He was not interested in the job at that time because he had committed to Dorati. The manager of the orchestra put some music in front of Starker to sight read, which he did, and said after a few minutes, "You will be very happy with us."

The next day Starker received a call from Dorati. He was very angry. Starker tried to tell him that he was not responsible for this mess and he had no intention of letting him down. Apparently, Reiner had called Dorati and said, "You get yourself another cellist. I want Starker in my orchestra." [34] Dorati said to Starker, "If you want to go to the Met, I cannot stop you, but get me another cellist." Starker replied, "I heard a cellist at the Met audition, and he was terrific." This man, Zirkin, was a professor at the Hindemith Academy in Turkey. So Starker's plans changed, and he became the principal cellist of the Metropolitan Opera Orchestra under Reiner, and Zirkin was offered the job in Minneapolis with Dorati. He had decided to come to America and try his luck. His bad luck was that he did not know that Starker was there that day and was offered the job at the Met instead of him. But during the summer, he and Starker became good friends and even played duets together.

Another time Starker played an audition when he did not know it was an audition. He was at Leventritt's house for a celebration. Leonard Rose just quit the job as principal cellist with the New York Philharmonic and signed a contract for solo concerts with Judson, a concert manager. At the party Rose asked Starker if he was interested in the New York Philharmonic job. The job was attractive to Starker because it involved much less work. But it also meant half of the salary he was getting with the Met. He said that of course he was interested, but he would not play an audition, and he would need to have more money.

A couple of weeks later Starker heard that the auditions for the cello position were being held. Rose called and asked him, "How come you were not at the audition?" Starker replied that he had no intention of auditioning for the job. Rose said then, "Tell me, do you know the Brahms *Piano Concerto* cello solo?" To that, Starker replied, "I have not played it. But if I should ever play for Mitropoulos, whatever he wants to hear, I am accustomed to sight reading." Another telephone call, and Rose asked if he could come and play at "such and such time." Well, it was after Starker's Met rehearsal. It was a bad winter day, and he couldn't get a taxi, so he had to walk from the Met on 39th Street to 57th Street with his cello in hand. It was a considerable hike with a cello. There were several orchestra musicians there: the concertmaster, principal violist, Lenny Rose, the conductor and the orchestra manager. He played a Bach *Suite* movement and a movement from the Kodály *Solo Sonata* for them. Then Lenny got up and asked him, "Do you know the Brahms *Piano Concerto* cello solo?" Starker said, "I told you that I have not played it, but I am accustomed to sight reading." Ironically, they could not find the music.

As the story goes, the orchestra manager came up to Starker and told him, "You will be much happier here with us. I know it will be difficult to tell John Mundy, your manager at the Met, that we are going to take you away." Then Rose jumped up and interrupting said, "No, please, I'll speak with Janos." The whole thing was a kind of mystery story.

At the time, Starker was making $400 per week playing in the Met orchestra. The New York Philharmonic was paying only $200 per week. For Starker it was a question of money. They would have to pay him more to lure him away from the Met. Starker could not afford to take the job.

Starker played the performance that night with the Met. The next morning he left for his ten o'clock rehearsal as usual. When he called his wife at noon, she said that she had taken a call from Laszlo Varga who was saying, "I don't understand. I was offered the job." When Varga played his audition for the New York Philharmonic, Rose jumped up and said, "We have the man." Actually Rose was only taking a year's leave of absence from the orchestra. In case his solo career did not go well, he wanted a job to come back to. Then Starker got a call from Rose telling him that they had decided against hiring another soloist and were not going to hire him after all. In the meantime he did not even know he was auditioning.

While Starker was in New York, he met a fellow Hungarian, Peter Bartók (son of Bela Bartók), a recording engineer for Period Records. He gained information about sales territories from owner, William Avar, and got the rights to use Starker's Kodály *Solo Sonata* recording. That was just at the advent of LP recordings, and hundreds of LP companies were coming into being. People were buying tape machines and setting up recording studios in their basements. They produced and sold five hundred of Starker's Kodály recordings and since there were minimal production costs, they actually made money. All of the big companies were gradually putting the old 78 rpm recordings onto LPs and marketing them. But Starker said that if he used the French recording, people would hear an electronic flaw, and it would not be acceptable. So Starker then recorded the piece again, this time for Period Records. His fame in American music circles began with that recording. He also recorded the Bartók *Rhapsody* and the Kodály *Sonata*, opus 4 with pianist Otto Herz, also the Vivaldi and Corelli *Sonatas* with Marilyn Meyers, and other works, making altogether twelve LPs.

Starker spent four years in New York with the Metropolitan Opera from 1949 to 1953 followed by five years with the Chicago Symphony, all of these with Fritz Reiner, conductor. During those nine years Reiner became almost like a father to him. Starker felt very close to Reiner. On two occasions Starker went to visit Reiner in Connecticut. Several times Reiner had dinner in Starker's home. Occasionally they had dinner together after rehearsals. He spent enough time to know Reiner rather well. He knew what Reiner represented and the things he had done in his life. Starker came to admire this man greatly and regarded him as the greatest conductor who ever lived. With so many years in a close working relationship, Reiner was a major influence on Starker. This relationship was one of the few strong associations in Starker's life outside of family and friends.

Starker found that the Metropolitan Opera Orchestra was made up of some of the top professionals in the country with Fritz Reiner, one of the finest conductors in the world. "His knowledge of the scores was unsurpassed. His musical authority was unrivaled. He was an emotional musician, and the emotions he expressed in music were higher than anyone else. He controlled an orchestra and singers with minimal means and maximum results. He could balance an orchestra while focusing on what was in the score, getting the finest results musically and technically.

"And some of the world's finest singers graced the stage," he says. The years he spent playing with the Metropolitan Opera Orchestra were musically among the most valuable to Starker. "Opera is the greatest learning experience of all. I was exposed to the greatest singers of the day: Richard Tucker, Jan Pearce, Lauritz Melchior, Jussi Björling, and others. Björling may not have had the natural beauty of sound that Caruso or Gigli or the bass Chaliapin had, but his breathing, his incredible phrasing and his ability to shape an unbroken line were simply remarkable. Maria Callas had an extraordinary ability to lay low for what was ahead, making a climax that was simply stunning! I was able to observe and learn from the musical coloring, breathing and use of the voice on the part of so many singers.

"After forty hours a week of instrumental playing in opera rehearsals, everything else seemed easy. I remember days when we would play *Carmen* in the afternoon, then go out for a Turkish bath on 42nd Street, grab a sandwich, then come back and play *Gioconda* in the evening." The Met provided an atmosphere in which the cellist felt at home artistically. The contract called for seven performances each week, including the Texaco Radio Broadcasts, with a proviso for extra performances. That meant that they had the right to call extra rehearsals and keep the players as long as they wanted. In those days they performed seven different operas each week, with sometimes nine performances in a week's time, a very strenuous schedule requiring the stamina of a horse. Although the orchestra played only twenty-two weeks in the city of New York and seven weeks on tour, this was the highest paid orchestra in the country.

Since the players worked only twenty-nine weeks each year, they were usually happy about the pay for the extra rehearsals and performances. For those like Starker who did all of the extras, they were not too happy about working more, but they did it. According to Starker's contract, as principal cellist he was given two nights off each week. If there were nine performances, he played only seven. If there were seven performances, he played only five. If

A BOATING EXCURSION WITH VICTOR AITAY, SINGER ROBERTA PETERS, BOW EXPERT HENRYK KASTON, VIOLINIST KAPLAN, STARKER AND OTHERS.

there was a *Ring*, *Die Walküre* or *Götterdämmerung* rehearsal in the morning, and it lasted until two or three o'clock in the afternoon, the musicians just had to sit there and play. Then in the evening, there was a three-hour performance of *Carmen* or *Tosca* or whatever— a grueling schedule.

Often the attitude of the orchestra in the pit, whenever the conductor was not present, was often one of play, sometimes playing a game of golf with bows and rolls of paper just to keep themselves interested.

There was a peculiar kind of seating in the pit orchestra. The first violin section was on the outside. Next to them were the celli. The third stand of violins were in front of the celli. The second violins were in the middle, and the violas were on the conductor's right. Nowhere in the world would you see that kind of seating. It was most unusual.

Starker's stand partner in the orchestra, Englebert Röntgen, had been the principal cellist with the Met for many years, a superb cellist. George Szell was the previous chief conductor at the Met. Röntgen was so stunned by Szell's demands that he had a heart attack. He could no longer take the pressure of being principal cellist, so he asked to be moved to the second chair.

Then started a sequence of several years when each year a new principal cellist was appointed including Fritz Magg, Lucien Laporte and others. Röntgen was so mad and frustrated after being first cellist for so many years that he consistently made life miserable for the principal player. As a result, each new player left after only a year. Starker was warned about him when he started the job at the Met. Somehow they worked things out.

A young horn player, Günther Schuller,[35] was playing assistant principal with the Met orchestra. This was his first experience playing *Die Meistersinger*. During the first rehearsal for the opera, he made a mistake and played a wrong note. Reiner stopped the orchestra. Everyone knew that Reiner could not stand mistakes. He put up his glasses and asked, "What's the matter?" "Sorry, Maestro," came the answer. "This is my first time playing *Die Meistersinger*." That was the worst thing he could say to Reiner. Reiner made it clear that he was not there to teach. He was there to make music. He used only professionals who knew the music and on whom he could rely. At that point there was dead silence in the hall. Reiner was known for making the most cutting remarks which just killed players mentally. After a few moments Reiner said, "You say you are playing *Die Meistersinger* for the first time?" "Yes," came the answer from the lad. Then in a pensive tone came Reiner's response. "My God, what a joy it must be to hear *Die Meistersinger* for the very first time! Start at number fourteen." The rehearsal proceeded. This was a memorable moment for all.

"I have never agreed that Reiner was a tyrant as some made him out to be," says Starker. "When he hired you, he watched you with an eagle eye for the first few months. If you could not function the way he expected, your days in the orchestra were numbered. But if you performed well, from then on, he never bothered you. He was looking for professionals because he was a professional himself. That is the greatest accolade I can give to any musician. Playing for him for nine years was a stunning, memorable experience."

The principal horn player was Richard Moore. He swore that Fritz Reiner would never catch him playing a wrong note. He had played previously with Reiner in the Pittsburgh Symphony. He had a love-hate relationship with Reiner. Moore had tremendous admiration for the man, but finally he came to hate him because of his demands for perfection. Says Starker, "As long as I was with the Met, this man never blew a wrong note. But the tension was such that after every performance he had to get himself totally drunk."

During his years with the Met Starker made some of his most important recordings. They were done in the middle of the night in a church after the evening's opera performance. Because the acoustics in the church were too live, they brought in carpets and placed them on the floor. He recorded the Bach *Six Suites*, the Beethoven *Sonatas* and *Variations* and the Brahms *Sonatas* with sound engineer, Peter Bartók. By the wee hours of the morning he would go home for a few hours of sleep and be back at the Met in the morning for a rehearsal.

A Soft Pitch for the Pit, Nights in the Orchestra

a story by Janos Starker

As a member in good standing of the New York Musicians' Union, Local 802 (by virtue of paying my dues on time), I regularly received their publication called *Allegro*. In the last few issues the director of public relations wrote a series of rather amusing anecdotes debunking isolated incidents in the famous Rudolf Bing journal, *Five Thousand Nights at the Opera*. While reading both the book and its comic antagonist, I couldn't help but peer down my own memory lane. I knew well the writer, whose pen today is mightier than his horn used to be. I always enjoyed his wit, his warm personality, his huge heart open to everyone in need.

I turned back my clock and stopped in 1949, when I was an immigrant youngster fresh in the U.S. After a short season in Dallas, Texas, I landed in the solo cellist's chair of the Metropolitan Opera. Edward Johnson was presiding over his last season, with Frank St. Leger and Max Rudolf at his side. Reiner, Stiedry, Cleva, Pelletier and others wielded the baton and on occasion even Bruno Walter came to visit us.

Then the big change occurred, and Rudolf Bing came to power. I remained until 1953, and twenty-one years later it seems that my view of the old Met on Thirty-ninth Street has a bit of a twist. Remember, you get an entirely different view of things when you sit in the orchestra pit instead of onstage, and I observe now that some who came to the opera without fame built it there. Others, who came with much fanfare, left when their fame was past its zenith. A handful of stars from those days are still there, shining high in the opera firmament. Many have gone on to heaven or hell, according to their dedicated fans or friends. Very few of those onstage or in the pit who left in relative anonymity had fortune smile on them later in terms of a career. I am one of those fortunate few, and in retrospect I look upon my years at the Met with pride, satisfaction and many smiles. The "good old days" far outweigh the "rotten old days." The haze over the unpleasantries is thickening, but the light is brighter every day over the crazy, funny, sometimes outrageous happenings that helped us get through some of those slow-tempoed, long-winded nights.

It shouldn't be surprising that my memory centers primarily on the pit and rehearsal room. In those days the blessings of democracy hadn't as yet reached the orchestras. We were hired and fired mostly on merit. Black liberation and women's liberation were unheard of beyond an occasional second harpist. The dream of musicians was a few extra weeks of work, longer rehearsals (as they were paid extra in the Met), a few extra per diem dollars on the road, fewer contretemps with dictatorial baton wielders, and of course the fall of anyone who had control over us—understandably human!

We had no say in matters concerning stage, budget or program, to say nothing of the board of directors. When a marvelous horn player swore revenge against a conductor, his revenge was, "That s.o.b. will never catch me playing a wrong note," and he proved it while I was there.

Then there was the woodwind player who had circulation troubles and had a foot warmer plugged into the music-stand lights, causing a blackout during a strategic moment in the score. But that didn't bother the two first violinists, former members of the Vienna Philharmonic. Once, on a bet, they played one week without opening the music, nine different operas while on tour in Cleveland. Not only did they not miss a note but they gave cues and sang the text in German, naturally.

As a matter of fact, tours were a ceaseless fountain of hilarity: two special trains of belated adolescents releasing the pent-up emotions of a supercharged New York season. Discretion prevents my recalling happenings involving real persons, so I remember instead the famed *Fledermaus* in Baltimore when a live bat, aroused by Strauss' music, scared the wits out of audience and performers. No wonder an innuendo gained currency that it was a publicity stunt.

The press always did and still does keep up with the Met on tour, but in those days some highly unpublicized events took place, invariably in the Eastman Theater in Rochester, where the spring tour ended each year. By coincidence the Teatro Colón in Buenos Aires began its "stagione" at the very same time, requiring the services of a number of Met members, chief among them our beloved prompter, Othello Cerone. Had fate extracted him from his hole, he could have been recognized as one of the true giants of twentieth-century music. His ability to cue six soloists and a chorus while giving words and pitch to all in Italian, French, even some German and at times English (with a ferocious accent), endeared him to all those whose lives depended on him. But the Rochester performances had to be devoid of his presence. The results frequently approached one of those memorable evenings with Florence Foster Jenkins.

There was the night, boring beyond endurance, when the question circulating the pit was, what would you do with a million dollars (pre-inflationary)? After all the Stradivariuses and Amatis were disposed of, business empires built and the whole game forgotten, along came a violinist who said, "I would restore all the cuts in the Wagner repertory all over the world and pay for the necessary overtime." Then he added slowly, "I would also leave something for my cats."

A different kind of rehearsal comes to mind when our appreciation for the science of conducting sank considerably. The case in point was a rehearsal with chorus and soloists on stage. Maestro Stiedry interrupted the music and vehemently instructed the singers to watch his beat, not turn their backs on him, and follow the tempo expressly asked for by Mozart. The chorus master emerged from behind the wings and tried, unsuccessfully for a while, to catch the attention of Mozart's devoted servant. Eventually the maestro turned toward him with an impatient gesture and yelled, "Don't bother me, the chorus was all right." "Yes, Maestro," said the chorus master. "Thank you, but we forgot to sing!"

It was this same maestro, famed for his Wagner interpretations, whose disdain for giving downbeats was legendary. One night, though, he startled us with the most authoritative beat ever received from him. The problem was that the music indicated a general pause. The silence was shattered by crashing timpani produced by a player who had recently joined our orchestra and had not time as yet to evaluate the significance of this maestro's beat.

I remember vividly my frantic inventions of excuses for arriving late, already the fifth time. While I was changing into my tuxedo as the overture played without me, dear John Mundy, the orchestra manager, interrupted my colorful story and said, "Don't, Janos—I know how unpleasant it is for you to be late." Twenty-two years later I do not recall ever again being late on any professional obligations. Then there was the night I found my chair removed from its customary location and placed smack in the front of the conductor with its back to the stage. I was told the reason later. It seems that the conductor had had enough of my watching the ladies onstage instead of his hands.

Those days we weren't intimately involved with the mechanics and the machinations of opera and its directors. We had the grapevine and knew who slept with whom, who would get what part in what opera, why and why not. But most of us did the best job we could, and fought for improved conditions. If asked to leave, we took our skills elsewhere and seldom cried foul. We had our favorites and underdogs. We cheered and booed like others and hoped for four of a kind in our endless poker games. Whatever our likes and dislikes were, we rarely envied those in power. We knew what it meant to have fun at the Met, what it meant to work with hundreds of people—the underpaid chorus, the abused ballet, the overpaid stage hands, the logically self-centered stars whose presence guaranteed sold-out houses, and on and on.

Opera is not a democratic institution. Reduce leadership and it falters on the waves of a stormy sea. I for one would like to salute all those who ran and now run the fragile ship and, above all, wish strength, continued health and dedication to my lifelong friends and soul brothers in the pit.[36]

J.S., *Opera News*, January 4, 1975

ᴧᴧᴧ

When Starker came to the United States, he planned to stay in orchestral playing for eight years or less and then pursue a solo career. Columbia Artists had expressed an interest in him when he was in Paris, particularly after he had received the coveted Grand Prix du Disque for his Kodály recording. But financial security motivated him to commit to orchestral playing. But with his career goals in mind, he submitted his resignation to the Met with a departure date of spring, 1953. However, Fritz Reiner invited Starker to play principal cello with the Chicago Symphony where he stayed from 1953 to 1958. During that time he frequently performed solo concertos with the orchestra, actually more frequently than any other cellist. "The basics of my repertoire were developed in Chicago: Strauss' *Don Quixote*, Hindemith's *Concerto*, Milhaud's *Concerto*, Prokofiev's *First Concerto*, Schumann's *Concerto*, Brahms' *Double Concerto*, Beethoven's *Triple Concerto* with Bruno Walter and with Reiner, the Saint Saëns' *Concerto*. The concerto performances were in addition to playing all of the symphony concerts. It was perhaps the most active and productive stretch of time in his life.

During each season Reiner conducted eighteen weeks. The rest of the season, including the summer, there were guest conductors. The conductors during that time included Monteux, Ansermet, Paul Paray, Bruno Walter, Charles Münch, CarloMaria Giulini, and Igor Stravinsky. Eugene Ormandy conducted some television concerts. Starker found the work with Giulini, Bruno Walter, and Ansermet unforgettable.

Many times Starker performed Strauss' *Don Quixote* with the Chicago Symphony. Before their first performance, he and Reiner spent an entire year studying the piece. They studied Cervantes' book, and since Reiner knew Strauss personally, he and Starker worked closely together to bring full meaning to the piece. Unfortunately, they did not record the work.

Starker also performed the Cassadó arrangement of Schubert's *Arpeggione Sonata* with the Chicago Symphony.[37] Cassadó's arrangement for solo cello and orchestra is not only a poor arrangement, but Starker recalls this performance as the only time in his life that he played badly. The piece was greatly changed from the original in this arrangement, transforming a classical piece into a highly romanticized one. However, Starker tells that now he uses some of Cassadó's ideas in performing the piece with piano. For example, at the beginning of the last movement, which is actually transitional between the second and third movements, Starker starts very softly, somewhat sneaking into the new idea. Cassadó marked in the music "lontano," which means from the distance. In the music the idea is gradually evolving until it reaches fortissimo. Starker tells his students in his cello seminars a story about a man coming home intoxicated after an evening out. He is tentative in his steps. As he is nearing the house he straightens himself up and comes in. At the fortissimo, one imagines his wife yelling at him!

Starker restarted his solo career with a recital in Orchestra Hall in Chicago, then his début recital in Wigmore Hall in London. The Wigmore Hall event led to a contract for ten recordings with EMI, a generous offer from recording impresario, Walter Legge. Then Legge arranged for Starker to sign a contract with Colbert, the artistic agent for Legge's wife, singer Elizabeth Schwartzkopf.

CARLO MARIA GUILINI, CONDUCTOR WALTER LEGGE, TOTUM FACTUM OF EMI RECORDS AND STARKER.

During the summers the orchestra performed outdoor concerts at Ravinia near Lake Michigan. As with most outdoor concerts, the performers have to deal with sound interruptions from occasional trains passing. Pierre Monteux had a system whereby if a train came, he would put down his hands and then resume the music once the train had passed. Igor Markevich was conducting one time when Starker was playing the Dvořák *Concerto*. They were nearing the cadenza in the second movement when they heard a train coming. It was perfect timing. Starker just waited for the train to pass. He looked up at Markevich who had a horrified look on his face as though Starker had a memory failure. Starker figured, "If he does not hear the train, then I might as well go on." No one had told Markevich in advance about the train plan.

Later, when Starker was playing principal cello with the Chicago Symphony, he became friendly with George Solti. This was due in part to the fact that Starker was one of several who were responsible for the symphony hiring Solti. Occasionally there was dinner in the Starker home followed by ping-pong with Solti, Isaac Stern and others. But they did not form the kind of bonds from which one promotes the other's career, a common behavior in music circles. Starker never wanted to give the impression that he would become friendly only in order to get an engagement. He never asked anyone for an engagement. He did not allow his public relations agent to even hint that he wanted someone to do something for him. Beyond a select few, Starker was always very private and respected the privacy of other musicians and, in a way, kept his life exclusive from other musicians. The notable exceptions to this were his lifelong friendships with his musical partners from his youth in Budapest. They remained always the closest of friends, even though they were often separated by many miles, meeting only occasionally.

When Reiner signed his contract with the Chicago Symphony, he had two conditions: he had to bring with him Starker as principal cellist and his alternate first horn player, Alan Fuchs. In New York Starker and Fuchs did not know each other very well, but on occasion they and a few other musicians got together to play poker. Then he and Starker moved to Chicago, and since they did not yet know the other players, they became friends. Occasionally, after performances Fuchs came to Starker's house for food and chat.

One night following a performance in the spring of 1954, Fuchs and Starker and several others were talking over a bite to eat, and their war experiences came up in conversation. They were very young during the war. There was the ever present danger of being killed. It was difficult for so many, being still youths, without father or mother. There were shortages in some places, food being rationed, etc.

Well, Starker smiled and said that his experience then was not very easy. He mentioned that he was in a detention camp near Budapest where warplanes were produced in the Messerschmidt plant. One day there were American planes carpet-bombing the area. People all around him in the V trenches were killed. One man completely lost his hearing. Despite the trauma of the event, Starker survived without so much as a scratch!

Fuchs asked, "When was that?" For Starker, this was easy to remember. It was July 31st, 1944, ten years ago. Fuchs then reached into his pocket and took out his diary. After a few moments of pondering, Fuchs said, "I was one of those bombers." Silence. Starker put out his hand, shook hands with him and said, "Thank you for missing me!"

Originally Starker planned to stay in Chicago only four years. "Well before the start of the fourth season, I handed in my resignation telling that I would be leaving in a year," says Starker. "But then came the Hungarian Revolution in 1956 when I imported a large number of my family members to the United States. I could not afford to leave the orchestra, and so I remained until my newly assumed debts were paid. Then I proposed that the Chicago Symphony allow me to continue playing principal cello, but only when Reiner was conducting. Reiner, however, refused to go along with such an arrangement, and I left. For a family man to leave a secure and honored orchestral post was nothing short of madness. But I never had any doubt that I could make a living as a soloist. It was simply that a career as a soloist was what I had been trained for, and that was what I had to do," says Starker.

It was in 1958 that Starker accepted the teaching position at Indiana University. "Reiner got very mad at me for leaving," Starker recalls. "At the time I considered him like my father, and I was one of the few people who ever left the Chicago Symphony Orchestra without being fired. Those five years plus the four years in the Met were among the most important in my life, making music on the highest level with a truly great conductor."

Completing his final season with the Chicago Symphony, Starker's fellow cellists gave him a tie pin. It marks an event in his last season with the orchestra. The maestro had paid his departing cellist a tribute before a performance of the Verdi *Requiem*. At the dress rehearsal, Starker's razor-sharp mind wandered long enough for him to lose count during a passage of unaccompanied sopranos. The cellist rejoined the music a bar too soon. Reiner cast a furious look at his wayward colleague and threw his baton to the floor. They did not make up for a while. But before they did, the cello section gave Starker a tie pin in the shape of a broken baton.

George Szell, Eugene Ormandy, Fritz Reiner, and Antal Dorati, all Hungarian conductors, at one time dominated major music centers in the United States. About Reiner Starker says, "Fritz Reiner was not necessarily the greatest performer of all time, but, in my opinion, he was the greatest conductor in terms of musical knowledge and technique. He was not only my favorite conductor, but he was the conductor I consider the greatest of the twentieth century. Bruno Walter, Otto Klemperer, Ernest Ansermet and Pierre Monteux were also outstanding. But Reiner was especially distinguished by his knowledge of the scores. Among hundreds of other works, he knew by memory Stravinsky's *Le Sacre du Printemps*, now considered the test piece for conductors. Moreover, he could balance an orchestra while focusing on what the score contained. He had control of the orchestra with minimal means, simply with his knowledge and his ear. He did the least stage acting of any conductor. If he repeated a program for four performances, three of them might not be necessarily exciting. But his performances were of the highest order, musically and technically. Sometimes when he had done a fabulous rehearsal, he felt the job was done so then perhaps the concert was not quite as interesting. But if the rehearsal was still not quite what he wanted, then he could give a staggeringly brilliant performance! I loved Reiner," he says. "I learned from him never to take anything for granted, never to let routine take over the music. Another important lesson I learned in Chicago. Pianist William Backhaus came to play Beethoven's *Concerto* with us. He had played concertos everywhere, but he worked hard in rehearsal, and every night in concert he got better. I thought, 'This is a model for me!'"

Starker's regard for George Szell is only slightly lower than his regard for Reiner. "The only problem with Szell was that he was too much a teacher. Even in the middle of a performance, he still taught the orchestra and the audience. That is a problem, especially for someone like myself, not to be a teacher while on the stage. Teaching involves making a point or bringing an issue to the fore. It may mean emphasizing a particular voice, stressing a bowing, or delineating a harmonic change or where the structure builds. Exaggeration is an essential part of teaching. If you do the same exaggeration on the stage, then you are teaching. But the audience is there for a performance.

"With Leonard Bernstein his exaggeration resulted not from teaching but from his personality. Although Bernstein came the closest of any musician I've known to being a genius, I did not consider him a great conductor. His genius came from the composite of conductor, pianist, composer, educator and writer. I do not believe that performing artists are geniuses, only those who are creative artists. Performers are recreative artists. Because of his excesses, I did not admire Bernstein as a conductor. He misguided many musicians by falling in love with notes, phrases and dynamics that were often unrelated. If a conductor learns the gestures but does not learn the score, that upsets me. In spite of this, he created many exciting evenings for millions and brought many people into the musical fold.

"Sir John Barbirolli was a good cellist with whom I played chamber music many times. I admired him primarily because he was an outstanding human being. It is one thing to admire people for their performances on stage, the books they write, the scientific discoveries they make, or whatever. It is another to view them as human beings. Most of the time I am short on admiration for conductors as human beings. They are too often interested in their own glory. On the other hand, I'm not particularly interested in hearing the dirt about these people. Let them conduct, and let's admire them for that. But forget them as human beings. The general public tends to either idolize or tear down those who are famous, but basically it is the job of the fourth estate, the press, to provide fascinating material for the masses."

Jean Martinon, French composer, was a very dear friend to Starker. He was someone Starker admired very much. They collaborated in chamber music, and one time Starker coached his orchestral string players. Martinon had written a *Cello Concerto* which was premiered in France by Pierre Fournier. When Martinon showed the score to Starker, Starker recommended some changes. He gave the premier performance in Ravinia with conductor Seiji Ozawa. He later performed the piece in Carnegie Hall, then in Washington and other cities.

Starker's inaugural appearance with an orchestra in New York was not with the New York Philharmonic but with the visiting Chicago Symphony under Jean Martinon. It was in March of 1966 when Starker performed Martinon's *Cello Concerto*. Harold Schoenberg of the New York Times called the piece eclectic. He said, "It was melodically inhibited and never seems to go anywhere, well-written as it is. But if nothing else," he added, "it is a formidable virtuoso piece for the solo cello. Seldom does the instrumentalist have a rest. He is on the go almost the whole way, picking a path through all kinds of complicated figurations, fancy running passages, abrupt shifts." Starker's performance "was dazzling. Is there a cellist anywhere who has so infallible a left hand? Or bow arm, for that matter? Mr. Starker is suave and subtle as always, with his perfectly equalized technique (no buzzing on the low notes for him), his aplomb and his almost terrifying equanimity, played the concerto like the great instrumentalist he is."

Years later when Starker was in Paris, Martinon invited Starker to perform with his orchestra, the French National Orchestra. When Starker arrived at the rehearsal in Paris, he found that someone else was conducting, Jasha Horenstein. Martinon's wife told Starker that he was out of town, doing some mountain climbing. Later over dinner she told Starker, "Jean was very hurt." Apparently he felt that Starker was not effusive enough when they performed together in Carnegie Hall. Starker said, "I brought him out, and we took the bows." That should be sufficient. But he felt that Starker was not complimentary enough. Perhaps since Martinon was conductor of the Chicago Symphony and also a composer, he felt he was deserving of more recognition. Unfortunately, he was insecure with his own work.

Starker was concerned because the next day he was going to fly to Hawaii to play the same concerto with another conductor, George Barati. His mind was on the next performance, and he wanted to remember everything that went wrong so that at the coming rehearsal they would not fall into the same trap. Then the next performance would be better. Maybe he did not do enough of "the Russian bit" on stage, the kiss on each cheek, hugging, and carrying on. If the audience is not applauding enough, then you applaud the audience to stir them up and get them excited so that they clap more. "This is one of the oldest tricks in the business," says Starker. "I learned in the Met how to get the audience frantic with excitement. I tested it a couple of times, but then I felt dirty afterwards and decided not to do it."

One time Paul Paray, French conductor, came to conduct the Chicago Symphony. It was a mind-boggling experience for the orchestra. He brought his own parts for the orchestra members to use. In the parts he had circled with red, blue, green, and pink colored pencil every so often a crescendo, a ritardando, a forte or some other instruction in the music. In the rehearsal he stopped the orchestra when there was a colored circle in the music. "Gentlemen," he said, "please crescendo." He stopped every time at the next colored circle and the next, and the next. At the next lamppost he said "accellerando," then "sforzando," then "Gentlemen, please, piano." It was all marked there in the music, but he felt the need to remind everyone. There was only about an hour and a half of music, and after a couple of hours of rehearsal they had covered all of the music. So then he started all over at the beginning again. He stopped the orchestra each time at the identical places the second time around. Three rehearsals went on like this, and the orchestra was in a shambles! He was always very nice. Pretty soon the orchestra automatically stopped at each colored circle before the conductor's indication, knowing that he was going to stop.

At the general rehearsal, the fourth one, suddenly out of nowhere he started suggested fingerings to the celli, and that went on for about ten minutes. The entire orchestra was waiting. Then Starker said, "Please maestro, if you want to give us a cello lesson, that is perfectly all right. We'll stay. But please let the rest of the orchestra go." Paray replied, "I do not understand." So Starker told him in French. And so went one of the more memorable experiences of the Chicago Symphony.

Disturbingly frank in his opinions, Starker has not gone out of his way to endear himself to some of the world's great conductors. "If I play with a mediocre conductor, I'm the nicest man alive, trying to help. If I'm playing for a top orchestra, and they are not giving their best, I'm furious. I raise my voice." He has had differences with Bruno Walter, George Szell, Eugene Ormandy and Herbert von Karajan. For this reason, his début with the New York Philharmonic was delayed until 1972. He played with the Cleveland Orchestra, but Szell did not conduct. Nor has he returned to the Berlin Philharmonic. Says Starker, "Karajan kept me waiting an hour at a rehearsal, and only then did he proceed to learn the score."

In 1950 in New York there was some discussion over who would conduct the recording of *Die Fledermaus*. Fritz Reiner was to conduct the opera with his record company, RCA Victor. In the meantime, in came Max Rudolph to take over as manager of the opera company. The Metropolitan Opera Company as an entity had a recording contract with Columbia Records. No one could solve this problem. If Reiner recorded for RCA, then they could not use the Met Orchestra. The Met wanted to record it. Rudolph Bing decided to use another conductor.

They found a central European expert, Eugene Ormandy, to conduct the opera. He actually volunteered his services for free. As a boy, Ormandy was a student at the Liszt Academy in Budapest, but some years before Starker. At that time his name was Eugene Blau. In 1950 he was the conductor of the Philadelphia Orchestra, but he had never conducted an opera. His manager, Arthur Judson, told him that he should establish himself as an opera conductor for the sake of his career. So he took the job. In the meantime Reiner recorded excerpts from the opera with RCA Victor and prepared the Metropolitan Opera Company orchestra and singers. Then Ormandy took over.

Ormandy was introduced to the orchestra as the great maestro, and the rehearsal started. As he began conducting, he turned around to Tibor Kozma, the assistant conductor who had worked with Reiner in preparing the orchestra. He asked him in Hungarian, "Is this the right tempo?" He did not realize that there were two other Hungarians sitting just under his baton, Starker and the assistant concertmaster, Victor Aitay. With the fourth time he asked this, they sort of "lost respect" for the great maestro. Instead of Reiner, who was truly the great maestro, Ormandy came to conduct, and, according to Starker, "he didn't know the score."

Then every time there was something of importance for the celli to play, Ormandy turned to the cello section indicating, "more, more." When he asked for more, they played louder. His requests became more and more annoying to Starker. Pretty soon the section was playing so loud that everyone was scratching with their bows. But they did not physically move around in the process. Starker was known for not moving around while playing. Years later Starker learned that the celli in the Philadelphia Orchestra moved around like the wind was blowing them. Only then did their maestro believe they were "playing their hearts out."

Finally, Starker went to Ormandy and asked if there were anything wrong with the cello section. "You keep asking for more, and we are playing so loud that we are blasting everyone's ears," he said. Ormandy's response was "Oh, no, no. I am so accustomed to my wonderful cello section in Philadelphia." At the time the Met orchestra was a better orchestra than practically any orchestra in the world. All the players were the most routined, all solo caliber players. There was no better cello section anywhere. Starker said, "You may be accustomed to having the celli on your right. We are sitting on your left." He started gasping for air and said, "Maybe it's the basses." Starker replied, "It is up to you to decide." The next day the orchestra manager told Starker to take it easy. Then the manager received a disciplinary letter stating that "some people are not collaborating with the conductor." Starker said to the manager, "I took it easy. I didn't do anything against him."

A Saturday performance was announced on the radio with Eugene Ormandy conducting. Actually, Ormandy conducted the first act, and then left to go back to Philadelphia to conduct a concert there. Tibor Kozma took over and finished the performance, but he had to be paid. Ormandy was conducting for free. Needless to say, this situation did not endear Starker to Eugene Ormandy.

It was in 1985, when he was sixty, that Starker first appeared as soloist with the Philadelphia Orchestra. His was an unhurried path to this début. Because of his misunderstanding with Ormandy in the fifties, which Starker considered an exchange in Hungarian between cellist and conductor over a matter of interpretation, Starker lost his chance to be soloist with the Philadelphia Orchestra until much later under the baton of Klaus Tennstedt. Characteristically, for this performance he chose the Hindemith *Concerto* (1940), a work of considerable challenge, but it was Klaus Tennstedt who was conducting, not Ormandy.

The review of this concert by Daniel Webster in the *Philadelphia Inquirer,* epitomizes everything Starker stands for: "In playing the Hindemith *Concerto,* Starker declared himself a perfectionist, a rationalist who had thought out all the dimensions of the music before touching the bow to the strings. The extremes of his dynamic had been determined in his mind, and the music's elements were ordered and proportioned in a way that missed being mathematical only because they were musically conceived. The performance had tensions that heightened every phrase. Starker maintained his proportions masterfully. He did not strive for mass when some pointed, refined sound would make the point as well, and he did not try to overwhelm orchestral lines that he saw as collaborative instead of as a matter of accompaniment. His playing was detailed. His ability to articulate rapid phrases clarified writing that is often blurred in perform- ance. The cadenza in the first movement, instead of launching him on a soaring self-congratu- latory flight, showed him controlling all the dimensions of the showy writing and placing them all in relation to the music that had gone before. This was not machinelike playing, for the middle movement included lyrical playing of considerable sweep, and the final movement grew with the contrast between the cello's flowing line and the plucked strings of the orchestral accompa- niment." [38]

One time Starker went to perform for the opening concert at the Edinburgh Festival in Scotland, playing the Elgar *Concerto*. Ormandy was conducting at the same festival. Then Starker returned to play the rest of the summer season at Ravinia with Ormandy conducting. At the next rehearsal Ormandy said to Starker, "I see that you don't like to play with me." Starker replied that he missed the first concert because he was performing in Scotland. He said he assumed Ormandy must have also seen his name on the program when he was in Scotland. Ormandy tried to find some way to express his resentment toward Starker.

Years later Starker was in Interlochen, Michigan, performing the world premiere of Bernard Heiden's *Cello Concerto*, also Tchaikovsky's *Rococo Variations* with Nicolas Harsanyi con- ducting. Harsanyi was a very close friend of Ormandy and said to him out of his excitement for the concert, "You should play with Starker. We have so much fun." Ormandy was known as one of the best accompanying, collaborative conductors. Ormandy replied, "I don't want to hear his name!" Then three months later Starker played the Rozsa[39] *Concerto* with Solti in Chicago. Rozsa was a very old friend and colleague of Ormandy and called him and said, "Eugene, you should really do my concerto with Starker." Ormandy burst out and screamed, "What is this, a conspiracy!" Rozsa later called Starker from California to tell him.

So Starker sat down and wrote Ormandy a letter stating that for many years he has had great respect for Ormandy's music making. "I am sorry that this feeling is not reciprocal. However, I would like to state that never in my life have I ever asked anyone for a concert or an appearance. I am sorry that my friends find it in their hearts to 'sing my praises,' but I had nothing to do with it." Yours truly, J.S.

Ormandy called up Harsanyi and said, "That bastard did it again!"

Just before Ormandy died, when Starker played with Tennstedt in Chicago, Starker learned that Ormandy was staying in the same hotel and wrote him a note. Maybe that is what sent him over the edge, he surmised. A few weeks later he died.

When Starker passed age sixty, some of the young conductors whom Starker admired became his close friends. Into and beyond his seventies Starker greatly admired Dennis Russell Davies and Gerard Schwarz. Starker felt that, "although sometimes a bit on the crazy side, they are outstanding musicians and honest, decent human beings for whom music is primary. They don't lose their heads because they are celebrated and successful." Conductor Gerard Schwarz has collaborated with Starker in Seattle where Schwarz is director of the Seattle Symphony, also at New York's Mostly Mozart Festival, in concerts with the New York Chamber Symphony as well as the Los Angeles Chamber Orchestra. "Starker has an incredible integrity," says Schwarz. "He elevates the level of experience for the players. I've worked with him for twenty-five years. That integrity of his and the fame that follows him make the players sit up and listen and work harder."

Fritz Reiner: in Memoriam

a story by Janos Starker

The lights had been turned off in Chicago's Orchestra Hall, but the sound of an ovation still lingered. After I'd changed out of my formal wear, I felt compelled to go to Fritz Reiner's room backstage. He sat in his chair, his wife at his side.

"Great concert, Dr. Reiner!"

He looked at me with a tired smile.

"Wasn't it! So why don't you stay?"

Nine years had culminated, the most tiring and yet most valuable period of my life to that time, nine years of making music with the greatest conductor of our time. There were other maestros, of course, but none like Reiner, who pursued the highest goal so relentlessly, so uncompromisingly, with such complete dedication to perfection. He was neither the subject of a personality cult nor a showman. He made music and demanded that others make it with him. He accepted no excuse for weakness, never forgave talent that lacked discipline.

He built orchestra after orchestra to a standard unattained before him or after. He said you cannot teach conducting, only music. He did that, and the world is richer for his students. He said the public didn't appreciate contemporary music, but he felt that he had to introduce them. He did that, and the world is richer for having experienced a new wealth of beauty. He said often what was committed under the blanket of music was a shame, and felt he had to show the truth. He did that, and the world is left with a huge void now that he is gone.

Thank you, Dr. Reiner. It was a great continuous performance. One we will never forget.

J.S.

FRITZ REINER

∧∧∧

Why Do Cellists Become Conductors?

a story by Janos Starker

The lady on my right asked, "Do they?"

I paused a moment before replying. "Do who do what?"

"I mean," the woman continued unruffled, "do cellists really become conductors? Isn't that what your friend asked?"

"Ah! Well, it is rather taken for granted that cellists will become conductors. You know about Toscanini?"

"Oh, yes! Now that you remind me, I do remember hearing that once he was a cellist. But what difference should that make? Wasn't Pierre Monteux a violist, and Koussevitzky a contrabass virtuoso? And Ormandy a violinist? I'm sure I heard that Klemperer, Reiner and Furtwängler were pianists."

"True," I responded. "On the other hand, you have heard that Sir John Barbirolli, Paul Paray, Camargo Guarnieri, Pablo Casals, Alfred Wallenstein, Antonio Janigro, Arthur Winograd, Enrico Mainardi, Daniel Saidenberg, Hans Kindler, Howard Mitchell, Frank Miller, Mstislav Rosropovich, and...."

"You mean to say all those conductors were previously cellists?"

"Let's say they are either conductors or they conduct. Some of them still play the cello as well as conduct. Others simply spend time reminiscing with friends and former colleagues about their past glories as soloists, and concentrate full-time on conducting. However, just about every cellist who has attained some recognition as an instrumentalists has formed a chamber orchestra or a community group. Either he's already conducting or is dreaming about a future with the baton instead of a bow in his hand."

At this point, a gentleman in the group addressed the lady on some "vital" matter or other, and our discussion ended as abruptly as it began. Only two days later, a friend I've known since school asked the simple question, "What next?"

When I say "since school" I mean from the earliest days of our dreaming about a concert career, through years of study, years more of work in opera houses, symphony orchestras, popular music, recording studios and teaching—right to the point where the dream was becoming a reality.

"After all," my friend continued, "what is there left for you to do? Certainly you will play more concerts in maybe a hundred new cities, and receive greater praise and larger fees. But then what? Are you going to play the same Bach *Suites*, Beethoven *Sonatas* and Dvorak *Concerto* all the rest of your life? Don't you want to conduct?"

"Of course I want to conduct! And I've done it already!" Suddenly aware that I was almost shouting, I took a deep breath and lowered my voice. "What the hell is the matter with all you people? If a cellist starts conducting, everyone says, 'Him too? Another frustrated cellist! He can't make it as a cellist so he tries to be a conductor.' If a cellist doesn't want to conduct, however, you say 'Now there's an odd character: he can't even conduct! Maybe he's not such a marvelous musician after all. Natural talent and gifted hands, but no brain.'"

At that moment I decided it was time to explore the phenomenon of cellists who, although the underdogs in many ways in the world of music, still manage to occupy center stage in more roles than one.

First, let's define the cellists we recognize. There is the cellist who plays in a symphony, opera or Broadway orchestra, and separately there is the principal cellist of such ensembles.

Also there is the cellist in chamber groups—quartets, trios and the like. There is the cello teacher. And there is the cello virtuoso—the soloist, recitalist and recording artist.

This categorization applies as well to other instruments. For example, the pianistic parallel of the principal cellist in an orchestra is the piano coach in an opera house: these comprise the largest suppliers of the conducting profession. Because my own life has encompassed all five categories of "cellistic" endeavor, I have some advantage as an observer of the mind and thinker of colleagues. But a large question begs here and now to be asked, and this is: why do people become cellists in the first place? I'll venture that it is mostly coincidence, except in families where the father or mother hands down the cello to a budding offspring.

Otherwise, if the firstborn plays the piano or violin, parental passion for variety assigns a cello to the youngest one—which is usually the case, I'd go so far as to say. Since the littlest one is typically given more attention by elders and is thereby spoiled excessively, he or she grows up believing that the louder you cry the more you get. Years pass until this child is needled by the nonmusical community: "What's in that big box you're carrying? A sub-machine gun?" Let's face it, comparatively speaking the cello is still an arcane instrument: most persons when they see a cello case tend to think bass-fiddle or guitar. Furthermore, most persons don't expect a child to be lugging such instruments, and so within the child there develops resentment and the desire for revenge as well as musical and instrumental talents.

Now musical and instrumental talents call for some examination. To repeat, the cello is an instrument comparatively unknown—or rather, new. Amati and Stradivarius built fabulous cellos, true, but far fewer than violins. While a present-day symphony orchestra may have up to forty violins, it requires only ten or twelve cellos (a ratio essentially the same in smaller musical ensembles). The larger demand for violins produced a larger demand for instruments to play on. From this larger pool of players, a proportionately larger number of outstanding violinists developed.

We do know of outstanding cellists, but quantitatively their number is much smaller. The nature of the instrument itself created performance restrictions. Since the cello was used as an alternating as well as alternative bass by early composers, both melodic lines and flowering, flourishing phrases were assigned to higher-register instruments. The poor cellist, ready and anxious to express himself on four comparably expressive strings, was relegated by great composers to a nether sphere where only the musical minimum was required from agile fingers and fertile minds. A cellist's abilities match those of any other instrumentalist, but far less is demanded of the cellist. Early players felt, why should they bother? And composers felt, when hearing dispirited playing, that it would be futile to write anything more demanding for the cello.

If slowly the musical community came to believe that cellos must be indeed very difficult instruments, since so few were able to play them well, the question remained for cellists: To play *what* well? A few ambitious artists, driven both by bravado and by boredom, began to imitate the violin. They played transpositions of violin music, wrote their own compositions of dubious musical merit, and eventually succeeding in planting the idea of the cello as a potentially expressive solo instrument. How much of this idea-planting involved sex appeal we will never know. However, because of the paucity of music to be played and a "why bother" attitude, cellists to this day have far more time to eye the fairer sex during concerts (and elsewhere) than other players. This is the real reason that cellists are reputed to be ladies' men: I'm convinced that statistics would prove cellists to rank first among musicians as heterosexuals.

Over a long stretch of time, the ambitious few did exert an influence: composers attempted to write a few major works for the cello. But to what end? The legion of less ambitious players fell far behind—not because they weren't fine musicians or lacked a genuinely artistic personality but because their intonation was a bit off, unfortunately, and their sound was, well, scratchy. Composers looked over the balance sheet, saw how many times a piano concerto was played, and then how many time a cello concerto (not to mention expertise). For who then the next concerto? Guess.

Persons in charge of concert programming heed comments by composers as well as audiences. They look at the repertory available, and say "Sure the cello's a lovely instrument. Personally I like it best of all—but let's buy a pianist or violinist: I mean, who wants the Lalo *Cello Concerto* when we can have the Tchaikovsky *Violin Concerto*?" It is *La ronde, Reigen*—limited demand, limited supply, limited repertory, slow development and slow appreciation.

In the catbird seat sits the cellist. What does he *do* in an orchestra? He has, like all persons, to make a living. In some few cases the beautiful daughter of a wealthy father will fall in love with the man supporting the big fiddle, and solve his boring problem of a livelihood. Ah, the true pursuit of "l'art pour l'art." But there just aren't enough beautiful girls—with wealthy fathers, I mean to say-and so the cellist has to make his own living. How? He auditions for conductors—the terror of which, sooner or later, he overcomes. But, throughout his lifetime, the cellist hates or envies that breed of musician.

Let me say to those whom good fortune has spared the adventure with an audition for a conductor, it is an experience eminently to be detested. The pity is that no fair substitute has been found. Apart from a few podium sadists with "Charles Addams-y" grins on their faces, no one on either side of the music stand enjoys these agonizing adventures. But the torture finally ends, let's assume, and a cellist finds an opening in whatever orchestra. From here on, his attitude dovetails that of any person in any job on a low rung in the work hierarchy. But the cellist's consciously (or subconsciously) sensitive soul of an artist is different. The cellist feels he plays better than anyone else in his section, and a conductor must be *deaf* not to recognize this. If only he, the cellist, held the baton, *then* players would be deservingly ranked! The cellist can find many colleagues in agreement with his noble philosophy, but only he, of course, realizes that the conductor doesn't know Mozart, is only so-so in Beethoven, and can't even memorize his scores. The day will come, swears the cellist, when *he* will show the world how music should be conducted!

Cellists have a great deal of time to squander on thinking. Always with exceptions to the rule, cellists have fewer notes to play in a concert than their colleagues do. And those few with even less music to play are so unoccupied that they read magazines or double in such profitable second professions as real estate, insurance, stock-marketeering and instrument sellers. (One has to admit, in fairness, that the parlous state of musical economics *is* a motivating factor.)

If the cellist happens to play in an opera orchestra for any stretch of time, he begins to watch the stage and comes to know all singers and dancers by their legs. He fantasizes on their physiques and has mental affairs with them. Soon enough this diversion bores him, and so he turns to the audience: Greets the steady patrons, shares backstage gossip with them, imitates the conductor, becomes *the man in-the-know*. But there remains the interminable rehearsals with very little do to. Granted that some German conductors call unfailingly on the basses and cellos whenever the score has black dots in those parts, our man then concentrates on the music reluctantly and mutters to himself, "What does that guy think anyway? *I* can read music. He has no confidence in himself!" Should the conductor not notice him, however, or threaten him in some way, then his estimate of the man's ability is further eroded. Of course, great conductors do occasionally come his way, and his reaction is to agree with them wholeheartedly: "See? He takes *my* tempo. Exactly what I would have asked from the flute."

Time passes, and the standard repertory becomes fixed in his mind. The "bass" part gives him a fairly sound understanding of a work's construction, and so he commences to whistle melodic lines and various entrances by solo instruments. Thereby armed he may even begin to give cues. Should a conductor be otherwise occupied with details rather than entrances, the cellist responds with scornful looks and destructive commentary on the conductor's ability. He even makes deals with other players to cue them in after long pauses, just to be on the safe side, and thus enable them to finish studying that fascinating picture-story of someone else's visit to a natural paradise. In short, the orchestra has within it a potential conductor.

He dreams about the maestro falling off the podium, and his own leaping up to save the performance. He buy study-scores and memorizes them. He practices baton techniques in front of a mirror, and hums aloud on the bus or subway with slight manual emphases. He acknowledges respectful glances from his fellow travelers with, "Got to work, you know."

By this stage the cellist will be found talking more and more to the boss, offering solutions for acoustic problems, suggesting new seating, planning last week's soloist. And then one day a break comes! A friend in the community asks if he will help at the next meeting of an amateur orchestra: "Our conductor is sick, but we hate to cancel our Friday night rehearsal." The cellist complies: his conducting base is established. He has become a leader of his own orchestra: The road to Boston from here is an easy one.

The soul of a principal cellist differs somewhat. After all, he is a member of the aristocracy: only the concertmaster ranks above him. He can, in some instances, if hired under pressure, have his name in the orchestra program in heavy black type. He plays solos, receives handshakes, gathers applause and criticism, is invited to parties. He becomes chummy with members of the Board, and their ladies, and comes to be considered an authority by them. His pointed comments may influence policy-making, the choice of guest conductors, even of soloists. He is influential; he shouldn't be frustrated; but who isn't?

At this point a peculiar acoustical phenomenon enters upon the scene. Fate and tradition have placed the principal cellist in a location where every small, meaningless detail can be seen and heard by the orchestra. Leopold Stokowski, who may have been the first discoverer of this phenomenon dealt with it in rather a crude manner. He moved the entire cello section from a place it enjoyed historically. I will not venture to judge the results of this arrangement musically, but it certainly eliminated any threat of competition from within. There was, however, only one Stokowski. Traditionally and continuingly, the principal cellist sits in his chair on the conductor's right hand and hears colleagues' mistakes and tells the latest Martian jokes. He looks up at the conductor with a forgiving smile to defang any forthcoming outburst, only to hear the Maestro ask the timpanist if he will move to the right so he can see him. "Impossible!," thinks the principal cellist. "The man has no *ears!* My ears are finer than his!" Give the principal cellist a few years, multiply this incident by hundreds of rehearsals and concerts, add the temperament of a section player, and another "conductor" has been seasoned to take over.

The public is prepared to welcome him; his contacts are strong and he has established his authority in other realms. His sex appeal may gain him the freedom and comfort to study music for a few years—even to hire an orchestra and a hall. Whereupon managers tend to oblige: They're not being forced to take any risks. The new "Maestro" is on his way to Elysian Fields. Mind you, though, the moment he steps onto an elevated podium his ears no longer hear the acoustic phenomenon he enjoyed when seated as principal cellist. As long as his memories of subordination stay with him, he will throw a tantrum from time to time and threaten to expel half the orchestra for a lack of discipline. Given time, he will discover a gradual improving in rank-&-file behavior; whereupon his underling, the current principal cellist, begins his transformation into a conductor.

The cellist in chamber music ensembles is a wholly separate species. Actually, he is a soloist, a stellar member of musical society. He works hard, usually assumes the role of the group's musicologist, and occasionally takes on managerial duties in addition. He studies scores, corrects bowings and dynamics, and actually conducts the affairs of his group. That group, however, hardly ever bears his name, and so he grows tired and finally sick of being called "the cellist" of Trio-X, Quartet-Y or Quintet-Z. He sits there with all that assumed responsibility and no one ever remembers his name. He quits, goes to another group, and traditionally becomes the most troublesome member because of his "star" complex. Having arrived here, a new "conductor" can hardly ever be diverted; his orchestra will be trained like a string quartet.

The soloist or recital cellist is the fighter and maverick of our breed. He fights the competition, managers, conductors and, above all, he fights for engagements and increased recognition. Any time another cellist plays with an orchestra, he charges political ties or family connections. When, however, he obtains an engagement, it is always on pure artistic grounds. He becomes successful, plays many concerts, but no matter the level he reaches on the musical ladder, his fee never matches those paid to violinsts, pianists or singers who are otherwise peers.

And he has transportation hassles: He must purchase extra plane tickets for his cello; in and out of autos, trains and planes he gets muscle pains from carrying that big box (but *no* one else dares touch the sacred thing).

He is discouraged by managers from his pursuit. Conductors explain infrequent engagements on the ground of too few popular concertos; they accompany him but seldom to his heart's desire. More and more, then, he dreams about playing *and* conducting. He grows restless at performing the same sonatas by composers unknown to the public, and those bagatelles required to demonstrate his virtuosity. He tires of fighting for the chance to play masterpieces that aren't good box-office (if the box-office even opens for him). So he forms a chamber ensemble in which he plays, but which he also conducts.

With contacts, he offers a musical variety beyond the bait of himself as cellist. This has proved to be a "natural" concert attraction. Shortly, the cellist's hands turn rusty and the "maestro's" program becomes entirely symphonic. He does this, remember, not because he lacks success in a limited field or is less than the best of breed, but because, after all, the scene is being joined by ambitious younger cellists ("We must give them the chance"). And, with his own immense talent and experience, he owes the world a greater range of his artistry, better expressed through orchestral literature....

Contrarily, cello teachers find themselves accidentally with a baton in hand; their invaluable advice has been solicited from a lofty pedagogic height. So who can blame them if they can't let loose of the baton; they are not, after all, supernatural.

I have yet to meet the musician who wouldn't like to conduct, and stand firm in the belief that, had any person in today's world who menaces the human race be given a baton and an orchestra early on in life, he would have been far happier and the world a better place to inhabit. A striking similarity between *conductors* and *dictators* has been noted by many, their physiques as well as characters. Surely it would be less consequential if one such were empowered to fire a few musicians rather than rockets or bombs.

But what of cellists who do not conduct? First of all, most of these rare exceptions have not conducted *yet*. There are the few, though—devoted and/or happy, satisfied with their lives-who find further self-expression in nonmusical pursuits: Do-it-yourself handicrafts, writing, painting, fishing... devoted ones who believe that someone has to fly the cello's flag, to carry on its tradition, to further its cause, and to open closed doors.

Too, the situation has improved: New works have been composed, and even finer cellists have developed. How long the devoted ones will maintain their steadfastness none can know, or even predict. Dangle a baton in front of any, and loyalty may succumb. At times they can be heard to say, "It doesn't matter what instrument you play, if you are a great artist your merit will be acknowledged. Look at Segovia; before him, the classical guitar was an all but unknown instrument." True, Segovia conquered the world, but the world lost a potentially great cellist because he chose not to remain with his first instrument.

What is there finally to say? Conductors of the world, beware of those who stare intently at you from the back of their cello stands! They are your competitors, not just in the future but now. They may be disguised as violists or other instrumentalists, but the mentality is kindred.

By no means an afterthought, any resemblance in the foregoing to conductors and cellists living or dead is wholly coincidental. I have lived with them, lived because of them, and love them all. Should any take offense at this sober, self-effacing, needful analysis of a significant subject, let them remember that it is preferred for me to remain a jolly cellist rather than a cankerous threat to the conducting profession. I, too, have a few slightly used batons in a bedside drawer and am, when all's said and done, only human.

J.S., Bloomington, Indiana, 1961

As soon as he left the Chicago Symphony, solo opportunities opened up to Starker, one being the city's summer ensemble, the Grant Park Symphony led by Milton Katims. The orchestra welcomed Starker to its lakeside band shell for a performance of the Dvořák *Concerto* beside Lake Michigan. Although the Chicago Tribune's volatile critic, Claudia Cassidy, was said to have been annoyed by Starker's withdrawal from the Chicago Symphony, she was won over by what she heard. "Not in my count of summers has there been a more beautiful performance on a moonstruck lakefront." She called the playing "eloquent, marked with a new authority, with new boldness, brilliance, and sweep... quite simply, a great performance."

In *The Chicago American*, Roger Detmer referred to Starker as "beyond debate the world's master cellist, a technician of supreme control and a musician of the rarest taste and refinement." Don Henahan of the *Chicago Daily News* noticed an "audience in which young girls were the most vociferous rooters," an audience not as large as that for pianist Van Cliburn, (a Moscow Tchaikovsky Competition winner of recent vintage with widespread media-induced fame, who had appeared earlier in the summer) but exhibiting "hero worship, easily as intense."

The engagements mounted. He would soon be warmly welcomed in London where he joined Walter Goehr and the Royal Philharmonic at Festival Hall for the Schumann *Concerto* and then commanded a solo spotlight during a performance of Bach's *Unaccompanied Suite in D*. Noel Goodwin said in the *Daily Express* that "a rare degree of imagination and purpose lay beneath the soloist's easy technical mastery of what is incidentally a virtuoso study of the instrument ... faultless phrasing and discreet expression drawn from the noble 'Lord Aylesford Stradivarius.'" The Schumann *Concerto* was less favorably received by the critics, most of whom blamed the composer. Charles Reid of the *News Chronicle* labeled it a "lame, tame piece." Says Starker, "The performer-composer relationship really helps. Schumann had no cellist of consequence to consult. If he had, his *Concerto* would be stronger and without some of its flaws."

There were countless venues on Starker's agenda between the Grant Park concert of 1958 and the 1959 concert in London, also between London and the 1960 engagement in New York's Metropolitan Museum. That one, however, held special importance. Although Starker had previously appeared in a small hall, the Met concert was considered his New York début recital. Critical response was enthusiastic. Paul Henry Lang of the *Herald Tribune* referred to the concert as "an artistic event of the first magnitude." "Starker was," he said, "a superlative cellist, equipped with an abundance of technique and a magnificent tone." Harold Schoenberg of the *New York Times* wrote, "Mr. Starker is a musician who is responsive to style. Whether dealing with the Brahms *E Minor Sonata*, the Debussy *Sonata*, Beethoven's *A Major Sonata* or the *Sonata* (1958) by Bernard Heiden, which was heard the first time in New York, the cellist was in sympathy with the text and the message. His phrasing has remarkable finish. Never is his playing flat. Rather it has (in common with all superior musicians) a constant alternation of release and tension. Some of this is calculated. An arm like Starker's can accomplish all kinds of shading in one bow. But the important thing is that it never sounded calculated. Rather it seemed inevitable."

In New York, Starker's partner was the veteran pianist Mieczyslaw Horzowski. To Schoenberg's ears, "Without a false moment or any suggestion of instrumental display, these two artists made music simply, elegantly and adroitly." At this time Starker was beginning to team up with his boyhood friend and pianist György Sebök who would not only share the stage with him for many years but also become his colleague at Indiana University. Early in 1963 the two artists performed in Chicago. Roger Dettmer of *The American* found their readings of *Sonatas* by Bach, Mendelssohn, Brahms, and a cello-piano transcription of Bartók's *First Rhapsody* "hypnotizing." He judged each "a musician of the foremost rank," and was struck by their rapport—a mutuality of purpose that one encounters, if lucky, never more than once in a decade. And "if one tended to be more conscious of Starker, it is because he has been a major concert artist longer, with the edge of authority that comes with international touring and worldwide acclaim. That is not to say, however, that Sebök was self-effacing or reticent. He played with extraordinary taste and sensitivity. No style is beyond his grasp or ability to communicate on the basis of last evening's evidence." Donald Henahan of the *Daily News* reported that "Sebök was not relegated to the background to strum the keyboard discreetly, as suits the vanity of some famous instrumentalists. In each piece of the night, he contributed powerfully."

For Starker, the choice of partnership has always been of vital importance. "It's problematic to pick up a temporary pianist when one is on tour," he says. "To find the right Argentinean or Brazilian or Japanese or whatever is not easy, and I haven't the nerve to do a lot of extra rehearsing on tour." For years, in Europe, he used the German pianist, Günther Ludwig, "always dependable, flexible, sensitive." "Sebök," says Starker," has played with me for fifty-eight years. We grew up together, we learned together. We experienced life together. We're soul mates."

Shigeo Neriki, a frequent co-performer in the past twenty-five years, is another colleague at Indiana University. "Neriki played for the students in my class. He grew to understand how I approach music and what I look for in the give-and-take of a recital," says Starker. "It becomes a matter of each knowing what the other does, then experimenting our way into an integrated interpretation. Now we have travelled four continents together. Musical and emotional rapport are such that heavy rehearsing are unnecessary. We share wave-lengths and simply try to run the program to refresh our memories."

Says Neriki, "I usually go to the concert hall before Mr. Starker to check out the piano and to see what kind of chair he will be sitting on. We spend an hour there together, then go back to the hotel and rest. I go to the concert hall about two hours before the house opens in order to spend enough time to get used to the piano and the acoustics. Mr. Starker arrives at the hall about fifteen minutes before the concert. We know what we strive for. Working with Mr. Starker is never a puzzle. He is clear. We talk. We practice. We adjust. He lifts me up to do my best. I think I do that for him. I think I help."

Starker believes in the collaborative nature of concert giving. "I want to be around musicians who are full-bodied human beings when I socialize, when I rehearse, when I perform." He wrote of the partner, not accompanist concept to a mythical friend in 1982: "An excellent accompanist must be a good pianist, an excellent musician and ensemble player. What is the meaning of the word accompanist? The dictionary states, 'to go with, to add to, or to play or sing an accompaniment for or to.' For centuries, composers published songs and instrumental works with piano accompaniment. There were composers who wrote works with such dominant roles for the chosen instrument, containing startling virtuoso display, that even without the perfunctory piano part, the work could pass successfully. In these cases the word accompanist could be applied. But what do we do when Beethoven and others publish works for piano and violin, piano and cello, etc.? Who is accompanying whom? Obviously neither part can stand alone irrespective of the number of notes played, plus the two people must express the composer's intentions together in partnership.

"These two types, partnership versus accompaniment, are comparable to the difference between the concerti of the seventeenth and eighteenth centuries versus those of the nineteenth and twentieth centuries. In the eighteenth century, the solo instrument dominated the orchestra, while in the latter centuries the orchestra has the symphonic role with the solo part as its principal feature.

"Obviously, when great virtuosos join singers or instrumentalists on occasion, these issues do not exist. No one calls artists like Gieseking, Bernstein, Ashkenazi, Barenboim, Lhevinne, etc., accompanists. On the other hand, when a yet unknown potential virtuoso-pianist appears on the stage with a famous performer, the savants of the press and public are quick to classify the person as an excellent accompanist, and from then on, the young artist may remain victimized as a trespasser to the solo ranks. It took long years for the public to forget Serkin's and Magaloff's associations with Busch and Szigeti. Without these artists, the great virtuosos would have had a difficult time functioning.

"Perhaps the most famous of them, Gerald Moore, whose contributions are legendary and his humor incomparable, has done more ill-service in perpetuating the word accompanist than anyone else. When he wrote his delightful recollections, he titled them, *The Accompanist*. But what a joy it was when Mr. Moore sat at the piano, and with a simple harmony change gave meaning to the phrase until then neglected. What an uplifting experience it was when in a repeated phrase he anticipated the desire to vary the expression, or he threw the challenge of a rubato within disciplined boundaries to the leading musical line. Real ensemble playing is not just playing together. It is living, breathing, and speaking notes and phrases with the same accents and beliefs.

"I appeal to you, the managers, organizers, printers, reviewers, and audiences. Make your references to the pianist, or someone at the piano, or the partner, and not to the accompanist. Above all, let us remind all the partners to be proud of their contributing more to the music than will ever be known." J.S., 1982

Martin Mayer, writing in *Esquire Magazine* in 1963, shared with his readers a description of a younger Janos Starker, "... a muscular, terrifyingly bright young man with black eyes staring out below his black eyebrows and an almost bald head. If there had been no Yul Brynner, Starker could have invented one. Technically he was a cellist of almost unbelievable skill, who had developed personal techniques of both bow and fingering. Musically his taste was severe, as befitted a man brought up on Bach and Bartók. He could play loud and soft, legato, staccato, and molto agitato with that angry, biting attack which is so much more convincing on the cello than on the other strings. He always made musical sense as well as musical sounds."

Rarely has there ever been anything but unanimity from the ranks of reviewers regarding Starker's work. Take, for example, the reactions to a 1972 performance of the Kodály *Solo Sonata* during the Ravinia Festival in Chicago's northern suburbs. The critical acclaim was euphoric. Dettmer of the *American* said that the sonata "under his fingers is not nationalistic Kitsch or sophisticated folklore, but a very major work by an almost major composer of the century. To hear it played as Starker played it last night, one realizes that he has added as much to the arsenal of virtuoso cello playing as Casals in decades bygone." Linda Winer of the *Daily News* wrote that he played it "with an infallible left hand, a tone someone called black silk, and a total mastery of this music of huge color demands." Robert C. Marsh of the *Sun Times* suggested the sonata might be subtitled "Everything you ever wanted to know about cello playing—but were afraid to ask," adding that it "contains all of the effects in the book, and a few that aren't, ending with an absolute whirlwind of virtuoso effects." Reminding the reader that the work features a Hungarian style, Marsh observed, "Starker sings these songs of his homeland with a special awareness of what gives them life."

For many years, Starker appeared repeatedly across the European continent, achieving, for instance, considerable success at major festivals in Prague, Edinburgh, Vienna, among others. After a 1969 concert during the Prague Spring Festival, a reviewer wrote, "What is important is that while playing, he seems to remain in the shade, simply a servant of music. One gets the impression that playing the cello is so easy. This evidently unaffected naturalness is always a feature of perfection. What one will remember about this kind of concert is just the music— beautiful, quiet, and emotional." The accolade came from the periodical, *Hudebni Rozhledy.*

Several years later, critics in Detroit had responded to his stamina. In one concert by the Detroit Symphony, Starker had taken on the Hindemith *Concerto* as well as the Brahms *Double Concerto* with his son-in-law Bill Preucil, violinist. Then they performed the Beethoven *Triple Concerto* with pianist-conductor Dennis Russell Davies. The reviewer, Mark Stryker of the *Free Press* said that attendance afforded an "opportunity to bear witness to Starker, who at age seventy-one has lost very little if anything off his fast ball. His technique remains unimpeachable, and his tone is still laser-like in its intensity, cutting easily through thick ensemble textures or soaring above the orchestra."

Writing about Starker's belated début with the New York Philharmonic in October of 1972, Harold Schoenberg in the *New York Times* verbalized his feelings as follows: "Mr. Starker's clean-cut style served this concerto (Haydn's *C Major Concerto*) especially well. He is a cellist who plays with a noble kind of severity, not in a dry manner by any means, but with a disinclination to slop over his instrument. He uses a tight vibrato that never departs from dead center, he shapes the musical material with utmost logic, he almost never slides into notes, and he is a fiend for perfect articulation."

Following a performance of Bloch's *Schelomo*, John Haskins wrote in the *Kansas City Star*, "There are various ways to attack the Bloch rhapsody and normally the cello soloist will take the overripe route. But that is not Starker's way with anything he plays. Faithful to the material, with a tone that is large enough and robust enough but never booming, he hews to the line of the score and demonstrates that expressivity need never slop over, that intensity can mean something besides a bow-whipping exercise in hitting the audience over the head."

Says Starker, "I don't believe in theatricality, in foaming at the mouth, in driving, driving, driving. Tricks may cause talk at the end of the evening. They may arouse conversation. But that shouldn't be the goal. If entertainment dominates, I have failed in my mission to bring music to the audience. Emotion should come through, of course. My mission, however, is to recreate poetry through music, not to speak about music in poetic terms. It is not to create a show, a circus."

Starker performed at Tanglewood in 1977, and in 1992 in Symphony Hall in Boston when he performed the Hindemith *Concerto* as well as Strauss' *Don Quixote* with Erich Leinsdorf conducting. Richard Dyer of the *Globe* found the Hindemith *Concerto* "dryasdust," then added that Starker is not an emotive player, and one wonders what Piatigorsky, a musician of entirely contrasting temperament, made of his style. "Starker's performance," he said, "set the piece forth, and you could make blueprints from it; the performance lingers in the mind, but not in the imagination." In the Strauss, his playing was in every respect commanding in intellect and execution, and in *The Knight's Vigil* he drew upon an almost vocal range of resource in drawing eloquence."

Starker's critics tell us that in his mid-seventies he plays with the same accuracy and musicality as he did decades ago. His hair is no longer black, and his eyes seem softer, but he remains a lean figure with an intensely searching glance. Following a 1999 Dvořák *Concerto* with the Pacific Symphony in Southern California, Timothy Mangan of the *Orange County Register* noted, "There didn't seem to be a wasted motion in it. It was like one of those perfect drawings by Al Hirschfeld, where a few lines catch the entire being of the subject... Starker gave the music plenty of room to breathe. Most cellists, even the good ones, jump all over this concerto and ride it for all it's worth, exploring every cranny, milking every nuance, exulting every peak, juicing up the vibrato to full power. Starker remained calm and poised, allowing the music to do its own storytelling. That's called trusting your material."

The most perceptive critics have acknowledged, accepted, and appreciated Starker's approach. Take these comments from Boris Nelson in the *Toledo Blade* in Ohio, written about a Starker-Neriki recital at Bowling Green State University: "Janos Starker remains the ultimate aristocrat of the cello—stern and disciplined, with an intense iciness on the outside and fire within that seems to leap out with the very first sweep of the bow. It has always been thus, and one should not expect anything else now. But there is something else, call it sagacity, if you will, which is adding a patina to his forever phenomenal playing. The sheer technical mastery is something awesome to behold. He plays the cello as many a violinist could wish for. The intonation is pure, on the head, the bowing an extension and partner of a most musical mind. For all the wizardry, there is the making of beautiful music—with every note in its place, its light or shade, its accent, its color, its sound absolutely right. For while Mr. Starker is one of the great virtuosi of all time, it is his musicality which is served by it, and so is the music."

In an interview with Evelyn Ames in her 1977 collection of interviews with thirty remarkable people, entitled *Mastery*, Starker tells, "I have never called myself an interpreter. I have always been a recreative artist. Can I do something different night after night, sometimes with the same piece, by re-creating a masterpiece? That's the motivation. It's also whether my re-creation appeals to or triggers the imagination of some people in the audience. I say 'some people' because in a hall of two or three thousand people, not everyone will understand my motivation or have the same perceptiveness that I have. I try to give enough to the people who are not familiar with the piece of music or the cello so that they still experience some resemblance of beauty and the joy of being lifted out of their everyday existence. My goal is to produce the highest level I possibly can under the circumstances with that piece. Pleasing the audience is secondary. The primary thing is, here is the work that I love, here I am, striving to totally enrich the music I am playing." This is the philosophical underpinning to his extraordinary career.[40]

Conversations with György Sebök

György Sebök, pianist, grew up in Szeged, Hungary, a major cultural center on the southern border of Hungary. The day came when as a sixteen-year-old his father said that he was the best pianist in Szeged. It was time to move to a place where people play much better than he. He moved to Budapest and became a student at the Franz Liszt Academy. It was there that he and Janos Starker met and became friends. They have been performing together ever since.

In order to gain more performance experience and a little pocket money, Sebök and Starker formed a trio with violinist Francis Akos. Says Sebök, "Out of sheer interest we frequently read through trio repertoire, not as an assignment for any teacher, but just for our own curiosity. I put a pile of trios on the piano, and we played through them nonstop. We would read, for example, a Brahms trio wondering, 'How does it sound?'" They organized a series of concerts for themselves in private homes in Budapest, performing the repertoire for piano trio, for cello and piano, for violin and piano, and for violin and cello. The Beethoven *Triple Concerto*, the Brahms *Double Concerto* and solo concertos were part of their performance repertoire. They performed all of the possible repertoire for their instruments, wanting more experience before being on stage somewhere.

They were students near the end of what Sebök calls the "Golden Age of Music" at the Liszt Academy. Hungary at the time wanted to belong to the West culturally and looked westward for musical influences, German and Austrian influences, French as well. Budapest was a shining center of music and culture. They were studying in the midst of a fantastic environment.

Says Sebök, "I say the end of the 'Golden Age' because our teachers were students during the middle of the 'Golden Age.' Imagine four students including Bartók, Kodály, Dohnanyi and Leo Weiner in the composition class! And then after they graduated, these four composers went on to become major figures in twentieth century music. Ironically, they proceeded to go in four very different directions with their compositions and their work in music.

"When we were students at the Liszt Academy, Leo Weiner was our chamber music teacher. He was undoubtedly the finest music teacher of the century and had a profound influence on his students, many of whom became prominent music figures throughout the world. The compositions of Bartók, Kodály and Dohnanyi speak for themselves. Kodály was teaching composition at the Academy when we were students. I was a double major, studying piano and composition. Dohnanyi was the Director of the Academy. Bartók was teaching piano there but rather reluctantly. He taught piano because he did not believe that composition was teachable. For him it was like talking about music, which is what we called 'words without songs,' such as what you read on a record jacket. That is not the same as making and experiencing music. One can teach things about composition, however. There were other outstanding teachers such as Antal Molnar teaching harmony, Waldbauer teaching string quartets, and others who were not so well known but were outstanding in their fields. The Liszt Academy had a very fruitful music faculty when we were there, and it was easy to absorb many wonderful things as students.

"There was a group of us friends who met daily over espresso and discussed culture. We had a 'Stammtisch,' a reserved table, at the local coffee shop where we talked about literature, painting, music, all manner of things, exchanging ideas. We were culturally a very excited little group. Obviously it was very fashionable at the Academy for everyone to think that he or she was a genius. We had enormous egos! If our teachers gave us some comments that were critical, things that were not very nice, we were not so offended as the younger generation today. Perhaps we were not as vulnerable. We were interested in things in general because we wanted to learn, even when there was negative criticism involved. If we received some negative comments from our teachers, we would just say, 'The old man is having a bad day.' We had enormous self-confidence and trusted the future, even though we knew the war was coming. In fact, it was already at the borders. It was imminent that Budapest would be bombed, our city would be ruined, and the Germans would come in and take over everything. To us, the end of the world seemed just around the corner. Many of us were drafted as eighteen-year-olds. I was drafted into the labor camps at twenty-one. Those who were enrolled at a university or academy could delay service for a while to finish their studies. Inevitably, the war did come, and then none of that mattered. We had a few very difficult years.

"We had the option of seeing the world and our future in two very different ways. Nothing mattered any more. Since we were very likely going to die soon, we could make orgies. Or we could take the position that since time was so short and precious, we felt compelled to learn everything there was to be learned, and as quickly as possible! We chose the latter."

Buda and Pest are two sides of the same city connected by beautiful bridges. With the German occupation, there was shooting on all sides. Then the Russians came and surrounded the city. The war was very near, actually a mile away in Buda. At the time Sebök was in a labor camp, and Starker was in the civil defense brigade.

After the close of the war in 1945, Sebök went to Rumania, riding in the cold of winter on the top of a train. Says Sebök, "Once I arrived in Rumania, my first wife's family received me wonderfully. I was very shortly invited to give a concert there with Enescu even though I had no proper clothes or music score. And for months I had not even had a piano for practice. The skin on my hands was thick and tough from work in the labor camps. To my surprise, Janos was already in Rumania, and at that concert with Enescu, he and I were reunited. He had gone to Rumania in February before the end of the war. For us it was as though the time in between, a bridge connecting two time periods, had disappeared."

By way of Austria and Switzerland, Starker and his first wife ended up in Paris. Sebök went to Paris shortly after, in December of 1946, for a competition. Says Sebök, "In Paris we lived for about six months on the fifth floor of a little hotel, for us a rather romantic student hotel. It seemed as though the future was wide open to us. I recall Janos sitting on the terrace, singing and strumming his cello like a banjo. Obviously we had no concerts. In fact we did not have anything! We had great fun and misery all at the same time, happy that we had somehow survived that mess in Budapest!

"The situation in France after the war was not easy, and we were very poor. Some of us began to wonder how things were in Hungary. After the biggest inflation in human history, we learned that the new money was then available in Hungary. The word was that Hungarian money was even more stable than the Swiss franc, and returning to Hungary began to seem more appealing to us. In the summer of 1947 several of us Hungarian musicians went back to Budapest. Starker's instincts were much better than mine. A couple of months later, Starker and his wife returned to France and then left for the United States where he played principal cello with the Dallas Symphony.

"I stayed in Budapest, however, and at a very young age I was appointed professor at the Bartók Conservatory. I made quite a nice life there for my wife and myself and became quite well known as a concert pianist. I frequently travelled for concerts throughout the Soviet Union including Hungary, Rumania, Poland, Czechoslovakia, everywhere in the Communist countries except Albania. I was an ambassador of Hungarian music, so to speak. But going to the West was an impossibility. Likewise, no one could come from the West into the Soviet countries. Wherever I performed, my travel was official state business. Although the atmosphere in the Soviet controlled countries was oppressive, I never felt that I was personally persecuted or endangered. I knew that if I wanted to speak that I would have to lie, so I preferred to remain silent and communicate through the music. Somehow I managed not to join the Communist Party. For ten years I enjoyed a position as a respected artist of the people.

"Everyone with relatives living in the West was looked on with suspicion. We were never allowed to communicate with people in the United States because of the general paranoia in the Soviet-controlled countries toward the West. For ten years Starker and I did not even exchange a postcard. Then came the Hungarian Revolution of 1956. For a short time it was possible to leave Hungary, very difficult but possible. During that time 200,000 people walked out of Hungary. The minefields were removed before the Russians returned. Getting passports for both my wife and myself meant that I had to resort to dishonesty and bribery, but we left Hungary legally with passports. It was necessary that I have a contract showing that I had concerts in another country. That was the only way that I would be allowed to leave Hungary, and then only for a short time. A Hungarian pianist friend living in Paris spoke on my behalf with Maurice Werner, a French concert manager. He said that I needed a contract for concerts in order to escape from Hungary. The concerts did not actually exist. They were only fictitious. As a result Werner had no financial obligation to me. Werner complied and sent me an invitation for a few concerts. In return I had to promise never to claim those concerts. That is how I was able to get a French visa.

"It was then that my wife and I decided to leave all that we had. It was a courageous thing for both of us to do because it meant starting all over with nothing. After all, we had established quite a nice life for ourselves in Hungary. We had a nice apartment with Persian rugs, lovely furniture, a grand piano, a job with recognition and respect and a modest income. We gave up everything, just packed a couple of suitcases and left! My wife was more eager to leave Hungary than I. The fear of being jobless was for me very difficult. But she was very optimistic and felt that I needed more than the life we had. In her opinion, I needed to have the whole world! So with two suitcases in hand, we left Hungary, knowing that government officials would come and confiscate everything we owned. To them we were considered traitors.

"In 1957 we turned back the clock to zero and began life anew in Paris. In all of France we had two friends, the Tauszigs in Limoges whom we had met ten years earlier. They were wonderful to us. I made a decision not to contact Starker or anyone else. I needed to make it on my own. Then things happened for me like a series of miracles. I was introduced to Rose de Pourtales, the niece of Guy de Pourtales, author of successful biographies on Liszt, Chopin, Wagner and Berlioz, also a music critic. Rose de Pourtales organized a concert in her salon. In the audience was the manager and opera director, Monsieur Dussurget. He was in charge of the Aix en Provence Festival. Following the concert he came to me saying, 'I have not heard a pianist like this for ten years. Would you like to work with me?' 'Of course, I would love to,' I responded. He introduced me to Erato, a recording company, and they offered me a contract for eight recordings. My very first record received the Grand Prix du Disque! So the misery of being unknown and the danger of having to 'sleep under the bridge' was very short. Then Maurice Werner approached me. He asked if I would take seriously the contract he had sent to me in Budapest, inviting me to perform concerts in France.

"The Tauszigs organized a concert in Limoges for Starker and myself. We met at the airport after a ten-year gap in our contact. At our apartment in Paris we played through a few pieces including the Brahms *E Minor Sonata*, the Beethoven *A Major Sonata*, and Hindemith's *Sonata*. It was like we performed just yesterday, as though no time at all had elapsed. Then we recorded together all the major cello-piano repertoire, things we had performed together as youths in Budapest; the five Beethoven *Sonatas* and three *Variations*, the two Brahms *Sonatas*, the Mendelssohn *Sonata*, the Debussy *Sonata*, the Bartók *Rhapsody*, several pieces by Leo Weiner, the Cèsar Franck *Sonata,* practically the entire repertoire for cello and piano. Then for about ten years we performed many recitals, lengthy concert tours throughout Europe and the United States, also in Japan. We were considered a duo. One time following a concert in London, my wife overheard a conversation between Joseph Szigeti and Kodály. Szigeti said that he thought we were the best duo in the world. That was about thirty-five years ago.

"With a special exchange visitor visa from France, I came to the United States. With this kind of visa, the United States guaranteed sending the person back after four years. Because so many were leaving their countries for the U.S. at that time, the United States was accused by the members of the world community of stealing brain-power. After the war, nuclear physicists and great artists were flocking to America.

"At the time I was very happy living in Paris and was not particularly looking to move. For me, going to the United States seemed like going to the moon. But with invitations from three universities in the U.S., one of these being Indiana University, I decided to look into the possibility. Being a very good psychologist, Starker did not try to convince me about coming to America, but he did have a hand in my decision. The fact that he was here, also Mr. Gingold, created a kind of attraction for me. I told Dean Bain that I would try it for a year. That was in 1962.

"I came to Bloomington as 'Artist in Residence' in 1962, and within six months I learned from Dean Bain that I was a full professor. I did not even know what that meant and was not concerned. Besides, for me 'Artist in Residence' sounded better than professor. I was not planning to stay, but one year became two. In fact, even after ten years, I still felt that it was a temporary commitment. I assumed that I would go back to Paris or Switzerland. Slowly we became more attached, even buying a house. I found that it was easy to travel from Bloomington, so we stayed. However, after four years I learned from the State Department that I was making my last trip abroad. The four years were up on my exchange visitor visa. Then a kind of movement started. The president of the university and the dean of the School of Music went to Washington D.C. to appeal my stay in Indiana. Senator Thomas Hartke put down a bill in the U.S. Congress on my behalf. He also initiated another bill saying that I could immediately have citizenship, not having to wait for five years. These two bills are in my scrapbook at home.

"A few years ago Starker and I performed a concert in Paris where we had not played together for decades. The French made such a celebration of our return that it was overwhelming! The collected reviews and articles about 'this great duo' performing again in Paris would make a book! A couple of years ago for the Eva Janzer Foundation we performed the complete Beethoven *Sonatas* and three *Variations*, one concert in the afternoon and one in the evening. Since Eva Janzer was a close friend of mine also, I serve on the committee for the Foundation. In March, 2000, Starker and I performed concerts in Paris and Budapest.

"Starker and I received a special honor at the same time. We both became 'Chevalier of Art and Literature' in France. That is like being honored by the Legion of Honor. When Chirac was Mayor of Paris, he gave me the Gold Medal of Paris. Also Starker and I both received a beautiful decoration from the President of Hungary for life achievement. From Sion, the capital of Wallis, which is a region in Switzerland, I received the Culture Prize. For the American bicentennial I received a beautiful honor stating that I am a treasure of the United States. Because of the festival which I established in Ernen, Switzerland, twenty-six years ago, I have been given honorary citizenship of Ernen in a ceremony on the Dor'platz in the center of the town. The president of Ernen said to the crowd of tourists, 'You should watch that! He is the third person in eight hundred years receiving this honor!' My wife said that if I should put on all of these decorations at one time, I should look like the Nazi, Göring.

"Starker and I both agree that at Indiana University we do not publicize ourselves. We do not display our decorations of honor or our glowing reviews. Also, when we perform music he and I are in complete agreement. But in philosophy or psychology or other areas we often disagree. In our younger years we would adamantly disagree on many things. By now since we are older and wiser, we know that if we have a basic disagreement on a subject, it is best that we avoid discussing it.

"We hold two different philosophies, ways of being and relating to things. He likes to believe that he knows something. He likes to define things. I am the opposite in that I prefer to think that I do not know something and am open to the unknown. It is a basic philosophical difference. Spencer said that our knowledge is like a sphere. Everything we know is inside this sphere. The surface of the sphere touches the unknown. As the sphere grows, we know more. But then we also realize more clearly how much more we do not know. I am terribly intrigued by the border where the known and the unknown meet. Einstein said that he found the most exciting things in life to be the mysterious. A hundred years from now I believe mankind is going to know much, much more. But the essential questions will not be solved. For example, there is an enormous science about light—physics, optics. It is much too much for one brain to understand. We know a lot about light, but what it is we do not know. Light does not see itself, and light is invisible. If there is nothing where light arrives, then it is invisible. We know much about how the human eye works, how the optic nerve goes into the brain. There the different groups of cells react to different things like movement, color, shape, and so on. It is like a very complicated television. But who is watching the TV? That we do not know.

"Philosophy has been important in my life since I was young. As a boy, I had a wonderful grandfather, a doctor. Each day in Szeged we walked and talked together in the early afternoon, discussing various aspects of science: anatomy, physics, astronomy, and everything else."

Says Starker, "Mr. Sebök is a philosopher and optimistic. I am an ideo-realist, an idealist but at the same time a realist. He is more of an idealist. That is the root of our disagreements. When we were in Paris we argued about politics, but never about music. Actually, we don't fight or argue, just quietly discuss things."

About Starker, Sebök says, "I believe there is no one in the world who knows better how to play the cello than he does. Likewise, the piano is my realm of expertise. And seemingly it works because my technique is the same as it was thirty years ago. The theory is that minimum energy gives maximum sensitivity. But at the same time I do not believe that what I now know is final. I am willing to change what I think at any time. If I should have proof that something I have believed for twenty years is wrong, then without any regret, I will immediately change my mind.

"When I say that Starker and I in many ways think very differently, that is inspiring for me because then I am able to see the other side of whatever I am thinking. Either I become convinced and change my mind, or I become stronger in what I believe. This kind of exchange is very rare. It is also rare to be partners and friends for more than half a century. He has had a great role in my life, particularly spending a lifetime performing music together. Discussing many things with him has been a great inspiration to me, not just directly within a piece of music but also generally in searching for the meaning in the music or a particular technique. We have often gone into great detail in sharing our thoughts. I find him a unique artist with a keen mind.

"I am remembering the fifty-year anniversary of Starker's parents. For that event he organized a big celebration. People came from all over the world. Everything was prepared in secret, a total surprise for his parents. Starker and I performed at the event as though we were child prodigies, wearing short pants and wigs. Mine was blond, and he had a black one. I don't recall what we played, but it was a big success, encore and all. It was very entertaining. After the performance when we were back stage, my wife urged us to go out once more saying, 'They don't want to hear you; they want to see you once more!'

"On the lighter side, for many years we have been ping-pong players. But as we get older, we have discovered that with ping-pong we have to jump around too much. So now we often play pool instead. Perhaps we enjoy standing around more and thinking about strategy. Since Starker owns the pool table and has had more practice than I, he is the better player. So he usually wins. Besides, he enjoys figuring out what shots I should take and takes great pleasure when I succeed. That way, if I win, it is because I am a good student of his. You see, he wins either way!

It seems that the way we are going, a few years down the road we are probably going to play chess. Then we can sit down!

"Sometimes we take a break from the pool game and sit. These are intimate times for us. We talk about old days, about his parents, my family, our childhood years, exchanging memories. I knew his parents very well, also his two brothers who disappeared. People often behave with another according to what the other expects or according to what one wants to project as an image. But when Mr. Starker and I sit down in his basement between two matches of pool and talk, we don't play games. We just become ourselves, opening our hearts to one another. For nearly sixty years we are like brothers: friends in life and partners in music, an exceptional relationship."

STARKER AND SEBOK WITH WIGS AND KNEE PANTS PERFORMING FOR PARENTS' 50TH WEDDING ANNIVERSARY PARTY

Dvorák Concerto

a story by Janos Starker

At noon the phone rang. On the other end my teacher asked, "Do you want to play the Dvorák *Concerto*, with orchestra?"

"When!"

"Tonight at 6 o'clock."

I was fourteen then, a cello student at the Franz Liszt Academy in Budapest. Six months before the call I had studied the work for the first time. "Sure," I said, without hesitation. Apart from the success of that début, I received in addition offers from a Korean guest conductor to settle in his country as solo cellist in his orchestra, to teach, and to marry. I was tempted, but mother vetoed the proposal. Obviously she felt that fourteen was not a marriageable age. When, twenty-nine years later, I did finally visit Seoul in the company of my beautiful non-Korean wife, any lingering doubts about a chance I might have missed dissipated. Mother knew best.

That Dvorák début in 1938 triggered off an endless series of adventures, some tragic, some comic. However, whenever and wherever the Dvorák *Concerto* was scheduled, the occasion was invariably memorable. Any concert cellist worth his salt can relate at least a dozen funny stories about Dvorák performances at after-concert parties. In the travelling cellist's repertory this is the most frequently performed work. Even in the hands of lesser players, it remains a master-piece, virtually impregnable although not always completed, as happened to me in Sao Paulo, Brazil.

Please note, performance stories fall into two categories: Those whose purely musical nature makes them in-jokes among performers (whether they sing, conduct or play instruments), and those of an ambient nature which can be shared with any and all who might care to know. That said, onward if not always forward, or upward.

Hungarian musical life was somewhat curtailed during the Nazi occupation, with the result that many of us young musicians found that the homes of well-to-do friends were the only outlets for concertizing ambitions. Our programs encompassed the entire chamber music literature, and, as insurance on the future, the entire concerto literature with piano accompaniment. Tickets were sold, and the proceeds democratically divided among us. Once, about eighty persons were listening, enraptured I like to believe, to my performance of the Dvorák *Concerto* when a doorbell rang loudly, followed by the sound of shuffling boots. My eyes, forced open from the act of concentration, saw two policemen. A slight tremor intensified my vibrato, but for lack of a better idea I kept on playing, and tried to ignore the intrusion of officialdom.

During the second movement, both uniformed men sat down on chairs offered them. During the finale, they rose and left the house quietly. Afterwards I learned that it was May First, a day on which the government forbade more than three people to gather. We had forgotten. Hundreds of others had been arrested that day in the city. But whether it was our hostess' charm or some lurking love of music, the policemen left our unlawful gathering without interruption of the performance. On occasion, I have dared to call this one of my most successful Dvorák performances.

Shortly thereafter, an orchestral concert was scheduled. Just before going onto the stage I left my beautiful cello alone, briefly, for a ritual visit to the w.c. In the nick of time I reclaimed it, strode onstage, bowed to the audience, and seated myself. I touched the open strings to make sure they had stayed in tune, only to hear an ominous buzz, indeed a rattle. I recoiled, and only then noticed a long crack atop the body of my cello. The lone recourse was to proceed, and squeeze the instrument between my knees as firmly as possible to subdue the rattle. No one observed anything amiss, except for my strange walk as I left the stage: Both legs had cramped severely. The crack was repaired the following week. No one ever admitted to kicking my cello while I was functionally preoccupied. But a number of cellists were suspects, to this day.

Soon after the war ended, I did time in Rumania. In the winter of 1945, the Dvorák *Concerto* again was scheduled. The day before the concert, Bucharest suffered a massive snowstorm. It continued for four days, paralyzing the entire country. On the fourth day, while we waited in a hotel for the storm to subside, the whole city began to shake, an earthquake near the oil fields. The concert of course was postponed, but I still wonder from time to time if the rehearsal had been that bad. Orchestra and conductor had given me qualms; but an earthquake?

Back in war-scarred Budapest, conditions were rough in February of 1946. I lived some ten walking minutes from the opera house where, then, I served as solo cellist. The only distance in those days was walking distance; few (if any) conveyances were functioning. My contract stipulated participation in those operas primarily which had an important role for cello. I had been engaged to play the Dvořák *Concerto* under Ferenc Fricsay, a conductor at the opera, at a Sunday morning concert. Both of us had planned the concert date carefully so as to be free from any operatic duty the night preceding. However, the phone rang around 6 p.m. on Saturday: two stellar singers were ill and the music had been changed to Puccini's *Tosca*, which happens to have the best known of all operatic cello solos in the third act. My presence was obligatory, a distress shared by Maestro Fricsay since he was the Tosca conductor that season.

It was bitterly cold throughout the city, and in the pit as well; coal-mining production left everything that year to be desired in Hungary. *Tosca* began with disgusted looks between conductor and solo cellist. After the first-act intermission, I sat down; or, to be explicit, fell down on my chair. A paralyzing pain had struck my lower back. Considering that I wasn't yet twenty-two years old, and never before had anything resembling such a pain, I was dumbstruck as well as disabled. Any movement caused suffering, although I could move my arms without hindrance. I must have turned chalk white because Fricsay whispered to me, "what's the matter?" I replied that I couldn't move. He looked disbelieving, suspicious of a trick to get home because of our morning concert.

After what seemed an hour, the second act concluded and I explained. But what then? My playing was needed in the third act: No one volunteered to play in my place nor was anyone else ready to accept a substitution. So we agreed that, once the solo ended, I should try to leave the pit, go home and call a doctor. It sounded easy. Throughout the second intermission I stayed motionless in my chair, then played the solo in the third-act prelude. After, I crawled out of the pit, literally, hoping I wouldn't scream out in agony during Cavaradossi's *Elucevan le Stelle*. But then came the ten-minute walk on icy streets, which took thirty that night with the cello under my arm. By midnight, painkillers had been administered and lumbago, my lifelong semiannual curse, diagnosed. Next morning I managed to get to the concert hall and to play Dvořák, but had to use my cello as a crutch whenever I sat down or stood. The reviews, after praising my talent, dwelt on a lack of involvement, a lack of motion, and youthful stage fright in front of an audience. Ahem, and amen.

For a period thereafter, positions in an assortment of orchestras prevented my performing concertos with any regularity. When I reentered the corrida of solo virtuosi, frequent requests for the Dvořák *Concerto* renewed "incidents."

The Prague May Festival of Music had requested the Prokofiev *First Concerto,* but the first rehearsal was catastrophic. There are, you see, two Prokofiev cello concertos and the conductor had learned the wrong one. When I refused to play the scheduled concerto (theirs, not mine), and the party hierarchy agreed to a program change after long deliberation, the Dvořák got substituted. The evening performance, in front of microphones broadcasting to the entire Iron Curtain bloc, went smoothly until the middle of the second movement. There, as if to rewrite Dvořák the conductor suddenly began to beat double-time, carrying the orchestra along, leaving me alone with a repeated phrase requiring a repeated answer by the flute. Fury rose within me, confronted by this horrid incompetence. In desperation I stretched my phrases to the point of collapse while I watched the conductor trying, and failing, to get the orchestra together. It was a matter of stopping altogether or intercede, and so I called out "Now!" We were able to finish both the movement and the concerto, just. Afterwards, an orchestra committee mollified me with the news that they'd passed a unanimous resolution never to allow the "maestro" to conduct a soloist again.

Again the Dvořák *Concerto* was a vehicle for a performance by solo cellist and orchestra unique in my experience. The orchestra was the Las Palmas Philharmonic, since disbanded and rebuilt by the Azores. As the long orchestral introduction began, only every tenth note was audible. The conductor, formerly a cellist in Pablo Casal's eponymous Barcelona orchestra, made the most musicianly gestures to his players, but his apologetic expression conveyed no hope that the notes would be played. Bows were moved left to right across stringed instruments, and wind instruments were held properly to lips, yet only an occasional gurgle escaped. Infrequently, someone tried to play but seemed frightened by his aloneness and so abandoned the enterprise. I played the solo part with a feverish conviction while the conductor waved his hands and followed me with ecstatic joy. My poor wife nearly fell out of her box in an attempt to see where from a few noises occasionally came. Later at supper, a band in the restaurant greeted me with the main theme of the concerto: They were members of the Philharmonic, as were the police and firemen bands, not to mention the rest of Las Palmas nightclub musicians. At their daily chores all were passably good, but in the Dvořák their playing could only have been complemented by that diva of legend, Florence Foster Jenkins.

Elsewhere and later, the Harvard-Radcliffe Orchestra asked me to play the Dvořák *Concerto* with them—a superb group of amateurs with a collective I.Q. that, put to the proper use, might solve all of the world's ills. They played stunningly well. In the University's venerable assembly hall, however, the heating system turned against Dvořák in the slow movement. A pipe blew and ferociously hissing steam escaped at one side of the stage. When the noise reached fortissimo, we stopped. Along with the ushers, orchestra members scurried to stuff the pipe, to quiet the intrusion, with articles of clothing and towels. At length we resumed our poetic effusion. One tradition-bound Boston critic, however, admonished me on the next day for a remark made while the steam was being fought: "Harvard ought to build a nice concert hall." Blasphemy, he implied.

On the leg of a long South American tour, two performances had been scheduled in Sao Paulo, of the Dvořák *Concerto*. Upon our arrival from Buenos Aires, a note awaited from the conductor, whose name I'd never before heard, asking permission to discuss the music prior to our rehearsal, on the upcoming same day as the first concert. This amounts to routine for the travelling artist since it reduces risk where rehearsal time is limited, and I agreed. Shortly after, a five-feet-four, white-haired gentleman—seventy-ish in age—arrived at the hotel room. He expressed fervent admiration of my artistry, and said that a long-held dream of making music with me was about to be fulfilled. Any discussion of a score by conductor and soloist without an orchestra—the singing, talking and gesticulation—is fodder for a Chaplin film. Every modification of a composer's markings provokes "oooohs" and "ahhhs," the delighted agreement of kindred souls who are, finally, discovering Ultimate Truth. An hour later the conductor departed, close to tears of joy.

At 10 o'clock the next morning, I took my place on the stage of an ornate and plush theater, but without the customary greeting from the orchestra, a tapping of bows against music stands when visiting soloists appear. Well, thought I, too early in the day for southern musicians. The maestro gave a beat and the long introduction commenced. In the very first measure played, I thought I must be hearing wrong. Dvorák wrote "Allegro" and there is a metronome marking of 116 beats to the minute. I may not be known for metronomic exactness, and on occasions even enjoy variety, but the maestro was beating only half-speed and the orchestra was following him. I thought reflexively that someone was making a joke; the Dvorák *Concerto* is after all, a repertory staple, and every musician knows it. I looked at the maestro to get his attention. Eventually, he lifted his nose out of the score, whereupon I motioned to him to go faster. He smiled and whispered, "Of course," but while his beat increased in size, there was no change in the tempo. I looked to the concertmaster but his eyes were glued to the music. I looked elsewhere but no musician glanced up from the music except for an occasional peek at the conductor. Never before in my life, not even in Japan, had I encountered such discipline in an orchestra!

When it fell time for my entrance, I began at my—Dvorák's—usual tempo. In the space of three bars the conductor and orchestra had fallen behind me a whole measure, and stayed there unperturbably. For a time I tried frantically to solicit help from the concertmaster, the solo cellist, the flute...anyone! No use. They played their notes and obeyed the conductor's beat, as though mesmerized. He was bound by a terminal arthritis, unable to move his arm faster. There was no other reason to stop and so, eventually, we reached the double bar of the first movement. The maestro looked at me with a victorious smile. "Good, no? Have you any wishes?" "Yes, one," I replied. "Might we play the right tempo?" "Don't worry," he responded, "We will follow yours."

The second movement, being slow, was less painful, apart from my occasional attempts at accellerando, which the orchestra annihilated. The maestro's arms simply could not change from one gear to another. The third movement, an Allegro Moderato, alas, recapitulated the travesty of the first. Any tempo adjustment indicated by Dvorák was ironed out by the conductor, which is to say, no change. One hour and five minutes after we started, instead of thirty-five minutes more or less, we reached the coda where an orchestral outburst ends the piece dramatically; or should. However, the tempo remained resolutely unchanging, right up to a terminal silence. The orchestra sat motionless; no applause, which is customary if not invariably owing. I was altogether perplexed since my playing had been, in spite of all, up to standard. I stood, and advised the conductor that the coda should go twice as fast, that he should beat one instead of two, that the entire work went at an unbearably slow tempo, that he had to do something. "Of course," he answered cheerily. "Don't worry, we will follow you. Anything else?" I knew it was hopeless and left the stage to pack my cello and get away. I heard the conductor speak something in Portuguese, and then the final twelve measures of the work played in a style unrecognizable, after which the orchestra got up and left.

The evening concert was to be televised and broadcast, both. Since the concerto was the final work on the program, I arrived at the intermission. Not one musician greeted me, something that never before that evening had happened. The performance started, and it replicated that morning's, exactly. The conductor's arms waved, lingered, and we all limped along like a car on low-grade fuel, unable to race our motor. I had to give up the fight, and entertained myself by practicing luscious sounds totally unrelated to any Dvořák *Concerto* I'd performed hundreds of times in the past. An immense relief seized me when I finished the last notes for the solo cello, and leaned back for the last "surge" by the orchestra. The maestro smiled at me, and started beating furiously in one as I had requested. Half the orchestra followed and finished with him, but half kept playing in two and persisted obliviously after twelve measures of cacophony. Then, noticing that their conductor was not beating, they stopped one by one, thinning out wretchedly. The last sound anyone heard was a violin, out-of-tune, as if shot down in mid-phrase. Dead silence followed. Under such circumstances a moment can seem like an hour. My mechanical sense-of-humor finally nudged and I threw my hands in the air, saying, "That's it, folks!" As if exploded, the crowd began to yell "bravo" and applauded madly. I stood and left the stage without shaking the conductor's hand, or the concertmaster's. Their faces went ashen-white. I even refused to bow. The conductor scurried to catch up with me, stuttering, "Sorry, sorry, they didn't follow me." At this I lost my temper and screamed, "That you can't follow me is excusable, maybe, but you managed to lose the entire orchestra when I wasn't even playing!" "Sorry, sorry," was all he could speak, but then added, "Could we play the last movement again?"

The cheering persisted all this while, until I realized that I had to return to the stage and acknowledge a bizarre success. I yelled, "No!" at him as I walked onstage with a phony grin. After my third return to the stage, each time backstage having to shove aside a whining "maestro," I resorted to the customary encore of Bach *Sarabande*. The orchestra seemed not to have breathed since the concerto dribbled away into nothingness. Bach calmed my nerves enough to observe the rules of the game, albeit reluctantly. I shook the concertmaster's hand and motioned for the orchestra to stand and leave with me. At least fifty musicians followed me to my room, where their spokesman explained in broken English that they resent the "maestro," who had been a third-rate pianist at best but now was in charge of all governmental budgeting for orchestras. In exchange he insisted upon conducting an occasional program. To prove how inept he was, the orchestra had voted to follow exactly what he did. They did not realize it would turn out so badly. They implored forgiveness, and swore during the concert next day to follow me. It was a fair performance, the repeat, with the conductor beating haplessly but the orchestra following me and their concertmaster, as professional musicians. Two days later, in another town, someone translated a rave review of the first concert. "Superb performance...total unanimity of purpose between conductor and soloist." The writer? A former student of the "maestro."

In balance, there are those unnumbered performances of Dvořák when the conductor has known the score, when the orchestra has played well, when the cellist has performed up to his standard, and when acoustics in the hall have allowed the solo instrument to be heard—nights when everything makes sense. The work, the struggles, the rigors of travel, all seem justified and vindicated. An audience cheers and an artist feels proud.

When relating stories, however, a self-imposed (if uncharacteristic) modesty cautions the artist not to dwell on happy tales that lack a punch line. Only a search for the truth allows me this recollection of a London late summer evening in 1956.

At the end of a day's third recording session, I put the cello into its case. We congratulated one another on a job well done—Walter Susskind who had conducted the Philharmonia Orchestra, Walter Legge who had produced the recording, and I. It was my first major recording with orchestra, for a major company, and—the dream of all cellists—the Dvořák *Concerto* was done. I was tired, although six more sessions devoted to other works were scheduled for the days ahead. A Rolls waited outside the studio to take me back to the hotel. After a long silence I said to myself, as if thirty-two years had tripled: I don't care if I die now, I have fulfilled my destiny. My version of the Dvořák is preserved for all to hear and it is good!

Since then almost a quarter of a century has passed. Yet the elation I felt then has seldom if ever been equaled, thousands of concerts and sixty-five records notwithstanding.

J.S., Bloomington, Indiana, 1977

⋀⋀⋁

"During the early decades of my career, I was sometimes described as being a cold performer," admits Janos Starker. "Music critics often seem to take a performer's playing temperature and pronounce a performance to be hot, warm, sweaty, cool or whatever." Starker counters, "Hearing something on a high level technically, some critics were so stunned that they considered it cold or pedantic. I was called a cold performer, I believe, partly because reviewers and audiences at that time hadn't heard performances that sounded like recording quality.

"People thought I was cold and immobile because they didn't see my face change or my body move while I played. Movement is fascinating. When you move with the music, nobody notices. People only notice motions contrary to the musical line. If you circle around the piano, then they notice it. If you go up with the high note and down with the low, they don't. I move to fit the musical line. If I play a downbow and the phrase starts with a downbeat, then I move to the right side. If someone plays a phrase on the downbeat and moves upward, then the person is emoting, which has nothing to do with making music. It's the difference between entertainment and art," he says. "The real musician avoids the obvious extremes of loud and soft, of fast and slow, sometimes so slow that you cannot breathe. It is the same with the gyrations of some musicians. When are they theatrical? When they do not match the music," he says. "I much prefer that people appreciate the work rather than the worker. But I am afraid that some of my colleagues perpetuate shameless musical lies on stage and think to themselves, why be pure when you can be successful?"

"Starker, like Heifetz, has one of music's authentic poker faces," says James Roos, writer for the *Miami Herald*. The performer's personality and viewpoint must come across to the audience, in Starker's opinion. "But I do not believe it is necessary to use theatrics to present a composer. Then people get a visual aspect of the music rather than an aural one. I hope those who attend my concerts listen rather than watch. Grand gestures—theatrics—bother my stomach a little. Nevertheless I tell students that if they aren't up to the task of playing well for an audience that paid for tickets, they should at least do something to justify their presence on the stage and give the audience its money's worth. That's stage presentation.

"I've spent a thousand nights in the opera, where I learned all the commedia dell 'arte tricks to capture everyone's attention and make sure they have much to talk about at the end of the evening. But in my opinion, this shouldn't be the goal. If entertainment dominates the music, then you have failed in the mission of bringing music to the audience. Use it when in trouble, because on stage part of the job is to entertain. Some of what I take issue with is a matter of good taste. It bothers me if a player allows stagecraft and show business to dominate over the music.

"Emotion is supposed to come through, of course. I consider my mission to create poetry through music, not to speak about music in poetic terms. Many of my distinguished colleagues have developed the ability to speak about music in flowery phrases. For me that is meaningless. I've spent a lifetime expressing poetry through music, and I did it at the time when I was considered cold. I'm a sentimental slob when it comes to soap operas. But in music, I'm emotional, not sentimental. What one listener hears as a cold sound may be searing to another."

Starker's tone can be so centered and concentrated that, combined with an absence of vibrato, the effect is simultaneously chilling and hot, as when he plays the opening of Ernst Bloch's *Schelomo*. "I do what the intensity requires; prolonged intensity loses its effect. Without changes in the level of tension, music becomes meaningless."

Starker is contemptuous of performers who favor a continuously warm sound instead of following the textures of the music. "With some people, making music is a matter of expressing themselves instead of the composer. Some famous artists sound the same no matter what they play. They use the same sound, the same vibrato, the same fingerings, the same bowings, the same color." This homogenization of sound and style disturbs Starker deeply. "If I hear Mozart played like Tchaikovsky, I don't like it. If I hear the purest of Beethoven's phrases, for example, played with a crescendo and downward slides, then I am reminded of a bad gypsy street fiddler."

It is not that Starker dislikes good gypsy music. "There are good and bad gypsy musicians. Growing up in Hungary I heard some of the greatest gypsy players of all time, tremendous artists and musicians. Some played unbearably, and some played fabulously. So to say that someone plays like a gypsy is not necessarily bad. It is only that gypsies use an awful lot of rubato, and the kinds of material they play often require rubato. To play Bartók's *Rhapsody* and Kodály's music, you use rubato because of the material. But to do it well, you must know the language of the composer."

Music performance traditions, the way things are expressed in musical thought, are closely related to the language of the region. Language clearly influences how composers express their thoughts. Musical expression is different with each country, be it music from Spain, Germany, France, Hungary, Russia, America, or wherever. Each country has its indigenous style of expression in music.

Any singing approach to music performance is clearly tied to the language. International exposure to French, German, Spanish and Italian... these languages are more widely spoken by foreigners than Hungarian, and therefore their music is more familiar sounding than Hungarian. Upon first hearing Starker perform Kodály's *Solo Cello Sonata,* opus 8, many people were stunned as well as captivated by the unusual nature of the piece as well as his performance.

The music of Bartók and Kodály, the most illustrious of the Hungarian composers, is clearly rooted in the Hungarian language itself. Every word of the Hungarian language has an accent on the first syllable with no exceptions. There are certain characteristic rhythms in the music of Bartók and Kodály which can be identified. For example the sixteenth note followed by a dotted eighth is typically Hungarian and is language related. Phrase groupings begin at the bar line with an emphasis on the first beat. The opposite is true in the French language where in a three-syllable word the accent will be on the third syllable. This characteristic does not happen in Hungarian music or in the language.

The Hungarian language has clearly shaped Starker's musical thinking. One would have to be a human chameleon to be able to take on the idiosyncrasies of every possible language, culture and playing style. Although we try to adapt to musical styles, we cannot escape our roots and how they influence our thinking. Starker definitely has a tendency to perceive phrases from the perspective of his native language. That suits how he plays, how he thinks about music, and how it fits into his overall concept of how music is put together. This is organic.

Starker feels that a professional must be able to perform at eighty-five percent capacity on any given night. The remaining fifteen percent should be a matter of inspiration. As far as he is concerned, the Holy Trinity of music making are simplicity, purity and balance. These we must adhere to.

Starker is one who feels things very strongly. He has a very sentimental nature balanced by his highly intellectual side. These two opposing forces at work within him come into conflict at times, creating a great intensity. That is part of the fascinating mixture of the man. Anyone who knows him realizes there is a strong emotional side to him even though he most often chooses not to display it in any obvious kind of way. Actually, he is rather understated, quite soft spoken. He seems to never raise his voice, but yet he clearly means what he says. He is quite sure of what he is saying, and his words are carefully chosen for their impact. Once you get to know him you realize that he is a very giving and warm human being.

What has set him apart from all the others from the beginning is his lean, incisive tone, his spectacular technical agility, and his patrician restraint in phrasing. He plays the cello like Heifetz the violin, with disdain for the most fiendish difficulties, with infallible intonation, yet with an emotional reserve some mistake for coldness. His ascetic style is the opposite of passionate cellists like Piatigorsky or the searching Pablo Casals. But he has since carved out a unique niche as a fastidious virtuoso, master teacher, and reviver of neglected music. As Starker is described in *Newsweek*, "He is no showboat, and he plays a well-tempered cello, rejecting the instrument's inherent seductive call to abandon in favor of restraint in volume of color or timbre." [41]

31. Bing, Rudolph, *Five Thousand Nights at the Opera*, Doubleday & Co., New York, 1972

32. See *Soft Pitch for the Pit*, p. 62

33. Druian later became the concertmaster in Minneapolis with Dorati, then the New York Philharmonic, later the Cleveland Orchestra.

34. Reiner and Dorati were related through marriage. Dorati called Reiner "Uncle."

35. Günther Schuller is a composer who incorporated jazz and ragtime into his music. He now heads the New England Conservatory of Music.

36. *Opera News*, Vol. 40, No. 18, Dec. 28/Jan. 4, 1975

37. Developed in 1823 by Viennese Luthier Georg Staufer (1778-1853), the arpeggione was a bowed, six-stringed, fretted instrument tuned like the classical guitar. It lacked an endpin and was held between the knees like a viola da gamba. According to the preface of the *Sonata*'s First Edition, Schubert wrote this piece for Vincenz Schuster, an arpeggione enthusiast who published the only method book for the instrument in 1825. The instrument remained in use for only ten years.

38. Webster, Daniel, *Philadelphia Inquirer*, "Music: Starker plays a belated début with the Philadelphia Orchestra," Friday, January 11, 1985

39. Miklos Rosza, 1907-1995, Hungarian-born film and concert composer

40. Newspaper quotes and information in this chapter taken from: Jacobi, Peter, *The Starker Story, A Life in America Since 1948*

41. H.S., "Cello Fellow," *Newsweek*, January 29, 1973

Part IV

The Teacher, Concert Artist and Recording Artist

"This is the golden age of the cello," says Starker. "It's a marvelous situation since there are hundreds of outstandingly gifted young cellists in the world today. Never in history have there been so many. In fact, in all instrumental playing, the technical standards have risen tremendously. The cello," Starker feels, "has lagged about a hundred years behind the violin. Paganini (1782-1840) provided the turning point in the development of the violin as a solo instrument. That was about one hundred years before Pablo Casals (1876-1973). Because of his immense popularity, Casals was instrumental in bringing the cello to the attention of the listening public. This was the turning point in the development of the cello as a solo instrument. Take for example Casals' recording of Dvořák's *Cello Concerto*, recorded in 1937 with George Szell and the Czech Philharmonic Orchestra. It is a historic landmark in setting the standards for cello playing, a splendid recording, great musicianship.

"But those one hundred years between Paganini and Casals encompass the time of many great composers. Unfortunately they wrote relatively little music for the cello virtuoso, and, as a result, the cello for too long was an unfamiliar solo instrument to the public.

"Casals was an early inspiration to me," says Starker. "He is the father of modern cello playing and has been a tremendous inspiration to so many cellists. But Casals' sound and approach to the repertoire were to me old style. To me they represented the nineteenth century. For too many years typical cello sounds meant to me either a kind of wailing or a scratchy sound, not centered, with vibrato applied indiscriminately. I thought there must be a better way. Then I heard Feuermann, who showed me the next stage of cello playing."

ON A CRUISE SHIP IN PUERTO RICO, PABLO CASALS IS GIVING STARKER A PIECE OF ADVICE, "BE SURE YOU VISIT ME NEXT TIME YOU ARE IN PUERTO RICO." MARTITA CASALS IS BESIDE HER HUSBAND.

On one concert tour, the first stop was in Puerto Rico where Starker played a concert with the Puerto Rico Symphony Orchestra. The photo was taken at the reception following the concert. In the photo Casals is pointing his finger at Starker, asking, "Why didn't you come to see me?" Martita Casals is by his side. They recalled together their first meeting in Budapest when Starker was a very young boy. Casals kissed him on the forehead. That was to Starker a symbolic blessing.

Although he recognizes Pablo Casals' tremendous impact on the popularity of the cello around the turn of the last century, Starker, on the other hand, has felt that Casals could have done so much more for the progress of the instrument. Says Starker, "Casals' musical tastes were quite traditional and conservative. Julius Röntgen was a composer whom Casals described as one of the great composers of the twentieth century, also Emmanuel Moor and Sir Donald Francis Tovey. But there were few other composers in this century whom Casals accepted. After Debussy, no one existed in Casals' opinion. Stravinsky, Bartók, Prokofiev.........nothing! Bad!"

Starker felt that many composers would have written for the cello had the famous Casals been willing to perform their pieces. Kodaly, for one, was held back six years in the publishing of his *Sonata,* opus 8 because of Casals' unwillingness to play his piece. In Starker's opinion, Casals delayed the development of the cello by perhaps twenty years. After his rejection of Kodály's piece, composers were reluctant to write for the cello, thinking that if Casals, the most prominent cellist in the world, will not play new works, what chance is there for me? So why bother writing for the cello!

Brazilian cellist Aldo Parisot suggested that it was Starker on whom Feuermann's mantle came to rest. "While Feuermann brought cello technique to the point where it rivaled that of the violin for ease and agility, he was a bit neglectful of intonation. Starker, on the other hand is impeccable in that respect, and sometimes a more mature interpreter." Starker said that had Feuermann not died prematurely, the cello's 'Golden Age' might have been reached twenty years sooner.

But then as the popularity of the cello started spreading everywhere, there were more and more cellists. For one, Paul Hindemith wrote for his brother who was a cellist. Then there were Russian composers who wrote for Rostropovich. Eventually more contemporary music came to the fore. For too long the development of the cello was delayed. Now, at the beginning of the twenty-first century, it is catching up with the violin. Without certain prominent people, such as Rostropovich, Piatigorsky, Leonard Rose, Pierre Fournier, Jacqueline duPre, YoYo Ma, Bolognini, Laszlo Varga, Starker and others, the cello could not have reached its current threshold of popularity and universal acceptance. Someone who Starker considers a very great teacher is Aldo Parisot. "When he is teaching, he never sits down," says Starker. "Cello in hand, he demonstrates while standing."

Because of the cello's smaller repertoire, when one compares it with the repertoire of the violin and the piano, it has been less likely that a conductor would hire a cello soloist. But now in history there are a great number of outstandingly gifted young cellists. The cello repertoire has been increased during the twentieth century. The "Golden Age" of the cello has arrived. This would not have been possible without those who have given their lives to promote the instrument.

Among his many contributions to the popularity of the cello, Starker once performed the *Double Concerto* by Miklos Rózsa with a violinist in Baton Rouge. He sent a recording of this performance to the composer who then wrote to Starker saying that as far as he knew, no one before had performed the concerto in its complete form. Before that, people would perform only what Heifetz and Piatigorsky had recorded; the second movement, which is a theme and variations. Actually it has been performed many times as well as recorded by Alice and Eleonore Schoenfeld, faculty members at the University of Southern California.

Miklos Rózsa was a Hungarian composer who moved to Hollywood where he composed one hundred and ten film scores. He wrote his *Cello Concerto* for Starker who performed the piece with the Munich Radio Orchestra. With that performance they did what is called a "mittschnitt." The rehearsal on the day of the concert, as well as the concert, are both recorded.

STARKER WITH COMPOSER, MIKLOS ROZSA

The best of these is later used for broadcast. Eventually someone bought this recording from German Radio and made a commercial recording.

Bernard Heiden, composer at Indiana University has written several pieces for Starker including a *Sonata*, a piece for cello and piano called *Sienna*, a concerto, a set of solo variations, a violin-cello duo, a quintet with two cellos and a cello quartet. Another composer, Ortega Salas wrote a piece for his wife for their tenth wedding anniversary, a concerto which Starker has performed. He feels that there are many advantages of being affiliated with a university, one of which is that his colleagues compose music for him.

Among his many recordings, Starker recorded five versions of the Bach *Solo Cello Suites*. "So when are you going to get it right?" was the obvious question asked of him during a recent visit to New York. "Ah, like the tenor in Parma," he replied with a grin, referring to the old operatic joke about the singer who had to keep encoring an aria until the audience was satisfied he had done it correctly.

He fondly remembers his first set recorded in 1951 in the middle of the night in a church on 14th Street in New York. He was then principal cellist in the Met Opera Orchestra. When the show ended each night he would go downtown with his instrument. "We would start recording around midnight and continue until about 4:00 a.m.," he recalls. "Then I'd go home for a few hours of sleep and be at the Met for a 10:00 a.m. rehearsal. That went on for about a week. I am still very proud of that set. It helped establish my career as a soloist in England where it appeared on the Nixa label."

"Every time I went with a new record company, they wanted me to record the Bach *Cello Suites*. My second set, for EMI, was not too different from the first in concept. My third, for Mercury, I think was more mature. By that time, 1966, I had played the suites around the world. In 1984 I was asked to do them for the Sefel label. That was digital, and the sound was more of a factor. The more recent RCA recording is for me reaching the destination of a lifetime, with tonal and expressive details and more emotional content."

As far as the question of performance practice goes, Starker says, "I have no intention of approximating how Bach's music was played in his own time. My objective is to give a late twentieth century view of Bach. There are many differences. In Bach's time the pitch was very low, there were gut strings, the bow was curved, there was no end pin, the equipment of the instrument was different, although the instrument I play, a Gofriller cello, was already in existence when Bach was alive."

"The cello repertoire," says Starker, "is perhaps wider than people think, but it is still limited," not like the repertoire for piano or violin, both of which are extensive. "When you concertize and play the instrument for a lifetime, in my case more than sixty years, you keep looking for new avenues of exploration. Take the Brahms *Cello Sonata in D Major, opus 76*. The music is familiar to people as Brahms' *First Violin Sonata, Regenlied* or *Rain Sonata*. In 1974 a musicologist came across Brahms' own adaptation of the violin piece for cello, which was gathering dust in the archives of the Vienna Conservatory for six decades. Brahms changed the key signature from G to D to highlight the cello's darker color and mellower timbre. There are two hundred minuscule changes in the score, which Brahms recast for his friend, the noted nineteenth century cellist, Robert Hausmann. Austrian pianist Rudolf Buchbinder informed me of the find, and together we gave the world premiere. The only piece I really envy is the Brahms *Violin Concerto*. I've tried it out on the cello, but it does not go very well. Of all the composers, Brahms is the composer I feel closest to emotionally. His music is introspective, not particularly showy but very powerful and rich in musical content."

Another piece Starker performs is the Bartók *Cello Concerto*. The piece was written for viola, the composer's last work. It was adapted for the cello by the composer's Hungarian disciple, Tibor Serly. In 1949 when Serly finished rounding out the *Viola Concerto* from Bartók's extensive but unordered sketches, he made a cello version. He said that Bartók intended to create one for Piatigorsky. Serly told Starker about it. At the time he was not a touring soloist. It wasn't until 1981, three years after Serly's death that Starker gave the world premiere of the cello version.

Over the past four decades, Starker has recorded nearly all of the mainstream cello works in addition to many lesser known pieces. "Today people appreciate my older recordings, perhaps more than at the time they were released. For many years my recordings struck some people as cold. The reason, as far as I am concerned, is that they were so astonished at how well I played the cello that they simply could not listen to the music. Now people are accustomed to my playing. Today there are hundreds of cellists who also play extremely well. Modern audiences are far more discerning when it comes to good cello playing today than listeners of thirty years ago. Now they are discovering the different sounds and concepts I have tried to convey and are not so preoccupied with technique."

Says cellist Aldo Parisot, "I heard from Feuermann's assistant that the famous recording he made of Schubert's *Arpeggione Sonata* required eighteen takes. With Starker, this would not be the case. He walks into the studio, and take one is already nearly perfect. If additional takes are required, then it is for musical reasons."

Harold Lawrence, music supervisor, editor and producer for more than three hundred Mercury Living Presence recordings says, "The fact that Starker seems absolutely at ease in the recording studio might be regarded as a sign of an easy-going personality. Between takes, he responds with charm and wit to people around him. He is a vivid raconteur, and he loves nothing better than to engage in a lively exchange of ideas on politics and contemporary literature. But it's fascinating to observe Starker switch instantly from the entertaining social companion to the intensely concentrated performer. Before we were through chuckling over a particularly amusing anecdote, Starker would already have snubbed out his cigarette and left the control room for the studio, leaving behind him a set of suggestions for the next takes. A record producer has got to be on his toes at a Starker session."[42]

Harris Goldsmith addressed in a Carnegie Hall program the "satanic virtuosity" of Starker with Stanislaw Skrowaczewski and the London Symphony performing the Schumann *Cello Concerto,* saying they gave "a reading of such exemplary brilliance that the work appears to be a masterpiece." Irving Kolodin in *Hi-Fi/Stereo Review* said of Starker in his recording of *Italian Cello Sonatas* (Boccherini, Corelli, Locatelli, Valentini and Vivaldi), "His playing of them is so extraordinary that it warrants purchase of the album ... The cellist throughout was in magnificent form."

Peter Aczel in *Audio Critic* wrote about Starker's presentation of *David Popper: Romantic Cello Favorites.* "If you think it was Fritz Kreisler who invented the short, schmaltzy, hummable, virtuoso encore piece for string soloists, I have news for you. David Popper, the greatest cellist of his time and a prolific composer for his instrument, had already perfected the genre a full generation earlier. Janos Starker, possibly the greatest cellist of our time, plays twenty of Popper's superb bonbons.... each of them more delightful than the one before.... Starker plays them as if nothing in the cello literature gave him greater pleasure. I have never heard better cello playing, and some of these pieces are monstrously difficult to play. The man's artistry is a perfect blend of scholarly musicianship and virtuosity."

R.C. in *Grammophone* says of the recording of the Schumann and Hindemith *Concertos* with Starker as soloist and the Bamberg Symphony Orchestra with conductor, Dennis Russell Davies, "Comparing Janos Starker in three separate recordings of the Schumann *Cello Concerto* confirms at least two significant facts: first, that what started out as a strong, finely drawn reading is nowadays just as strong and finely drawn, but far more flexible than before; and second, that in a span of some thirty-five years (my first listed comparison dates to September, 1957), Starker's tonal fiber, technical agility, and expressive nuancing have, if anything, increased.

You'd never guess that this is the work of a seventy-year-old." And as for the Hindemith, in it "Starker is again a master of elegance; his tone is finely tensed, his sense of rhythm impeccable...." [43]

Starker recently recorded the Elgar *Concerto* and the Walton *Concerto* with Leonard Slatkin and the Philharmonia Orchestra and collaborated on a new concerto with composer Chou Wen-Chung. The Starker recordings amount to a legacy.

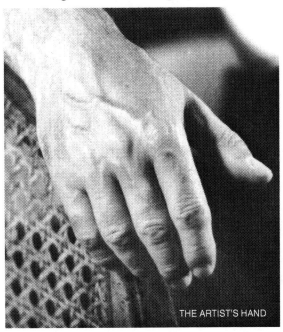

THE ARTIST'S HAND

Take One — Take Nine

a story by Janos Starker

8:30 p.m.

The house lights dim, the artist comes on stage. Applause reminds him of a responsibility to give his very best to the audience assembled—people who have travelled to the hall and bought tickets expressly to hear him. He must give his best under prevailing conditions. And what are these? A hall subject to every kind of acoustic anomaly caused by cold, warmth and humidity. Perhaps the concert has been preceded by travel hazards in cars, trains and planes. Or, perhaps with insufficient rehearsal, sometimes with an orchestra of poor quality. His instrument could have reacted to change in temperature and altitude, not to mention the artist's own physical and mental response to any given combination of factors.

So he performs. The music is drawn from his repertory. He knows it intimately and has played it previously many times all over the world. However, because of the compound conditions involved, small accidents happen. A finger slips, or a note doesn't "sound" right. As the artist adjusts to conditions beyond his control, some phrasings change, dynamics are altered, tempos vary; but the *overall* concept comes through. His communicative powers function. His personality, combined with a consistently high standard of playing, wins him appreciation by his audience. Little accidents and incidents are over in a moment and forgotten. Sheer musical enjoyment remains with the listener. "Take One" was a success.

10:00 a.m.

In a recording studio, the artist takes his assigned place. All around him are the orchestra, conductor, sound engineer, producer and assorted others, all geared to create a recording of the highest possible level and quality, a recording to be heard throughout the world, to be scrutinized by critics and reviewers, and above all to be listened to repeatedly by music lovers and musicians.

On a recording, the magnetism of an artist's presence does not exist. A shared experience with audience under the same roof and conditions does not prevail. Fleeting discrepancies in a live performance are magnified to the degree of annoyance or distress during repeated hearings of a record, as the listener grows more and more familiar with the qualities of an artist. Before the advent of magnetic tape, recording techniques permitted only slight adjustments, and the intention therefore was to "photograph" celebrated performances by an artist. These "photographs" were, in this sense, not retouched. They showed the artist at his momentary best, like a woman without make-up. Thus, only a tiny fraction of thousands of early recordings are able to withstand the judgment of time and the rising standards of performance.

Today the artist leaves the recording studio feeling as though he has given testimony under oath—testimony about a certain composition as it appeared to him during a particular stage in his artistic life. In the studio, he has on his side all the acoustical advantages of a concert hall built with the greatest care. He has highly trained sound engineers and technicians working with him and, above all, a musician-producer who through constant labor with tape has developed an ear capable of detecting the slightest tonal changes, variations in tempo, and momentary inaccuracies. The tape machine permits innumerable stops and starts to correct even minute musical errors. Any artist is thereby given the opportunity to achieve a performance he considers truly his own—provided his concept of a work has been clearly and decisively defined—by repeating movements, sections, even single measures within reasonable time limits. (Since it is costly to keep an orchestra in session for repeated takes, the artist whose technique requires too much time to record will find himself less often engaged.) The takes are then assembled into a final "master." However, if a concept isn't decisive, tempos and dynamics will vary on different takes and in the end product will betray the lack of unity. The artist will not recognize his own playing, let alone give any impression of a coordinated performance. All this could be compared to the police artist's composite drawing of a wanted fugitive.

The clearly defined concept of a piece being recorded differs in many respects from the version an artist plays in concert. This is of course abhorrent to some puritans, those who maintain that only the composer and his message matter. They reject any calls for adjustment because of the vagaries of a concert hall on the one hand, and the specific demands of the microphone and disc on the other. In order to avoid any misunderstanding about such adjustments, one must attempt to be exact.

Music consists of horizontal (melodic) and vertical (harmonic and dynamic) elements in various combinations. Different artists are defined by their respective mixes of these elements. On records, vertical elements must outweigh horizontal. Stronger accents and more distinct, clearer harmonies are essential. Excessive speed created by tension and temperament often leads to problems. Slow or lingering tempos become dull, and rests become dead silences instead of spiritual communication. Dynamic changes have to be exaggerated and accentuated, although extremes need to be avoided. The nearly inaudible whisper of sound means nothing on records although it may be overpowering in the concert chamber. The climactic *fortissimo* that may be overpowering in concert can sound like sheer noise on a record. Technical details require far more attention. A blurred attack, an ill-timed slide, mechanical noises from an instrument are heard much more acutely by the microphone than by an audience listening at a distance from the point of origin. A wide vibrato creates faulty intonation on discs rather than tonal warmth. The high-fidelity stereophonic record projects music with such intimacy that even the sounds of breathing become part of the performance, an approximation of the artist's visual presence.

Tensions can be applied in spurts while sections of music are being recorded, but overall structural considerations have to be of such a strength that, regardless of the number of stops and retakes, the unity of a composition will not suffer.

No one can say whether any artist is able fully to submit himself to the notated demands of the composer, whether in live concert or in recording. Nor can anyone say in good conscience how much of a performance is the composer's and how much is the recreative artist's. Recording, as we know it today, is a recent art, and a collective art at that. The producer, unsung hero though he may be, is nearly as responsible for a recording as the composer and the performer. We will need more time until the art of Take Nine can be judged by its own norms on its own merits.

Just as no one questions any longer the artistic values of cinematography, and none in theater fears its competition, no one should regard recordings as a threat to live music. They are two distinctively different artistic expressions, albeit related in the ultimate goal of recreating, to the best extent possible, works of the master.

From all of the foregoing, one might be led to suppose that my recording likes are limited. I bring, however, concert-hall experience into the home listening environment. To be sure, acoustics are far from ideal, and perhaps an oboe has a thin sound or the harp is not precisely tuned. Still, I accept the total experience—trying not, in short, to criticize details but instead to appreciate, say, the superb piano sound of Rubinstein's recordings, the fascinating clarity and brilliance of Horowitz, the extreme control, and extreme lack of it, heard on Richter's.

Likewise there is the tear-provoking beauty of yesteryear's Beniamino Gigli, Fyodor Chaliapin, Elisabeth Schumann and Lotte Lehmann. Then there is the absolute dedication to the written score, never surpassed, of my idol for so many years, Fritz Reiner, exemplified by Strauss' *Also Sprach Zarathustra* (RCA album 2609) and final scene of *Salome* (Odyssey 32.16.0078), Bizet's *Carmen* (RCA album 6102), and Bartók's *Concerto for Orchestra* (RCA Victrola 1110), *Hungarian Sketches* and *Music for Strings, Percussion and Celesta* (RCA 1620).

As played by Henryk Szeryng, there are the Bach *Unaccompanied Sonatas* and *Partitas* (DG 319270-2).

Practically anything Heifetz ever recorded gives goose bumps—the Miklós Rózsa *Violin Concerto* (RCA 2027) which stuns on every hearing, and the Dohnányi *Serenade in C* with Primrose and Feuermann (RCA LVT-1017).

Then there is the Szigeti performance with Bruno Walter of Beethoven's *Violin Concerto* (Columbia M6-X-31513 album).

The Bartók *Quartets* as played by the Juilliard String Quartet (Columbia album D3S-717).

The Dvorák *Cello Concerto* recorded in 1937 by Casals with George Szell and the Czech Philharmonic Orchestra, a historic landmark in the setting of standards (Seraphim 602240).

There are so many more examples, beyond convenient or practicable enumeration, a journey into joy, limited only by the time available to listen and revel in memories.

J.S., Bloomington, 1963, expanded 1969

ᴧᴧᴧ

Janos Starker's career stands in proud defiance of the Shavian theorem, named for George Bernard Shaw, "Those who can, do; those who cannot, teach." Despite a performing career as distinguished as any colleague, nothing defines the relationship Starker has with his instrument better than his teaching. Says Starker, "I personally cannot perform without teaching, and I cannot teach without performing. When you have to explain what you are doing, then you *really* discover what you are doing."

Starker discovered at a very young age that his own understanding of the possibilities of his instrument grew as he helped students. Articulating musical and technical thoughts so early in his life proved enormously helpful. "I had to explain *why* something does not work, or why you put the thumb *there* instead, evaluating, analyzing, explaining. For this, I am enormously grateful," he says.

"I unequivocally consider teaching more important than anything else. But, on the other hand, if I don't perform, I lose contact with reality, which I consider necessary for a contemporary pedagogue. This does not necessarily mean that one must be famous in order to be a good teacher. Certain people by nature and temperament are teachers, and I happen to be one of them," says Starker. "I learned from great teachers who gave me the keys to understanding music. I always felt that I had strong principles. If a person truly believes in principles, then he or she is obliged to share them."

Shortly after the war, when Starker was having considerable difficulties in playing, he developed his concepts which took shape in his book, *Organized Method of String Playing*, published by Indiana University Press. The visible and published part of the method is the left hand exercises. It is a thought process with regard to music making via cellistic skills. It systematizes issues pertaining to cello playing and music making into four categories. The first category contains basically all of the issues pertaining to the body, the mind, the timing, and muscular functions. The second category includes all issues pertaining to the right side of the body; right arm and shoulder, upper arm, hand, fingers, bow changes, bowings, etc. The third category deals with the left side of the body, the left arm, upper arm, hand positions as an extension of the instrument, vibrato, and anticipation and delays in various actions. The fourth category is the musical application for the sake of which we do all of this.

Teaching for Starker is a different kind of approach than that of other cello teachers. It is not just a sprinkling of holy water, saying, "Do it this way, because that is how I do it," as in most master classes. It is instead a matter of conveying concepts based on immutable principles. There are four kinds of teaching, according to Starker. These include beginning instruction, remedial or restorative teaching, repertoire teaching and interpretive teaching.

"The results from teaching fundamentals are not necessarily visible or audible immediately," says Starker. "Sometimes years later I will get a letter from a student saying, 'Now I understand what you were telling me.' The great reward from teaching is to make a student's imagination work. I am far less interested in talent than in a student whose brain allows for continual development. I want to make sure that my students are prepared for any demands that music will make on them throughout their lives. It is my wish that young performers should develop an awareness of tone color and dynamics as well as the ability to realize their personal thoughts through the music, making them integral to the total musical picture."

"Starker provides a role model that is extremely inspirational for students on any level," says Chicago Symphony Orchestra cellist, Donald Moline. "Not only is he a technically perfect player, but he is a very analytical person intellectually. He can articulate lucidly, which is the essence of great teaching." Starker says that he can tell his students exactly, in a nuts and bolts technical fashion, how every nuance and effect in good playing is achieved. "Of course there is magic in the musical experience, but the magic is explicable. From an analytical point of view, one can explain the magic," he says. "But I do not expect my students to play like I do. In that way I am open-minded. I do not believe that the only way to present a piece of music is the way I do it, even though as a performer I must be not only very convinced of my interpretation but must also be very convincing. However, it is my natural inclination to try to see everything from every conceivable angle. That lends itself better to teaching than to performing."

Starker is demanding, everyone agrees. He expects the best and most from his students. They work to their limit, and then more. "The teacher is supposed to set unreasonable goals," he says, "but only for those who are able to handle lifelong frustrations and the brutality of a public career. The students I accept will unquestionably become members of the professional community. They will be members of orchestras, small ensembles, and teachers. In every generation a few will become concert artists. All are heading for professional existence." As a teacher Starker asks for discipline in performance and in career preparation. Each lesson is a test. Is he or she making progress? Starker seeks results.[44]

"But a teacher cannot teach something that the student is incapable of doing. It's the job of the teacher to find out what the student can do and to enhance that capability. Teaching is supposed to inform, but you can only bring forth what is in a student's nature and then enhance the love of music by giving them the right information. By nature some people will be ensemble players, some will be orchestral players, and a few will be soloists. The teacher's job is to help students learn all of the principles and skills of instrumental playing and music making.

Regardless of whether a musician performs as a soloist or a member of a small or large ensemble, or assists a budding instrumentalist in learning the "trade," the significance of knowing and understanding the issues is beyond the value of natural gifts. The goal of utilizing one's gifts, great or small, is universal. When talent and fortunate circumstances coincide, there may be no need for theories in order to arrive at great results.

When it comes to practice, Starker recommends that a session should include several kinds of practicing to address the different demands of performing. There's experimental practicing in which one learns proper technique. Add some playing for the purpose of building stamina and keeping in good physical condition. Spend some time learning the notes of a piece. Then work on learning to perform the music, not to practice but to think of yourself performing. People spend too much time on the things they already know how to do, he says. The important thing is to pinpoint the trouble spots, and work on those.

According to Starker, an understanding of the musical style of a particular composer is best learned by studying a broad range of music. "You don't learn to play the Beethoven *Sonatas* well because you manage the fingerings and bowings of a piece. If you're not familiar with Beethoven's string quartets, piano trios, and symphonies, you cannot truly play Beethoven. The same is true for every other composer. Years of orchestral playing can make one a complete musician. It is in the symphonic repertoire that one learns the language of the great composers, much more so than from instrument teachers."

Style is not a matter of finding the one correct way to play. Starker is dedicated to helping students discover good choices. If one has an overall understanding and familiarity with a composer, then there will be a variety of choices. "A student may come to a lesson well-prepared technically but not have the foggiest notion of the musical essence. First you teach the skills required for instrumental playing. Then you teach the artistry of making music. You help them to develop musical taste."

Starker has a doctor-patient relationship with his students. When a student arrives with a problem, the diagnostic procedure begins. After Starker spots the difficulty, he prescribes several remedies. If the student follows the suggested directions, a cure is usually forthcoming. However, if a particularly difficult problem or a new version of an old problem appears, the doctor is intrigued and tries even harder to find the solution. He is able to analyze and isolate the trouble spots, then relate the problem to the student, showing how to make the correction. "Ah, too much tension. We cannot play when we are tense." Then comes an experimental phase. "Try this, try that." If his suggestions do not work, he keeps trying until the answer appears. He says, "There are many ways of arriving at the same destination."

Starker's technical and analytical advice includes details as specific as which muscle should contract or relax. One student sent him a postcard with a drawing of the human back, every muscle identified by name. A desperate question came along with the card saying, "Which muscle did you say to tighten?" [45]

One of the most fatiguing things in cello playing is the extension, the stretch between fingers of the left hand. If one can keep the hand compact, there is much less fatigue and strain on the muscles. To watch him, Starker appears to keep his hand always in the most comfortable shape. He avoids stretching "like the plague." Casals' fingering system required often fingering the lower positions diatonically, thus using a lot of stretching between fingers. Starker uses the stretch infrequently because the readjustment of the hand after the stretch alters the intonation. He believes the extension is an unnatural function, so he avoids it as much as possible. Nevertheless, there are situations when for musical reasons one needs to use it. He finds that if stretching distorts the sound, then he would rather shift. When extending is the best or even the only option, for Starker the stretch lasts only as long as it is absolutely necessary. Then bring the hand immediately back to normal.

Says Starker about use of the body in cello playing, "One of the saddest things in my life is to see a number of instrumentalists who have destroyed themselves because of overexertion of the muscles. They have reduced the years that they can play. It is not uncommon to find a pianist or violinist playing into his nineties. More than with the violin or piano, there are immense physical demands in playing the cello. It takes a great deal of finger pressure to press down the strings, particularly in the higher positions where one does not generally use counter pressure from the thumb. Also the strength it takes to produce audible sounds with the bow arm requires simply **physical conditioning, stamina, and conscious, thoughtful use of the body.**"

According to Starker, musical sounds are based on waves of tension and non-tension. Persistent tension or pressure loses its effectiveness. In order to provide this exchange of tension and non-tension in music, we must set up the body in such a way that it does not block, so that it can produce unhindered circular (not angular) motions, occurrences of tension and release of tension.

Starker's vocabulary is full of metaphors and colorful descriptions. When a student has trouble with a treacherous shift, the pedagogue says, "Take your time, and enjoy the trip." Or in explaining a bow concept, he may say, "It is like spreading peanut butter on your bread." (It takes some pressure.) If a tempo is too slow, he has been known to say, "Son, that is a middle-aged tempo." One time a young woman fainted during a lesson when he was talking about the importance of controlling the input and expulsion of air in a disciplined manner. The woman told him she was pregnant. He scolded, "Why didn't you tell me?" "I was afraid you would not think I was a serious student," she replied. He dismissed the incident with, "Silly girl," and went on with the lesson unperturbed.

This teacher claps, grunts, gestures, and commands to make his points. One time a student was having trouble articulating the correct bowing for the opening theme of the Dvořák *Concerto*. "Sing the opening theme," Starker bellowed. "I can't. I'm too embarrassed," the student admitted." Starker came back with "An artist cannot afford to be embarrassed! Sing!" The student sang and discovered through her singing the mistake in her concept. Through her increased awareness, her playing improved immediately.

Starker might be intimidating to some students, but he tries not to discourage them. Sometimes he does not use his Gofriller cello at lessons for that reason. "Some students are intimidated by my sound. Others are egged on by hearing the possibilities. I show them different ways. Sometimes I imitate what they are doing, exaggerating their ills and demonstrating the alternatives."

Piatigorsky discovered in his teaching that sometimes it was beneficial for him to make mistakes in demonstrating a passage. Suddenly, the student started shining, producing much better results than ever before. It was then that the student discovered that the teacher is not perfect, and he could be himself. Piatigorsky discovered that with this approach, he would enhance those qualities in a player in which he already excelled. This is not necessarily Starker's method. Starker is not interested in the one thing the student does the best. He will emphasize instead the things the student does not know how to do so well, teaching them instead every aspect of music making. "There is a very important pedagogic definition," says the cellist, "when a student reaches a certain level. At that point you congratulate the player on getting there and then say, now let's move from this level to the next."

Starker once gave a definition of a great music teacher as "one who cares for the individual and is willing to spend a lifetime learning the elements of every aspect of his art so he can transmit the message of the great composers." He sees his job as teacher "to inform, to show my students how to use their brains, and then through guidance to lead them through the problems to a self-designed solution." Students come out of his studio knowing how to be their own teachers.[46]

Regarding the use of his editions, says Starker, "I want to make my ideas available for people who listen to my recordings and wonder how things are being done. Bowings, fingerings, interpretive ideas, these are performance details that I have experimented with and arrived at through thousands of concerts. They work for me. So deviate from there, and develop your own ideas. Instead of just adopting a few things, rather, use this as a basis. Then, if you want, change it."

Since 1958 when he began teaching at Indiana University, his cello seminars have attracted string players from all over the world. One time Starker was giving advice to his young artist students in a seminar in an atmosphere that crackled with excitement and intensity, according to Shirley Stroh Mullins, string specialist from Ohio. A young slender woman who had just performed appeared to be under great stress while awaiting the verdict from the great man. Starker began, "My dear, the most important thing you must do is...." People leaned forward, waiting to hear his words of wisdom. Starker leaned closer to the student, smiled, and said, "You must eat more pasta." [47]

He went on to tell a joke about himself. It begins with Saint Peter standing at the Pearly Gates. Three cellists come knocking, hoping to get into heaven.

"Who did you study with on earth?" Saint Peter asks the first.

"Leonard Rose," says the cellist.

"Sorry, you will have to go to hell," Saint Peter answers.

"And you?" he asks the next, "Who did you study with, young lady?"

"Rostropovich, the great Rostropovich!"

"Sorry, you will have to go to hell, too," says Saint Peter.

"What about you," Saint Peter asks the last cellist, "Who was your teacher?"

The cellist replies, "Janos Starker."

"For goodness sake," says Saint Peter. "Come right in. You have already been through hell!" [48]

Despite his stern reputation, Starker is generous with his advice: "Learn as much as possible from every area of music making possible. Get the broadest possible education so that you are functional in every area. Be a complete musician, not like the great virtuoso who cannot play second violin in a string quartet."

Starker is quick to remind his students that we performers come and go, but the masterpieces remain. Thereby our primary objective is to remain as faithful and subservient to the master-pieces as possible. It is the performer through whose eyes the viewing of masterpieces is presented. But the performer is secondary to the creator.

The door to his teaching studio bears his card with the title, "Distinguished Professor," before which someone has penciled "Very." To this, Starker appears pleased. "The kids are always writing something there. Sometimes, they put Un instead." Evidently, his austere mien is not taken too seriously. Starker's students adore him. "He's like a father to me," says one. "Lots of us feel this way."

But certain things, such as giving less than one's best, whether a student or a great artist, infuriate Starker. Sloppy playing covered up by histrionics, poor preparation, foolishness when a gifted student does not concentrate.... these to him are inexcusable! He hates excuses. A student who came in to a lesson poorly prepared and said she was disgusted with all of the opera rehearsals commented, "I know that opera backwards and forwards." Starker, who had played the opera dozens of times at the Met, remarked, "I wish I could say that."

Because Starker is a world traveller, his students never know where he has just been or where he might be going. Returning from Africa where he had played concerts in a short-sleeved shirt, he mentioned that he would soon be in Venice. "How lucky you are! I'd love to see Venice," a student commented. "So would I," was the reply. "I'll see the inside of a cab, a hotel room, and a concert hall."

He has been successfully combining performing and teaching careers for decades. Such a life demands near superhuman stamina. But he quotes a favorite maxim, "If you have to practice twenty-five hours a day, just get up an hour earlier." For him the combination of playing everywhere and living in Bloomington is the most perfect thing in the world.

Starker has had much to do with the development of the musical standards at Indiana University School of Music. It has attained the kind of manifest prominence to have been voted the number one music school in the United States by the American Association of Colleges and Universities. It has seventeen hundred music majors. When Starker moved to Indiana, there were about five hundred majors. By the time the new facilities had been built, the numbers reached a thousand. The success of the school is credited largely to Dean Wilfred Bain, a distinctively powerful visionary who hired such faculty as Joseph Gingold, Menachem Pressler, György Sebök, Franco Gulli, Eva Janzer, Starker and others. The university is known to have over a thousand performances in a year. All of the disciplines are represented by outstanding people. The Institute for Advanced Studies was recently established, the first Fellow being Leonard Bernstein. There are six orchestras in the school with many orchestra concerts. Chamber music events are ongoing. Often on Friday and Saturday nights there is a fully staged opera in the opera house, not to mention lectures by prominent world figures, Nobel prize winners, etc.

When Starker's "Bloomington existence" started in 1958, the dean of the School of Music asked him what he should say if one day a member of the state legislature should come and ask, "Where is this highly paid professor of cello?" To this Starker responded, "If anyone objects, then I leave." He guaranteed that each of his students at Indiana University would receive twenty exposures to him each year including private lessons and master classes. Usually he held about ten master classes each year on Saturdays. There were several decades when Starker played over a hundred concerts each year. At the same time he was a full-time professor at Indiana University. In the summers, sometimes in the winters as well, he taught at the school in Banff. For six years he was also a full-time professor at the Folkwang Hochschule in Essen, Germany. This job he took over from Tortelier who could not tolerate the air of the "Ruhrgebiet." (Essen is in an industrial region where the air quality is quite unhealthy.) Tortelier then got the summer job in Lucerne, Switzerland, where Starker had formerly been teaching. Following his years in Essen, Tortelier moved to Nice, France, where he spent the rest of his life.

Starker was in Europe three or four times each year. Just before a tour of concerts and then again at the end, he would teach his students in Essen. It worked out that he spent about twenty days in Essen. Each day he taught six hours, taking a maximum of twelve students. He guaranteed that he would give each student ten lessons plus some master classes.

Each time he was on the plane heading for Essen, he did all of the mathematics, figuring the hours he would spend with each student. He figured twenty days in Essen at six hours per day, total one hundred and twenty hours, a full-time job. On that basis he accepted the contract. For this he was paid such a fortune that he thought he was the highest paid teacher in the world for six years.

He also took his German assistant, Maria Kliegel, a woman who was studying with him in Bloomington, with him to Essen. One time when he was in Sienna, Italy, he was approached by the wife of the president of the Deutsche Bank. She said to Starker that there was a very gifted young cellist, Maria Kliegel, who should study with him. She sponsored Maria's study in Bloom-

JANOS STARKER   MARIA KLIEGEL

ington. When she finished her studies, she became Starker's assistant. Later she was the first prize winner in the Rostropovich Competition and won several German prizes in addition. Then she moved to Essen and stayed there to teach Janos' class of cellists when he was away. "This young lady," according to Starker, "is one of the finest German cellists."

Starker had built up the cello class in Essen to seventeen or eighteen students. His original plan was to stay only as long as the cello class was sufficiently large. When Tortelier left, there were about seven students. So his class became larger than they had expected. Maria Kliegel then took over for him. She taught there for a number of years, later teaching in Köln.

For several decades Starker played over a hundred concerts each year in addition to maintaining an incredible teaching schedule, often teaching eight or nine hours each day. The concerts and all that they entailed never appealed to him so much. He always felt that the most important aspect of his life was teaching.

Starker found that the life of a concert artist is a lonely life. "At times I found myself in a hotel room in some faraway place: Mozambique, Rio de Janeiro or Kalamazoo, or wherever. For the first twenty-five years of my concert life, travelling was very hard and very lonely."

Later Starker found that wherever he went, he came upon dozens of students in every town! This was glorious and delightful to him, one of the greatest joys in his life! But sometimes it would "drive him up the wall." He would have simply no privacy. On the other hand, there were times that he felt that he never wanted to become this kind of person, a touring concert artist. But it was his choice.

Starker's interest in his students professionally and personally is quite up to date. He keeps in contact with hundreds of former students, pleased to know about their careers, families and successes. He is extremely proud of his large number of former students. "My kids," he calls them. They are cellists playing in orchestras and teaching in universities all over the world.

He plans to continue teaching, "as long as I have something to say and can demonstrate musically like my teacher did, as long as I can play a phrase with a good sound and in tune." He is not in favor of the Ivan Galamian and Dorothy Delay kind of teaching where the teacher sings the line and says, "More, more." The teacher should be able to give some aural representation of the music, at least a phrase so the student can know how it is supposed to sound.

After years of struggling as a concert artist going to faraway places, he decided to travel only first class and stay in the best luxury hotel suites. It was not for his own pride or to prove that he was a successful artist. Rather, he figured, "If I am not in my own home, and I have to stay in a small room, then what the hell am I doing this for!" The comforts of a larger, more luxurious living space gave him a feeling of peace.

Starker chose to live in Bloomington because he did not want to be a part of the usual music cliques where "everyone goes around socializing constantly." In Bloomington he could pick up the telephone and say, "Let's play chamber music," inviting Joseph Gingold, György Sebök, George and Eva Janzer, or other friends. For Starker it was "a gorgeous feeling to fly to Tokyo, London, Paris, New York or wherever from the airport in Indianapolis. The scenery changes, interesting experiences, then I am back in Bloomington. If I wanted, I

EVA JANZER, JANOS STARKER'S FIRST STUDENT. THEY WERE BOTH CHILDREN WHEN SCHIFFER ASKED JANOS TO SHOW HER HOW TO HOLD THE CELLO AND BOW. THEY MET WEEKLY FOR LESSONS FOR SEVERAL YEARS. LATER IN LIFE, SHE TAUGHT AT INDIANA UNIVERSITY.

could have a vacation home in Switzerland, France or wherever. But I am not crazy. If I do not have to travel, I don't want to."

⋏⋏⋎

In 1971, on the twenty-fifth anniversary of his leaving Hungary, Starker returned to the country of his birth. Following a concert in Stuttgart, he travelled to Budapest and arrived on a Saturday at about 4:00 p.m. By 7:30 p.m. he was on the stage of the Liszt Academy where he had played many a concert as a student. There was a rehearsal going on when he arrived, and he did not have much time to contemplate the situation. He was simply in another town, playing another concert. It just happened to be his hometown. Without any fanfare or official recognition he gave his performance. Afterward the audience cheered. This was perhaps the best concert of his life!

In 1976 Starker took his two daughters for a visit to Hungary. While they were in Budapest, he decided to take them to see the pond in Gyömrö where together with his parents and brothers he spent the summers in his childhood years. Unlike the seemingly long train ride of many years before, the trip was only about a twenty-minute taxi ride. It seemed like nothing, particularly when the trip did not require lengthy preparations, packing, planning, and then spending two summer months away from home.

When they arrived at the pond, Starker found the little cottage with boys and girls dressing rooms, just exactly as it had been fifty years earlier. Even the same nails were still on the walls. That is where they used to hang their pants when putting on their swimsuits! Children played on the sandy beach and swam in the water, playing their water polo games just as Starker and his brothers had done so many years before. The fruit trees had changed. Many had died. Some had been replaced with other fruit trees. There were more cottages than he had remembered. Starker was filled with nostalgia, reminiscing over childhood days and the pain of war years.

Conversations with Aldo Parisot, 1998

Aldo Parisot, Brazilian cellist and for many years professor at Yale University, has been a good friend to Starker for a long time. He had wanted to meet Starker since 1948 when he heard a recording of his. Friends told him that Starker wanted to meet Parisot as well. But they were both busy, Parisot with his concert tours and Starker with his orchestras. For many years their paths did not cross.

Parisot and Starker happened to have the same British manager, Wilfred van Wyck. Parisot was in London in 1957 for a recital in Wigmore Hall when his manager said, "Guess who is in town tonight, Janos Starker." Parisot suggested inviting him to the concert. So Janos attended the concert. After the concert Starker approached Parisot to shake his hand and asked, "What are you going to do?" He made no comment about the performance, no words of congratulations or appreciation for the music. He asked "What are you doing tomorrow?" "Actually," replied Parisot, "I have to fly to Holland tomorrow for a concert three days later." Starker suggested that he postpone his trip one day so that they could get together for lunch in the hotel. Also he wanted Parisot to come with him to the recording studio, Angel Records. He had just had fabulous success with his Kodály recording and wanted Parisot to hear some of it.

After lunch they were walking toward the studio. Parisot remembers hearing Starker say, "Why do you play Bach so free?" In return Parisot said, "How come you play Bach so square?" This was the end of their musical conversation. Parisot says that was one of the funniest experiences of his life. Ever since then they have been the very best of friends.

Every year since 1970, at the invitation of Parisot, Starker has given a cello seminar at Yale University. "Starker is without a doubt the greatest cello virtuoso of this century," says Parisot. "There is no one who has ever played the cello the way he does. When he was young, of course, he was a phenomenon. He is still a wonderful cellist today, the finest I have ever heard. That includes Emmanuel Feuermann, Piatigorsky and all the others. On top of that he is a magnificent artist with wonderful musical ideas. Of course I do not always agree with his interpretation, but there is no doubt that I have the greatest respect for his musicianship.

"As a teacher he is just phenomenal! He is an incredible teacher. I have been in Bloomington many times. We have sent students to each other. I have witnessed his teaching many times. He has an uncanny teaching ability. He knows the instrument so well. Every physical motion he makes with the right hand or the left, he knows exactly how to explain it. He has solved the most complex problems for many players on the spot. The result happens immediately. After his explanation, the student will feel the physical sensation immediately, and the problem is solved right there in the class. I have witnessed this many times.

"There are times when a teacher will explain spiccato, and the student will go home and practice it for months, and if he is lucky enough, he will discover it. In Starker's class he explains it in such a way that the student can do it immediately! This is just one example.

"No one could attempt to write about the history of cello playing without devoting about fifty pages to Starker. Although I admire many of the fine cello teachers today, I regard Starker to be the greatest of them all. As a clinician Starker can diagnose and cure the disease of tension almost on the spot." Starker has been tapped as a diagnostician for many different instrumentalists over the years, not just cellists. When he was playing with the Met Opera Orchestra, he was helping some of his colleagues, such as a violinist who had back and arm pains. In some cases he was able to help lengthen their careers ten to fifteen years through his diagnoses.

"Many people feel that he is a very hard man. I always tell my students to go to Starker to study. If he is rough, just take it because it is worth it. But actually, inside he is a pussycat. He is a very warm person. Besides, he's awfully funny! The reason that he sometimes scolds is that he is actually a rather shy person, and he is rather embarrassed when he does not know the person. Once he knows you, he is one of the warmest human beings. On my list, he is number one!" Ironically, both Starker and Parisot claim the other to be the greatest cello teacher.

The Artist-Teacher

a story by Janos Starker

The "Legend" tells about the great master of the violin, spreading his wisdom to anxious youths for an exorbitant fee:

A future legend scrapes together the sum required for a lesson and is admitted, trembling, to the presence of the sage. The sage, ensconced in the comfort of an easy chair, reads his favorite newspaper.

"What have you prepared?" he asks.

"Mozart," says the young genius.

"So play," says the Master, and continues reading his paper.

About 15 minutes into a brilliant rendering of the concerto the Master looks up and says, "Don't scratch."

The young man, shattered, continues. As the concerto comes to an end the Master says, "I told you not to scratch... Start again," and continues to peruse his paper.

As the time of the lesson draws to its limit, the sage utters, "Well, scratch if you like," and bids the student goodbye.

This "message" remained for a lifetime in the minds of pedagogues, and led to the frequent remark that there are those who teach and those who give lessons.

Not long ago the question was posed to a teacher of some 53 years—myself, "Can you define your teaching philosophy?"

At first I recoiled.

What nonsense! The number of my students count in the hundreds, and they in turn account for thousands of follow-up generations. And then there are those who have participated in my classes around the world—string and wind players, pianists and others—and they number in the tens of thousands. These participants contribute to the world of music on stages as soloists, ensemble players, orchestra members and principals and teachers in schools and universities.

I have given hundreds of interviews and lectures and published writings on music and methods. I have stated my principles so often that it seemed anything more would be redundant.

Well, shortly after the question was posed, I scanned a few of the widely circulated music magazines—*Strad, American String Teacher, Klavier*, etc.

I was struck by the large number of articles by some of my former students and by some of the prominent and not so prominent members of the musical community, about subjects that I had read about 50 years ago, questions and answers others dealt with 200 and 100 years ago.

I realized that principles must be restated again and again (if nature allows you to live long enough). Then also I realized that teaching must be looked at from the point of view of the teacher as well as the student, and that one must be aware that today's student is tomorrow's teacher. A few stock answers came to mind. "The teacher must collect information and dispense information to students." It is basically as simple as that. No teacher is capable of teaching someone something that the pupil has no ability to perceive. All the teacher can do is to assist, or accelerate the attainment of basic skills.

Therefore the teacher is really only an aide, and there are good aides and bad or mediocre aides. But is it all that simple? What allows an individual to become a "teacher" in the real sense of the word? What is the difference between giving a lesson or a class and teaching? Maybe by defining these manifestations one can outline a possible philosophy thereby arriving also at the definition of "artist-teacher." First of all, one needs to establish categories of students:

1 - Beginners in need of elementary instruction.

Here the imitative approach is the most effective—that is to show the motions, placements, induce sensations and trigger aural and visual recognitions. When the student asks questions, depending on the nature of such questions, principles should be addressed in a limited fashion.

2 - Intermediate students requiring remedial instruction and repertory studies.

Here the issue of lessons versus teaching arrives. Repertory studies imply the study of specific pieces and thus fall in the category of coaching, or lessons. Teaching requires the imparting of general principles applicable in all repertory and instrumental playing.

3 - Advanced students requiring, first of all, assessment of their mental, physical and musical abilities. These assessments must establish the limitations and attained level of skill in order to design a path to solidify and expand the goals of these students. Here psychological issues dominate teaching.

Those who are hindered by doubt need help so as to build self-confidence. Those lacking self-critical faculties require criticism that may on the surface seem destructive.

However, these approaches must be coupled with factual information—specific data about how to cure existing ills and obtain desired results. The highest priority must be given to the inducement of thinking in order to force them to make individual discoveries of functioning principles, thereby reducing the risk of training automated imitators. The teacher's solutions to his or her own difficulties may be discussed, but never used as guidance for students with differing problems.

In all these evolutionary classifications the underlying musical principles, such as *purity of sound, simplicity and verity of interpretation of the written text*, should be stressed in order to lead the student to develop an inner need to strive for those principles.

Parallel with these objectives the elements of the art of performance, including stage presence and theatrical but musically motivated gestures, are brought into focus; then the student displays a readiness to master the necessary details.

It is during this phase that the assessment of potential in a player requires guidance toward the variety of musical activities possible. Here the teacher must be able to stress the learning of repertory which leads to solo, chamber music or orchestral playing and to teaching. Given the proper training, none of these choices will exclude success in others. Energies will simply be channeled toward realistic goals.

Class teaching should be divided into two types: *Master Classes* where players are instructed in the improvement of prepared pieces, and *Individual Coaching* which differs from the master class only in that no listeners are present.

Master classes need occasional tension-releasing activities such as the relating of anecdotes because the player finds himself or herself in a public performance situation with a critical but sympathetic audience. Criticism by the teacher often brings on excessive nervousness which hinders reception of information. A mixture of positive and negative observations may be needed in order to reach constructive results.

And then there are the sessions we call *Seminars*: Here the players are incidental and the focus is on the participating listeners. Problems of instrumental playing and music making are discussed and various approaches and solutions proposed and talked about. These sessions require the teacher to become a performer as well, demonstrating, speaking and hopefully keeping the attention of the group for the prescribed length of the session.

It remains to define the concept of the *Concert Artist.*

First of all, whoever dedicates his or her life to public musical activity ought to be an artist. The extent of a concert performer's activities can be local, national and even eventually international. These classifications are seldom, if ever, based on truly essential artistic elements. Rather, they result from a multitude of talents which are the same in all professions requiring public appearances—consistency, stamina, stage presence, charisma, drive, and so forth.

When a music school obtains the services of one or more performers whose activities are international, a host of problems must be faced and a number of issues settled. International concert artists are booked years in advance. The number of performances require travel and rehearsals and generate hardships unimagined by most people.

International concert artists live an existence comparable only to the concept of the "twilight zone," appearing in floodlit halls, receiving ovations, flowers and adoration from the crowds and then carrying their suitcases and instruments through crowded airports and railroad stations. They must face cameras, microphones and interviewers and then, in order to prepare for the next day's performance, order room-service steaks or hamburgers in loneliness. Loving and hating their chosen professions as these strains change day by day, concert artists are proud of their achievements yet fearful of the physical limitations imposed upon them as individuals.

When such an artist accepts a teaching appointment, motivation can be manifold. Though it is rarely the case, security is thought to be the primary reason. In truth, the remuneration of a professorship often equals less than one or two months of earnings from concerts on the road. The real motivating force is apt to be dedication to the belief that one's principles are worthy of continuity via teaching. The artist-teacher who is propelled by dedication to principle will do his or her utmost to combine these two activities in order to serve both with equal loyalty.

Once at home, the interests of students, institution, and colleagues reign supreme. And only then can the concert artist step out of the "twilight zone" into the real world of learning, teaching and wage earning. *Only then will it be possible to take care of the highest level of the educational process—that of assisting already accomplished players,* and here, the aim ought to be never accept limits.

Having attained some success already, accomplished student musicians have obviously chosen to continue studies because they have still-unanswered questions. The limitless search toward the dreamed-of perfection, and the hallmark of professionalism and consistency, requires the setting of unreachable goals. The teacher must be aware of inherent dangers in this phase. Only those students who display a capacity to bear lifelong frustration and temporary satisfaction can be exposed to such brutal demands.

When on occasion the eyes of such a young musician gleam with the self-satisfying realization that he or she belongs to a small, but elite company, it is then that the *Artist* may also truly be called *Teacher*.

Janos Starker, Bloomington, November 11, 1986

Conversations with Joseph Gingold, 1997

Joseph Gingold, professor of music at Indiana University, said of his friend, "With Janos, there are so many categories where he proves himself worthy: as an artist, as a musician, as a teacher, as a phenomenal cellist, and as a good and devoted friend."

Mr. Starker and Mr. Gingold planned to record the Kodály *Duo*. Said Mr. Gingold, "Mr. Starker did not arrive in Bloomington until one day before the recording session. Because he had been away on a long tour all over Europe, we did not have a chance to rehearse. A couple of years earlier we had performed the piece. It is not productive to play the piece alone. For a duo, you need your partner to rehearse with. I was very concerned. But Starker said, "Don't cancel the session. Let's just play it through, and see what happens. It will be fun just to play together." Well, we played the first movement through, and Janos said, "We already have a perfect recording. Maybe one splice, and that will be it." There was one splice. Naturally, I relaxed completely from his words of encouragement and the fact that he seemed happy with the playing. Jani is very difficult to please when it comes to music making. But the recording went well, and we were happy.

Gingold found Starker to be a fine human being and said, "Starker was a wonderful family man, a great husband and son. He gave his heart and soul to his father and mother when they were alive. He set up his father with a little tailor shop so that he could be productive. He did not want to just hang around the house as though he had nothing else to do. He was as a tailor what Starker was to the cello. He took great pride in even sewing a button on someone's coat. It made him happy.

"As an instrumentalist, Janos is today the greatest influence in the area of string playing that anyone can imagine. He will not settle for anything less than perfect. He hates anything that smacks of insincerity. He cannot stand anyone who cannot play according to his standard. His standard is so high that it is hard to imagine. He has my admiration and love because of his sincerity."

According to Gingold, "He sometimes gives the wrong impression of what the inner Starker is like. He is not a smiler. He is very serious. Some of his students are scared to even say hello to him. His inner self is buried within, and he is always thinking about music. He is never quite satisfied with anything he has done. There are instances when I have seen Janos unhappy. Perhaps one or two notes in a concert did not please him. He does not please easily. He is a very tough customer to please. But show him someone who is a natural musician, someone who loves what he is doing, and Janos is in his element. Janos loves what he is doing. And he does it so magnificently!

JOSEPH GINGOLD

"His recordings of the Bach *Six Suites* are heavenly. As far as I am concerned they seem to come from Bach himself. They are so perfect. Janos plays the cello as Heifetz played the violin. I cannot pay a higher compliment because Heifetz was the greatest string player who ever lived. And Janos is right up there with him. Such heavenly music making comes out of his cello.

"His qualities as a friend...Janos is a true friend in every sense of the word. I do not know if there is a more wonderful friend in the world than the one I have in Janos. Recently I had some problems with my violin. My son had the instrument and would not return it. Janos stepped in, 'working his head off' on my behalf. The violin was eventually recovered for me, thanks only to Jani. He worked with such determination and with the brains of a lawyer. I am proud to be called one of his friends. It means so much to me. He is without a doubt a friend who is with me as long as I live, truly loyal. I have seen him use his heart and soul, helping out wherever he could."

Authenticity, or Authority from Intuition, Endless Experimentation and Conviction

a story by Janos Starker

When I was contacted recently about my participating in an August conference for the American Society for Aesthetics (1998), my mechanical response was, as usual in the past forty years, "If I am in Bloomington, I will do what I can for Indiana University." It only dawned on me later, what on earth am I supposed to do for the American Society of Aesthetics? The response was, "Whatever you like." My thought process went haywire. Yes, I have spent a lifetime searching for beauty as a performer and spent a lifetime trying to eliminate ugliness as a teacher of music. But I find myself among learned men and women who spend their lives explaining what I and my fellow performers do right or wrong.

What can I, whose musical and general education were not traditional, to say the least, contribute to the society's elaborations? Well, I will give you some of my thoughts, and then, as you probably expect, I'll play for you.

My life was spent playing thousands of concerts alone, with piano and with orchestra, either in front of them or inside of them. I must have spent roughly 6,000 hours teaching and roughly 50,000 hours practicing and probably 20,000 hours rehearsing for whatever activity I was involved in. I throw in these numbers because it seems to me that statisticians are among the leading menaces in our society. What do these numbers prove? That I ought to know a great deal about music. But about aesthetics?

There was a class of music aesthetics in the Franz Liszt Academy where I received my music education. The teacher was dry and boring, so I dropped the class. At the age of fourteen I dropped out of high school, and at the age of fifteen I dropped out of the Academy when my cello teacher retired and the political winds were against people like myself. I never graduated but was celebrated moderately, first as a prodigy, then as a professional. However, I continued to learn from chamber music teachers, private tutors, composers and the like. Some taught me to hear, some stressed the sanctity of the composer's wishes, some stressed individuality but with discipline.

You may ask what effects these influences had on me in the sixty years that have elapsed. Well, that is a tall question. When I read the variety of views on performing practices, authentic performances, the morality of adhering to dead composer's wishes, a wide panorama of experiences comes to mind. Let me enumerate a few. As a six-year-old I sat in concert halls and listened to Pablo Casals, Bronislaw Hubermann, Jascha Heifetz, Zino Francescatti, and some pianists whose names may not mean a great deal to you. My views and expectations changed. To me playing Bach on the violin meant ideally Adolph Busch on violin and Edwin Fisher on the piano. World War Two ended, and suddenly all of the idols tumbled.

A visit with George Enescu revealed how Brahms himself played his sonatas, with Enescu smilingly reminiscing why you cannot do it today. A few years earlier Dohnanyi, at the piano, played with me his concert piece, just leading me on, and thirty years later complimented me on my recording, notwithstanding all of the *changes* I made in his work. Sir Walton conducting me in his concerto and not noticing that I am playing an open A string instead of an A flat in the main theme! Stravinsky continuing to conduct after the orchestra has stopped in the recording of *Rakes Progress!*

At least ten composers have appreciated and adopted my proposed changes in the works they wrote for me. No, I do not have limitless respect for the written text. Magdelena Bach made obvious mistakes in her manuscript of her husband's *Cello Suites*, some debatable. Beethoven produced inconsistencies, and so did many others. Schumann wrote passages for instruments with other instruments in mind. Orchestration often ignored the relative inaudibility of some instruments. Some composers molded their writing on existing standards or attempted to stretch their capabilities. Some succeeded, some did not. Subjective judgment? Maybe.

Two more examples about composer's intentions I ought to cite. Bartók in his *First Rhapsody* notes, "When playing both movements, use the first ending." He himself skipped the first ending and played the second ending. And my favorite, when I asked Kodály about a questionable note in his *Solo Sonata*, whether it was a G or a G sharp, he answered, "Yes," and continued to sip his champagne.

These and other similar happenings led me to make many changes in works of the centuries. Although Shostakovich's son begged me not to add a bar at the end of the concerto, saying his father would turn over in his grave, I did so anyway. I am convinced that, at least in the cello repertoire, the contemporary practitioners were not up to the task of enlightening the composers of what works on the instrument and what doesn't. I am not referring to playing difficulties.

But what has all of this to do with authenticity. Not much unless that is what you are looking for. That has never been my goal for multiple reasons. Whenever I played with or for musicians who were Liszt students or their contemporaries, invariably they found everything played in our day *too fast*. Was that due to advanced age or faulty recollection? Your guess is as good as mine. I believe both, and I have noticed that my views change with age.

The quote, "Tradition is last night's bad performance," rings truer and truer. I have therefore decided that I will interpret, reinterpret, and even try to "recreate the Bible," so to speak. I will present the views of any period of history as a musician in our time, with an instrument built centuries ago but equipped for our time. I did feel like an idiot when performing the Bach *Suites* in halls of 4,000 seats or more, though the satisfaction came when my highest aspiration of creating *silences* succeeded.

And so the dominating factors became the search for simplicity, purity, balance, contrasts, positive and negative sounds, and the tension-release function. I refrained from theatrical displays and self-flagellation, though I did learn the skills of commedia del arte while in the Metropolitan Opera Orchestra. I even taught those skills so as to use them when the mechanics to produce high level of music failed.

I resolved that instead of authenticity, authority is supreme, authority that comes from intuition, endless experimentation and conviction. The intuition is tempered by learning as much as possible about the composer's total output, not just the music at hand. I adhere to the school that considers music as a language, not so much as French, German, Russian, etc., but as Bach's, Beethoven's, Mozart's, Tchaikovsky's, etc., language and discover with delight when someone uses a colleague's language, though from a different country or even a different time.

Obviously I am travelling through territories of aesthetics and philosophy, but just as an individual performer who gets leery when masterly performances or Masterworks are exposed to an autopsy instead of just lauded or panned. I am one who gets leery when performers use poetry to describe their intentions instead of creating poetry through music.

And just to clear the air about my personal feelings when listening to so-called authentic performances, some I like, some I don't. My dislike is due to basics. Either go *whole hog* with authentic instruments, pitch and surroundings, or don't pretend. Don't explain intonation, just play in tune. Don't explain ugly sounds. Just avoid them. And, above all, be honest, and judge with your trained ears and heart, not with your conditioned brain. The possibility of agreement on these subjects is about as likely as agreement between Arabs and Jews, or even worse, in the Knesset. That is why forty-eight years ago when I first recorded the Bach *Suites*, I remembered that my same performance was branded too fast, too slow, too cold, too over sentimental, etc. So I was fastidious with intonation, rhythms, contrasts, and I was disciplined in the use of rubatos and vibratos. For decades I was considered the model. Now, with reconstructed Bach with the Swingle Singers, *Cello Suites* are played on guitar (not just the lute suite), horn, tuba, trombone, trumpet, viola, bass, bassoon, even on the claw-hammer banjo, and, of course, the multimedia presentations. The search is still on. It will go on, and I am rejoicing that my beloved instrument, the cello, is getting more and more attention. Hooray for authenticity or the lack of it. And now I will try to present you with Bach's music as I behold it in my eyes and ears today. (And with this Starker performed a Bach *Suite*.)

Starker's Instruments

As a twelve-year-old, Starker played a Piatellini cello, a fine old Italian instrument loaned to him by a wealthy family in Budapest by the name of Toszeghi. As a youth he frequently played chamber music with Mrs. Toszeghi. For several years he taught her son, Anthony. At that time Anthony's primary studies were in medicine. He was not a great music talent, and his parents did not feel that he was deserving of such a fine, old Italian cello. So they loaned the cello to Starker. He played it for about ten years until 1946 when he was in Vienna. At the time the cello was not sounding right. Starker did not know about adjusting the sound post, so he returned the cello, shipping it back to Budapest.

With about $80 worth of flour, sugar, and fat smuggled from his parents in Budapest, Starker bought his first cello, an instrument made by Martin Stoss, a Viennese maker. It was with this instrument that he recorded the Kodály *Solo Sonata*, opus 8 in Paris for which he received the Grand Prix du Disque. With this cello he performed with the Dallas Symphony.

While he was in New York in 1949 playing with the Metropolitan Opera Orchestra, George Lang introduced Starker to his violin teacher from Juilliard, Madame Fornaroff. When Starker played for her, she insisted that he needed a better cello. At the time he was playing the Stoss cello. Madame Fornaroff took Starker to the instrument dealer, Emil Hermann, and said, "This young man should have a really fine cello." At the time Hermann and Wurlitzer were the two most famous violin experts in this country. First of all Hermann gave Starker an Andreas Guarnerius cello, but then he changed his mind saying, "That cello is not right for you." Hermann then gave him the Lord Aylesford Stradivari cello.

Hermann told Starker that Piatigorsky bought the cello with the understanding that within one year he could return it if he did not feel comfortable with it, and he did. Even though Piatigorsky was well over six feet tall, the cello was too big for him. But this cello had an incredible sound. Hermann asked Sacconi to push up the bridge so that the string length would be normal. Starker took the cello home but with the understanding that if there should be a customer for it, he would return it to Hermann and then pick out another. When that happened, Starker took home the Gorbuth Strad, another time an Andreas Guarnerius cello made in Cremona in 1707. Later he gave his Joseph Schuster cello plus some money in trade for the Guarnerius cello. He kept the Guarnerius in Europe for his European tours.

Ironically, when Starker met Piatigorsky in Paris in 1948, Piatigorsky was playing the Lord Aylesford Stradivari. At that time Starker tried out the cello.

In 1958 Starker was living in Bloomington using the Lord Aylesford Strad, when Hermann sold the cello to a millionaire in New Jersey for basically a tax scheme. This man was the founder of the first mutual fund company. He paid the same fee to Hermann for the cello that Piatigorsky had paid for it, $40,000, and then "gave it back." By that time the cello, for insurance purposes, was worth $35,000 more than he paid. By donating it to Ivan Galamian's String Society, a nonprofit corporation, he was able to deduct from his taxes the real value of the instrument. In reality he paid $40,000 for the cello and deducted $75,000 from his taxes. They had an agreement that Starker would continue to use it. If at a later date Starker wanted to buy the cello, the parties involved agreed that he could do so for about $25,000. Through all of this, the cello never left Starker's hands. At the time Starker had just begun his job with Indiana University and was just getting started with his international career. Because he and Eva were going through a divorce, he did not have any money with which to buy the cello himself.

Galamian agreed to be the "clearing house for this manipulation" because he was promised an annual sum of $5,000 from the investor in New Jersey. This money was used for scholarships for his summer music camp. Also he knew that eventually he would get $25,000 from Starker when he was in a better position to buy the cello. In 1965 the man from New Jersey was ill and forgot to send the $5,000. Shortly after, he died. The Galamian String Society sent Starker a letter telling him that they decided to sell the cello and he had the first call for it. It was a good time for Starker since his career was going well, and he thought he would buy it. They notified him, however, that the selling price was $75,000, not $25,000. As a result there was a big hassle with Starker, Hermann and Galamian, who was haggling like a market clerk, pushing up the price. The three of them eventually agreed that Starker could pay $37,500 for the instrument, half of the fictional value, to be paid off in five years.

When Starker returned home, he received a letter from the board of the Galamian String Society. Actually, it was from Galamian's lawyer, stating that the selling price was $40,000 with five percent interest on the remaining balance. Starker was so mad and disgusted that he gave back the cello. That day he saw an ad for a Matteo Gofriller cello, made in Venice in 1705. The price was $17,500. He immediately bought it from William Moennig in Philadelphia. That was 1965. The cello had been owned for forty years by Ivor James. James was a professor at the Royal College of Music and member of the London String Quartet. Later when Starker was in London, he went to Hill, an instrument dealer in London. Hill said to him, "Three years ago, in 1962, we had three Gofriller cellos in the shop selling for four thousand pounds, and no one wanted to buy them. Now everyone wants them."

STARKER AND PIATIGORSKY

A few years later when Starker was in Bern, Switzerland, he saw the Lord Aylesford Strad at Werro's Violin Shop. Werro thought that no one wanted to play it because it was so big, so he cut down the top half of the instrument to make it smaller. He left the bottom of the instrument alone because of its incredibly beautiful bass sound. Then it was a misshapen instrument. After this transformation, the instrument was "troubled," in Starker's opinion. Eventually someone in Switzerland bought it.

One time when Piatigorsky was in Chicago, he and Starker played duets together, Piatigorsky with his Batta Strad and Starker playing the Lord Aylesford Strad. Starker played the Lord Aylesford Strad from 1950-1965 and made 95% of his recordings during this time with it. He also used the Rothschild Strad and the Gorbuth Strad for recordings. With the Gorbuth Strad he recorded the original Brahms *Sonata in E Minor* and *Sonata in F Major* in 1951. With his Guarnerius, he recorded the Beethoven *Sonatas.*

Of the Lord Aylesford Strad, Starker says, "Stradivari instruments have a sound of their own to which the player must adjust. I consider Gofriller to be more like a Guarneri del Gesu violin which allows the player to produce his or her own sound."

In about 1975, Starker saw again the Piatellini cello that he had played as a boy. A student came from Switzerland to Indiana University to study with Starker. He sat down for a lesson holding the Piatellini. How ironic, the cello should visit him in Bloomington! The family in Budapest who had loaned Starker the cello when he was a boy sold it so that their grandson could buy a viola. This grandson was also at Indiana University but studying viola with Primrose. The boy's father was then a highly respected doctor in England. As a young man and a pre-med student, he had taken cello lessons from Starker who was then somewhat younger than he. What a small world!

Before Starker bought the Gofriller, he had a copy of the Lord Aylesford Strad made for himself. It was made by Eugene Knapik in Chicago. Later he sold it to a student who lives in South Carolina. This cello appeared in his studio again when a student came for a lesson! He had contemporary copies of both the Gofriller and the Guarnerius cellos made in order to have exact-size instruments to use in his teaching studio. The Gofriller copy was made in 1976 by Capella, a maker in Porto, Portugal. Garavaglia, a very gifted maker who works for Kenneth Warren in Chicago made the Guarnerius copy for Starker in 1984.

Repair work at Indiana University was done by Ole Dahl, an employee in Kenneth Warren's shop in Chicago. Once each month he came to Bloomington to do repairs. Eventually he started the instrument-making school at the university. After Knapik died, his widow gave his wood-working tools and various pieces of wood to the instrument making school at Indiana University.

Starker sold the Stoss cello during the time when he was playing the Lord Aylesford Strad. The sizes of the two instruments were too different. Starker gave it to Kenneth Warren in Chicago to sell. Seven years later when Starker was performing in Columbus, Ohio, he was invited to a dinner party. The host brought one of his students to play for Starker. He was playing the Stoss cello!

Starker owns a smaller sized French cello made by Pierray in 1709. Starker also owns a nineteenth century French instrument which looks like a Strad and a five-stringed cello of probably German origin. He says there is only one instrument in the world which he covets, the

Batta Stradivarius which belongs to the widow of Gregor Piatigorsky. It is the only cello he considers better than his own.

Starker owns around twenty bows. He says, "One continually searches for the ideal bow. I have tried all of my life not to make myself dependent on the uniqueness of a bow. Bows change as the years go by, losing elasticity due to wear and weather conditions. Furthermore, the player's hands are also changing. There are times when one prefers a light bow, other times a heavier one. My experience has been that the size and weight of the frog affects my response to and appreciation of the bow. I have several German bows, eight or nine French bows and several modern bows. These days I tend to favor using modern bows."

He frequently travels with his cello. Says writer Jane Dunlap Norris, "If you think it's tough being a world-renowned cellist who travels the globe, imagine what it's like being his cello! Get an airline ticket for the passenger cabin, and you'll learn that the skies are not always so friendly. There's no telling what name your ticket is under, anything from Mr. Cello to Cabin Baggage. But it's probably not the same name as the one on your boarding pass. No in-flight meal, the headphones are too small, and they won't let you out of your case for a second! To top it off, it doesn't matter if you're almost three hundred years old and can prove it, they still won't give you a senior citizen's discount!"

Luckily, over the years, catching planes with his cello has grown easier. He can enjoy the discount that his cello can't, and buying a seat for a musical instrument isn't considered the oddity it used to be. "Sometimes I'll put my hat on the cello, and it will look like a person asleep," he says, "People find that amusing."

"But if you're Janos Starker's cello, the rewards outweigh the travel tribulations. Your owner is regarded as one of the greatest virtuoso cellists of all time, praised by musicians and critics for his technical mastery and expressive style of playing. People may think you're difficult to move around, but in Janos Starker's hands you can move *them*, even to tears." [49]

The Merry-Go-Round

a story by Janos Starker

The plane banked. Below were the Ionian Sea and the Greek islands, aglow in the last rays of a retreating sun. The seat-belt sign flashed on, which somehow triggered a second reaction, both unrelated and unsettling.

How, I thought, did I get here?

Many colleagues, I'm sure, who travel the international concert circuit have puzzled similarly. While the plane was making its landing at Athens airport, I remembered an anecdote told to me recently by a fellow musician.

"Do you know the shortest history of an artist?" he asked.

"No, but go on...."

"Let's say that Mr. Smith is a violinist of terrific talent, O.K.? And Mr. Blunt is a very powerful concert Manager. Blunt speaks."

Act I. Who? Smith?

Act II. Ah, Smith. Well, yes; but you know how difficult it is.

Act III. I must have Smith! I don't care how, but I must have him.

Act IV. I must have someone like Smith, you know.

Act V. I must have someone like Smith, when he was young.

Act VI. Who? Smith?

I repeated this story to an artist friend—he just happened to be in the middle of Act III, in demand everywhere—and his manager. "Act VI" was followed by a short silence, then forced laughter. Perhaps at that moment all three of us thought of past experiences, and looked hesitantly in the direction of the future.

After a short stop in Athens to refuel, our flight continued. Aloft again, I wondered how to tell uninitiated persons what lies hidden behind the facade of glamour—the real truth about the six acts of an artist's life. The whole truth might possibly spare those "on the way up" disappointments and frustrations, although some may question the need of any exposé. After all, to reach the heights one must experience firsthand the fears and insecurities, the fighting and winning and losing. Otherwise the final reward will lack the satisfactions of achievement.

What follows is not, therefore, to those who will eventually live out all six acts, but rather to those who watch and wonder. And also to those who stop, who never venture beyond Act I or Act II. Know, however, that to reach even Act I is a long and arduous undertaking; once there, Smith (by whatever name) should feel immense gratification. Whoever approaches Mr. Blunt on behalf of Smith must have reasons to believe that his client, his discovery, his protegé—whatever—is a potential concert artist. Smith must have put in years of hard work, have received pedagogic certification, possess an excellent talent, and have made occasional concert appearances. Interest in any budding artist is whetted by adulatory adjectives printed about his performances, plus a medal or two won in competitions. Maybe Smith logged time as a member of an ensemble, and heard the question repeated by colleagues, "Why don't you play solos more often?" Most important, however, is Smith's own determination to succeed.

He is truly gifted and has studied the violin from age six (his father loved the fiddle and wanted his son to be a great concert artist). As a boy, Smith worked and even played in public, all the while cursing his fate when he saw other boys at their games, and was taunted or teased about being a sissy. But when the applause swelled, he felt happy and proud; his tormenters suddenly looked at him with envy, and with a peculiar kind of awe. Girls? They occasionally found him to be the most interesting boy in their peer group. So he worked on and on, until his discovery that music and the violin were inseparably a part of him, not merely the fantasy of his father.

He wanted to play better, then best—as none before had ever played. It seemed to him that the artists he admired early on began more and more to play worse and worse. At this stage, he was almost ready to compete with anyone, ready to conquer the world. But how? By this time, Smith was a serious student, perhaps even an orchestra member. His recognition increased and the competition dwindled away. Yet the world, monstrously large, didn't seem to notice (much less care) what Smith was doing. The world already had its group of familiar idols to worship.

Finally Smith was mentioned to a manager, and introduced. Here Act I begins. If this manager respects what he meets and hears, he will suggest the next procedural step—the début recital, probably in New York. The obstacles in that path are money and principles. Everyone knows that famous artists get impressive fees; ought it not to follow that less famous artists get less impressive fees—but fees in any case—regardless of talent level. This sounds logical, but in most cases doesn't wash. Smith therefore must, in addition to whatever other problems, obtain financial assistance from somewhere. All manner of sources are tapped for a loan, parents, relatives, friends, organizations—with an automatic assurance that any such loan is as secure an investment as a blue-chip stock. All that Smith needs is to be heard, whereupon the world of music, critics, record-company representatives and managers will flock to his room after the concert. Smith will be required only to choose from a plurality of contracts, and bless the best one with his signature.

The début is arranged. Costs have been estimated, funds pledged, and a program not only carefully chosen but exhaustively prepared. Finally, Smith goes on stage. The audience is primarily comprised of his relatives, friends and a few outsiders who cadged free passes (all hail to those who dare to break with this last custom and buy seats!). If the Philharmonic and the opera and other stellar attractions aren't scheduled that evening, even a few critics may wander in. What can follow is rich in variety.

Smith may be applauded and feted by his family, friends and well-wishers. But if his performance shouldn't measure up to the expected or acceptable standards, then a few lines may appear in the newspapers but the whole affair will be forgotten in a day or two. The blue chips will fade, with Smith left to wonder what next and how to pay back the loan.

He can find employment, hoping to try again in a few years. Some of the Smiths conclude that they have tried, failed and should seek a new kind of endeavor—other, that is, than concertizing. In most cases, however, Smith will believe that the public and critics alike are idiots who lace sensitive ears and the perception to recognize greatness. He imagines a legion of magnificent recreative artists dying unappreciated and so manages to soothe his frustrations.

He may cut a few lines from the reviews and construct the following kind of interest-provoking but misleading excerpt:

"His playing is excellent, a marvelous Brahms *Sonata*. His phrasing and tone, of the highest order."

Smith might print a lovely brochure, including a dramatic photo of himself, and keep trying through the years, playing here and there, until the hard reality of earning a living ultimately consumes all of his energy.

What happens, however, if our Smith plays magnificently? He is now ready to start the second act of the scenario. Reviews are excellent, if less than adjectivally unbuttoned. That is understandable; he is new, and so often young flickering stars fall suddenly behind the horizon. How many reviewers want to stick their necks out? There will be plenty of time to unleash exuberance.

The music world takes note of him. "O yes, Smith. Quite good, I hear, but young isn't he?" After his début concert, Smith may even receive offers: Perhaps a few concerts, even perhaps a contract from a manager. A contract—the fulfillment of dreams! "We will do our best," the manager assures him. "After all, you play the concerts but we get a percentage of your fees." From this moment forward, the Blunts take over—persons who sponsor and sell artists in every city of every country on the globe. Mind you, the Blunts of the music world (or the Mrs. Blunts, as the case may be. It's amazing the number of women in this field) have an uncommonly difficult job. Sometimes they like music, sometimes not. Now and again they also know music, but that's not essential. Many salesmen don't know the intricacies or minutiae of the product they are selling, but they must know buyers and *their* needs, and how to fill an order. A Virginia cigarette salesman may not smoke and still be successful. So Blunt may be a jazz expert, or an ardent wrestling fan, whatever else, but still can be a fine manager of musicians.

Before pressing on, however, some clarification of the Blunts may be helpful, since the role of managers is many-faceted. Each has a list of artists he sells to societies and orchestras, plus a list of artists under exclusive contract whom he "jobs out" to other, local-area Blunts. The latter buy for societies and orchestras, but also present artists, touring orchestras, ballets and spectacles under their own aegis, for profit. Frequently these presentations incur financial losses, but the Blunts average-out a series of fixed fee attractions; their overall profit margin absorbs losses. What the Blunts are is an apparently contradictory, surely confusing composite of manager, agent, representative and impresario. Certain powerful concert managements employ a lot of Blunts under a single corporate roof.

So our Smith has his own Blunt working for him, and vice versa. Every Blunt in the world has to satisfy the musical wishes of his territory. Although the masses manage, untroubled, to survive without classical music, every community has a group (proportionately small, sad to say) that loves "good music." These groups want concerts by orchestras, chamber ensembles, solo artists. Each listener within the group may differ in tastes and whims but as a congregation they can, together, persuade a larger segment to believe that music is a necessary part of their civic culture. Even disinterested persons will attend concerts, and may even come in time to like classical music, thereby enlarging the nucleus of art's true devotees.

If Blunt himself loves music, and has in the bargain a solid background coupled with high principles, he will make the effort not only to sell but to raise standards. He will cater to prevailing wishes but subtly shape an expansion and refinement of these in the future. In any case Blunt offers Smith to the world. Where upon Act II may be performed over and over. "O, yes, I hear he is good, but there are so many. Another time." Blunt has quite a job selling Smith's qualities to clients who don't even know the name, by which I mean the ladies on local committees, board of directors or orchestras, conductors and managers of these organizations—the people ultimately responsible for Smiths actually performing in their jealously guarded sanctuaries.

This may sound desolating, and even imply a virtual impossibility of finding engagements by thousands of artists around the world, unless their names are Heifetz or Rubinstein. Nonetheless, new contracts *are* written, and someone is always on stage. Conductors, managers, board members and critics all listen to auditions, read the newspapers, hear the latest recordings, discuss current music with friends, shop for artists and prepare the future seasons. Furthermore, fellow artists constantly plug their comrades. This professional promotion is arguably the strongest single force in Smith's graduation from Act II to Act III. Praise from a colleague is not tainted by considerations of personal gain, and thus is both prized and widely respected.

A hundred times a thousand details go into the planning of a season. Stars above all are required, expensive though they may be. Proportionately, the amount of money spent for such stellars may seem unbalanced, but without famous names, neither persons nor organizations can build subscription audiences, which are the backbone of a sound budget. But who are the stars? Members of the cast of Act III. They are the envied ones—artists whom everyone wants to see and hear. Stars are so sought after that they cannot begin to fulfill demand, and so are able to dictate conditions—which concerts they'll play, and which not. Programs are built around them while the rest are fill-ins from the ranks of aspirers.

How does our Smith become a star? We must backtrack to Act II. We have a Blunt. We have shoppers. Smith is heard by a conductor. He is also heard by Mrs. Pshaw. Mr. Jones reads the *New York Times* or the *Cleveland Plain Dealer*. As a new season is being blocked out, the usual budget is set apart for the usual number of concerts. The stars, first; perhaps two can be had, but a third one hoped for is unavailable. Cautiously, someone suggests, "You know that fellow Smith? I heard him the other week and he sounds like _____ years ago." The revered name is whispered to avoid insulting the icon. Other persons offer other names. It happens, however, that Blunt has mentioned some difficulties in regard to Star Number One, and then goes on to speak of Smith, of how highly he regards him. It can prove useful to buyers in the future to gain Blunt's good will; by taking Smith now, they will be owed a favor next year. The fact that an Act II artist receives a lower fee comes as a relief; budgets are always tight.

Finally, then, our Smith is chosen and now has a concert date. The same scene is duplicated elsewhere until Smith finds himself with twenty or thirty concerts in a single season. He is successful! Or is he? In one city, the cheers are loud but the reviews bad. In another, the reviews are excellent but the audience merely polite. Smith is certain that all his performances are basically of a quality, on every level, and that his artistic beliefs are consistent with his experience of the moment, subject always to change as he progresses. Wherever he goes, although colleagues may argue about him, may criticize this detail or that, they all fortunately agree that Smith is on his way up. Fees, though, are still low. And he must engage an accompanist, pay for management, publicity, brochures and cross-country travel.

In some cities, he is almost a star, and reengaged, feted, wooed. In others, his appearances are perpetual débuts with all the elements of hard sell, rebuffs and whisperings. Time passes. But the whispers begin to increase in volume until one day Mrs. Pshaw says, "That Smith! I tell you he is just as good as _____!" In her city, Smith is promoted to stardom. Elsewhere, though, in other cities of other countries on other continents, Smith remains an unknown, an Act II *persona*, or a comer. But he *is* good, and getting better—one of the anointed few.

What does he possess that marks him for success while many more will play forever in Act II? You often hear a wonderful artist, a fantastic instrumentalist who plays faultlessly. You admire this artist, yet others do not. Or you hear an artist, enjoy the performance, but still feel some quality to be lacking. You have little desire to hear him again and don't secure tickets when he happens to return. The explanation? Nature distributes talents. In Smith we find all the musical attributes: an exceptional ear, excellent fingers, perfect coordination physically and mentally, a first-rate memory, a mind both curious and studious, diligence and the will power to concentrate on work. He has spent years practicing, studying everything of musical importance—other instruments, composition, the history of music. He has played chamber music and in orchestras. But others, too, have done all this and possess in addition the natural talent.

Smith, however, has imagination and a sense of color. He strives for construction and balance in a work of music. His tone has warmth and beauty. He is ready. He has high standards, and often plays above them but never below. Yet others, many others, have these attributes. They themselves *and* the world at large should realize that they're artists of the first magnitude, even without star billing. Without them, the world of music would be a vacuum. They carry on traditions. They create and maintain standards in their various communities. They supply the true climate in which a handful of immortals can thrive.

Smith himself may be nervous before concerts, but once on stage in front of an audience, he feels completely at ease. No one is aware of his fears or worries. The audience watches and believes him, noting idiosyncrasies, however small or large. People talk about his features, manner, gestures and every movement. Smith has Personality, good or bad, as the case may be, but pervasively convincing; not perhaps for everyone, but certainly for the majority. He is determined and unflinching. Whether he is passive or aggressive in his approach is immaterial since, on occasions, one can find more aggressiveness in passivity than in straight forward pushing. If he suffers a setback he shakes it off. He doesn't cry about bad luck but works all the harder, plans better and so gradually moves up. This quality of determination invests him with an air of authority. Now a second Smith may reach Act II although missing, perhaps, in a few of the prerequisites—technical, musical and mental. A third Smith lacking many of the prerequisites could still reach Act III because of personality, politics, press agency, professional connections, social power or a striking appearance. But the third Smith's glory is likely to be temporary, and his arrival at Act VI abrupt, premature and without transition.

Our focal Smith has all of the desirable assets in happy balance. As time passes he finds himself flying all over the world to play, with more offers of engagements than he can possibly fill. His peregrinations become planned years in advance, and managerial letters change in style. Now they inquire about his needs and requirements, while he in turn exercises the prerogative of changing, cancelling choosing at will. Smith's promise of a future appearance provokes anticipatory sighs.

In time, however, Smith begins to tire. Taxes become so high that he decides to play fewer performances for increasingly steeper fees. Fewer and ever fewer budgets can afford him. He makes recordings and collects royalties, his name a legend. When his fiddle is sounded, listeners know immediately that they are hearing Smith. He has become recognizable, and his playing is consecrated as a school. It is "the Smith sound" or "the Smith approach." Everyone else is compared to him. He may be criticized, and must be; no single person can possibly appeal to all tastes. But criticism is no longer detrimental to Smith. As the *ne plus ultra* he instinctively discredits whoever may dare to speak or write objections to his style. It is now almost that Smith alone is qualified to judge Smith. To most, his evolved artistic goals and ideals may be incomprehensible. Overwhelming adulation may indeed derive from factors other than Smith himself would choose to be known for. Yet such dichotomy matters little. Everywhere people plead to hear him.

And so Smith, and a handful of his acknowledged peers in the entire world, advance themselves to Act IV, while the Blunts look for substitutes. Not only can Smith *not* be everywhere, he does not want to be. A new generation of potential Smiths rears its head, and new Blunts take charge of them. Smith's own authority is unchallenged, but the years have taken a toll on his physical resilience and musical discipline. For a while longer he is forgiven everything since the magnificence of his artistic concepts remains visible as well as audible. Each new generation discovers, however, new insights, values and standards...and their own Smiths. The counterpart of his own youth arrives on the scene, and Smith is moved on to Act V.

The class is silent. Professor Brown discourses on all the different tempi he's heard in the finale of the *Kreutzer* Sonata. His face is illuminated, he sighs deeply, and excitement appears to take hold of his body as he recalls a concert from the far past.

"Smith!," he says slowly, reverently. "No one ever played that movement as he did!"

Johnny Prep whispers to the girl next to him, "Who? Smith?"

J.S., 1962

42. Roos, James, "Cellist Starker Revives, Masters Difficult Scores," *Miami Herald*, April 1, 1992

43. newspaper quotes taken from: Jacobi, Peter, *The Starker Story, A Life in America Since 1948*

44. Jacobi, Peter, *The Starker Story, A Life in America Since 1948,* p. 30

45. Mullins, Shirley Stroh, "The Intriguing World of Janos Starker," *The Instrumentalist*, November 1986, Volume 41, Number 4, pp. 16-17

46. Jacobi, Peter, *The Starker Story, Life in America Since 1948,* p. 31

47. Mullins, Shirley Stroh, "The Intriguing World of Janos Starker," *The Instrumentalist*, November 1986, number 4, pp. 16-17

48. ibid

49. Norris, Jane Dunlap, "Starker bridges composers voices, audiences," *Daily Progress*, p. 3, Charlottesville, Virginia, March 28, 1997

Part V

**Starker's Humorous Cartoons, His Parents,
Tales about the Master by Former Students**

The Roll Call of the Blessed Ones

by Janos Starker and Jorge Sicre

In 1985 Starker published his cartoon book, *The Roll Call of the Blessed Ones* (text by Starker, drawings by Jorge Sicre, cellist in the Cleveland Orchestra). It presents a satirical look at many of the world's great conductors and virtuosos. In this section you have a sampling of Starker and Sicre's cartoons. If they whet your curiosity, buy the book.[50] Starker quotes George Steinberg when he says, "Parody is not an attack; you cannot parody anything that you cannot love. This book is dedicated to those included and omitted, whose lives are spent in the single-minded pursuit of music, maybe the highest of all human endeavors; a pursuit that enriches the lives of millions as a by-product." He goes on, "This book has been ten years in the making. Many of the blessed ones have since joined the heavenly philharmonic, international pantheons, or just social security systems. We salute them with love, admiration, and eternal gratitude."

The book is, according to William Safire, "A hilariously penetrating look into the world of musicians by a couple of the inside greats. Put this book between your knees, start sawing away, and you'll discover that these two cellists are not just fiddling around."

Starker's intent was to poke fun at individuals, whose superb output presupposes self-security and a sense of humor. Well, poke fun he did with his cartoons of these major musical figures. And up to this day there are people who are hurt either because they are included in the book or because they are omitted. Unfortunately, this little cartoon book created enemies all over the music world. He expected that people have a sense of humor. He wrote only about admirable,

JANOS STARKER

ONE WHOSE INNER HEAT
FREEZES THE AIR
AROUND HIM
(AVAILABILITY LIMITED)

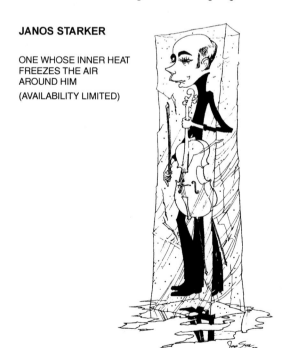

SIR GEORG SOLTI
THE ANSWER TO THE UNIVERSAL ENERGY SHORTAGE

MSTISLAV ROSTROPOVICH

THE BERNSTEIN OF THE CELLO:
A ONE-MAN EAST-WEST SUMMIT

great artists. Making fun of them was something else. He made fun of himself as well. Some do not have the good humor to see that Starker included only people who are dominant in the musical world, those who have done fantastic things and those who have some kind of special characteristic about which one can laugh. Fritz Reiner was one who could laugh wholeheartedly about a joke on someone else, but if it was something involving him, then he had no sense of humor. A person has a good sense of humor if one can laugh at himself. "One frequent quote about me is that I am deadly serious about what I am doing," says Starker, referring to his performances and his teaching. "But I never got deadly serious about myself in the whole process. I assumed that those people who get up in front of an audience and become the idols of the stage, celebrated and honored for their performances, that they kept a sense of humor."

At the end of the booklet he said, "There are thousands who are doing the job for the benefit of humankind. We can only admire them." But he antagonized some by using the words, "the world's greatest artists," describing those included in the book. "I admire so many for what they do. And if they are not the world's greatest but they contribute to the welfare of music and musicians, that is the important thing."

He found far greater human beings who perhaps did not receive great successes or high acclaim. There are some who are not known by the great public at large, friends "who have helped me retain my sanity and my qualified appreciation for the human race. But those who have in their power to do something for the benefit of others but do it invariably for their own glorification, then I am rubbed the wrong way. So when Karajan one time came to rehearsal an hour late and had not learned the score, then I said so in the New York Times." The question was put to him, "What is the worst concert you have ever played in in your entire life?" To this he replied, "That is easy, with Karajan and the Berlin Philharmonic." This did not exactly endear him to the members of the Berlin Philharmonic. He was not interested in making a bigger career for himself through his relationship with conductors or other instrumentalists.

Another time he said, "The New York Philharmonic and the Orchestra de Paris are the worst orchestras in the world because they have the best memberships in them, but they behave like school children." A year later Zubin Mehta made the same statement. Then they realized that Starker had said that, but why? Conductors still tell Starker's closest friends, "Why did Starker publish that cartoon book? The whole world of music is mad at him."

To this he responds, "Whatever I feel is unjust, I speak against it. It is as simple as that. Some of my friends say that I made a pretty damned good career against myself." His outspoken personality coupled with his reclusive nature determined that he did not cultivate relationships with other musicians for the purpose of promoting his career. He chose to live in the rural Midwest rather in the cultural center of the country, New York.

Says Starker, "This human being is cursed with the kind of mind that sees things from seven different ways! But to me the important thing is if I can get up after a concert and feel clean. I don't care if they like it, or if they don't like it. I just do what I believe is right whether it is music or some other kind of expression."

Starker's Parents

Starker eventually brought his parents to the United States. When the war ended they also became Hungarian citizens as did Starker. But then it was a lengthy process to get passports and permission to leave Hungary. The problem was no longer whether or not they were Hungarian but rather that the Communists refused to give out passports. That process took nearly three years. They received their passports the same time as Starker's in-laws. Eva's parents managed to get out of Hungary just before the Hungarian Revolution, but not Starker's parents.

Once they had passports, Starker's parents applied for American visas. But a Hungarian-born American diplomatic servant in the visa division in Budapest, a Communist-hating American, discovered that Starker's father had held membership for one year in the newly powerful Communist Party. When his father learned in 1947 what the Communist Party was doing, he did not renew his membership. But because of this affiliation, his parents were refused American visas.

There was a lull after the Hungarian Revolution before the Russians arrived. During this lull his parents managed to go by train to Prague. With a great deal of money and effort, Starker managed to get them British visas and flew them to England. That was in late 1956. At the same time Starker appealed to his congressman in Chicago on behalf of his parents, convincing him that they were not Communists.

During the four months his parents were living in England, Starker received a call. At the time he was in rehearsal with the Chicago Symphony in Orchestra Hall. He was told that his father was deathly ill, and if he wanted to see his father again he had best take the next plane to London. He put away his cello and with a small bag left for the airport. He had not seen his father since 1947. Starker spent two days with him in the hospital. Fortunately, he recovered and actually lived quite a happy and productive life until 1976.

MARGIT STARKER

A month later Starker was in London for a performance of Dvorák *Concerto* with Solti conducting. The day before his performance, he put his parents on the plane to Chicago. After all they had been through, they were in a poor state of health but glad to be alive. Very soon his apartment in Chicago was home to his parents, his in-laws, Starker and his wife and their daughter, Gabriella. That was a full house! Shortly thereafter he was able to get a small apartment for them. After a while Starker's father wanted to resume his work as a tailor, and his parents both wanted an apartment of their own.

In 1965 Starker's parents celebrated their fiftieth wedding anniversary. For this event Starker rented a ballroom in a Chicago restaurant, inviting all the people they knew from New York and Chicago. It was a surprise party. Starker had told them that he was sorry that he had to be out of town. He would try to get to Chicago on time and would try to make it.

He arranged for some friends to take them to a fine restaurant for dinner. When they arrived

SANDOR STARKER

at the restaurant, they were welcomed not only by Starker and his wife and daughter but also by fifty or sixty dear friends. Among the guests in attendance at their anniversary party was the congressman who arranged for their American visas.

At the dinner there was a throne chair for each of them. At the event Starker asked that they be remarried, saying that he was not born yet when they were married, and he wanted to be certain that he was legitimate. He published a newspaper like the *New York Times* telling what happened on the day they were married, with photos of where they lived in Hungary, containing articles on what it is like to be an artist's mother or artist's mother's husband, what it is like to be their granddaughter. Mr. and Mrs. Starker received letters from the President of the United States as well as the Mayor of Chicago. During dinner a trio played chamber music. Later everyone enjoyed dancing. György Sebök and Starker dressed up in short pants and wigs and played his mother's favorite tunes from thirty years earlier. Starker devised a lottery from which people won many prizes, the best of which was a vacation trip to Florida for Sandor and Margit Starker. It was an unforgettable evening for everyone.

How to be an Artist's Mother

by Janos Starker

A little over five feet, grayish, with a lovely smile crowning a motherly figure, Mrs. Sandor Starker greeted us in her home. First she apologized for the lack of a solid speaking voice (a consequence of a throat operation years earlier), and then she offered us everything under the sun, or rather everything in her refrigerator, bar, and pantry. We settled for tea and then explained the purpose of our visit.

When Mrs. Starker reached the historic point in her marriage, her coming 50th wedding anniversary, we asked if there was any advice she might give to other mothers who raise child prodigies, concert artists, or generally successful children. We also wanted to know how it felt to be the mother of a son who reached the goals the mother hoped for.

Mrs. Starker opened her sparkling eyes wide, puffed excitedly on a cigarette, (third since we entered) and said, "How can you ask such silly questions? There is no difference between a mother who raises musicians, or a mother who raises just...just children."

I couldn't help interrupting. "You say, Just...children, so there must be some difference."

"Musicians are crazy, I mean crazy in a nice sort of way, but I wouldn't love my son less if he would be a plumber or something. Well...?" Mrs. Starker had a twinkle in her eyes. "I might be a little less proud, you know!" and then suddenly her whispering voice, which by the way, was more powerful and penetrating than some of the stage roars I have heard, became clipped, "Would he be a plumber I would see him more often. I could kill him sometimes when he doesn't call or write for weeks, and I can't sleep at night worrying how he is, where he is, has the plane landed, is he driving 100 miles an hour? Is his stomach all right before concerts, did he play well, is he mad because of some stupid conductor, does he have enough money, or most important, did he practice?"

I asked, "Tell me Mrs. Starker, how did you make your son practice when he was little?"

"Oh, it was easy. I didn't have to force him at all. He could only go to the movies after he practiced three hours, so you see I didn't force him at all." She smiled merrily. "He liked to find excuses to interrupt his practicing, like eating and drinking, so I made little sandwiches and cookies and put them next to the music stand. But that wasn't really forcing him! I did give him a whack here and there, who doesn't? That is the trouble these days. The parents let their children get away with murder. They are much too worried about what the psychiatrist will say.

Psychiatrist, schmichiatrist! Give them a good whack, and later a kiss so they know you love them too."

"And your husband?" we asked.

"My husband? He was busy working, to earn a living so we could eat and dress. How could he have time for the children's education? But why should he have worried about that? I took care of my children, and never minded. When I got mad, I told him that the boys must be his sons, not mine." She laughed. "So what else do you want to know?"

"How did you know that your son really had talent?" I questioned.

She puffed on cigarette number six.... "That's not so simple. You see, every mother thinks her children are the greatest, and so did I. But all I really wanted was that my children should have a good education, and they shouldn't have to work like their father."

"But, Mrs. Starker, we hear that your son works a great deal?"

"Ya, but that is different. He is making music, and music is the most beautiful thing in the world. How some people can live without music I'll never understand? All my children played music, and all children should play. Not everybody will make a great career, but if you don't try how are you going to find out? You got to have a chance. My older grandchild plays the piano and sings a little and the younger grandchild plays the violin a little. Are they going to be good musicians? I don't know. But when I hear them I tell myself if I had them in my hands I could make artists out of them!"

"You mean to say, Mrs. Starker, that you would be willing to do the same thing all over again?"

She looked far, far away, waited a little while and then slowly said, "You know, if it wouldn't be for my two boys those animals took away from me, I wouldn't change my life, whatever happened in it, for no money in the world."

J.S., October, 1965

✦✦✦

How to be an Artist's Mother's Husband

by Janos Starker

He looked up from behind his glasses though his right hand continued the motion automatically, the motion of sewing buttons on a piece of garment. "Can I help you?" he asked in a deliberate and slow manner. He was a fragile looking man, dressed in shirt sleeves and a Scottish vest. He had the vestiges of white hair brushed across his bald pate. In the back of his head the brush wasn't too successful and a few long, lonely hairs were flinging around in the slight breeze of a fan.

"We would like to talk to you, Mr. Starker, about the momentous occasion of your 75th birthday, and your golden wedding anniversary," I said.

He had a quizzical look of a man who had all the surprises a human being can have in a lifetime.

"You want to talk to me? That's something new," he said. "People usually interview my son. He is the celebrity. If they come to talk to us, the parents, my wife speaks. Bless her soul, she sure can talk. Me, I listen mostly."

"Mr. Starker, how come you are still working? Wouldn't you rather retire and enjoy yourself?"

"Enjoy myself, I am enjoying myself. Sure, my son tells me, 'Father, you don't have to work. Stay home.' But it isn't so simple. I have been working more than 60 years and took care of myself and my family. You don't think I would change now? I must earn my living, and my wife must take care of the family. Now we are just the two of us to take care of. As long as I can move my hands I don't want to feel that I am useless. Besides, you just try to spend a few hours with my wife and you will understand that it is better to work than stay home."

"Mr. Starker, you sound strange for a man who has lived 50 years with the same woman."

"Why should I sound strange? I love my wife today as I did 50 years ago. She is quite a woman, but she can talk, oh my, can she talk!! You can't argue with a woman like that. No logic helps. She makes up her mind, and nothing can change it. Like with the children. We had three sons. She wanted them all to be musicians. So she got teachers and instruments—everything. She kept after them so they would practice. When the first two didn't do too well, she started on the third."

"What happened to the other two boys?"

"Well, they were talented in many other ways, but the war took them away from us." His eyes started to turn red, and he quickly said, "Let's not talk about that."

"You said something about the third boy, Mr. Starker?"

"Ya, him. She was successful with him. But I tell you he could have been a great tailor too. When I still had my business I thought he would help me one day and take over my work. You know how every father dreams about his son being one day at his side, and building his plans further."

"But, Mr. Starker, you are certainly not sorry that your son is not a tailor?"

"Not a tailor? what's wrong with being a tailor? It is an honest profession, and it can also be an art. Of course, I'm not sorry. He is famous, and sometimes even we the parents get a little of the glory he receives. But he has a hard life. He works, travels, and runs and runs. If he sits still the trouble is not enough concerts. If he has enough concerts he is never home and has no peace. So he is famous. You see what I mean? I am proud to be at his concerts and to listen to his records, but if he would be a great tailor, I could see him more often and he wouldn't have so much trouble. And don't forget, I wouldn't have to listen to his mother's complaints—why he isn't here, and why he doesn't write or call."

"Mr. Starker, what do you say is the difference between being married to an artist's mother and just a mother?"

"Listen," he said. "There is an old proverb that says that one sleeps the way one makes one's bed. I married an ambitious woman. She wanted our sons to make great careers. But don't forget, she never neglected me. Sure, sometimes it feels like I married an institution, with all those people in the house, but most of them are nice people. A little nuts, but nice. And I must say I'm glad that at least it is music my wife got me involved with. I like music. Imagine if my son would have been a modern painter and I would have to know about those scratchings people admire these days. My dear boy, you marry a woman for better or worse. I did. We had it all. God keep her, and God give me the strength to live with her, and provide for her." He took the scissors and cut the thread.

As we quietly left, we couldn't help thinking that wisdom and human greatness are not reserved in the much publicized African jungle: it is all there in the little tailor of Clark Street.

J.S., October 1965

Tales about the Master Told by Students

Starker is intensely loyal, devoted to family, friends and former students. It is not unusual for certain students to enter that special sphere in his life reserved for his kin and lifelong friends from his Hungarian childhood.

Starker has felt that the kind of master classes that most people are doing, "the sprinkling of holy water," for him is not teaching. "These are only for the highly prepared, gifted students. After they perform, the artist teacher says essentially, I like it better my way, play it a little faster, more expression here, more vibrato there. Then comes the poetry like imagining the sun is shining, or that you want to die, be sad and such." Starker's approach in master classes is rather one of teaching concepts which students can take with them and apply for a lifetime.

All of his students will attest to Starker's mastery of the instrument, the greatest that anyone has achieved so far in history. To maintain that level of playing takes much dedication. That is one reason why he did not have time for many things. He was very dedicated to his career and maintaining a very high performance level while at the same time promoting the same performance level in his students.

After the war, Starker, realizing that he was one who survived out of the many who did not, felt it was his duty to pass on what he learned from some of the greats in music history. Since then he has impacted thousands of young cellists. His students now fill positions in orchestras and universities and conservatories in cities all over the world. He was not content to hold a full time teaching position at one university. He taught simultaneously in the United States and in Europe while at the same time performing hundreds of concerts each year throughout the world.

Starker has former students in prominent positions in cities all over the United States. For example, in five prominent Ohio universities the faculty cellists are all former Starker students. The principal cellist in the Metropolitan Opera Orchestra, Rafael Figueroa, winner of the Piatigorsky Competition, is a former Starker student, also Gary Hoffmann, winner of the Rostropovich Competition, Alan Harris at the Cleveland Institute of Music, Helga Winold, Indiana University faculty member, and Tsuyoshi Tsutsumi, winner of the Rostropovich Competition who also teaches at Indiana University. In the most prestigious music schools in Germany, including the Musik Hochschule in Freiburg, Germany, Starker's former students are now holding leading cello positions. They include Diana Contino, Margaret Bergen, and Kristoph Henkel, also Maria Kliegel at the Musik Hochschule in Köln. She was the first-prize winner of the Rostropovich Competition. Cellists all over Japan and South America, many in Europe including France, Spain, Germany, Hungary, England, Norway and Finland are former Starker students. His former students number in the thousands. Like the ever widening wake behind a boat, his effect continues to spread in ever greater reaches.

Conversations with Maria Kliegel

Maria Kliegel, professor of Music at the Hochschule in Köln, Germany, is a former student of Janos Starker. She was in the second semester in the Musik Hochschule in Frankfurt and found that she was dissatisfied with her studies. Inside she had the feeling that she was just playing and with no idea about how she was doing things. Her teacher could not explain how things should be done, and she found that she was not improving. These things disturbed her. She felt that she needed to find another teacher. Many of her young colleagues were saying great things about Andre Navarra. In the summer he was going to hold a master class in Sienna, Italy. That caught Maria's fancy. She pictured herself sitting in the piazza with a glass of red wine, talking with the maestro, and having a good time. She could not imagine a better way to spend part of her summer.

Maria had a lady friend who lived in Sienna, Katia Dohrn, the wife of a banker and quite well educated in music. Mrs. Dohrn knew many famous musicians including Rostropovich, Henryk Szeryng, Janos Starker and others. She had told Starker about Maria, saying what a great talent she was. He said in reply, "If this young girl is really so talented as you tell me, she should not go to a master class with Andre Navarra. She should come take a class with me. This summer I am giving a class in Canada at Shawnigan Lakes School for the Arts."

A week before Andre Navarra's master class was to begin, Maria was in Sienna, very near the seashore, in the home of Mrs. Dohrn, when she learned about her friend's conversation with Starker. To Maria this was somehow quite intriguing. But she had already booked a room in Sienna, and all of her thoughts were on the piazza and the red wine and having a good time there. Mrs. Dohrn said that she thought it would be very helpful if Maria would go to Canada and work with Starker. She even offered to pay for Maria's trip so that she would have no concern over expenses.

After a sleepless night, Maria made up her mind to go to see Starker, and two days later was on a plane bound for Canada. She was "scared out of her mind." It was her first experience in Canada. She was fearful about being in a faraway place in a foreign country, but she was thrilled at the same time.

She soon found herself performing the Dvorák *Concerto* for Starker before an audience of cellists who listened with rapt attention. It was the first time in her life she had ever played in a master class and found that she was quite nervous. She knew that most of the people in the audience could play the piece as well as she. After she finished the first movement, she looked at Starker. He said nothing, only lit up a cigarette with his gaze fixed on Maria. The room was in total silence. Everyone was on edge waiting for the word from the master. Finally he said, "Sing!"

"How am I going to sing this?" she thought. "I have to sing forte! And then there are the double stops in the third and fourth bars. How am I going to do this? I found that I could not move. I could not sing. I could not do anything but sit there frozen with fear."

"Sing," he said. "Go ahead and sing." He looked at her with his dark, penetrating eyes, seeming to look into her very soul. She had to do something, so at last she sang the opening few bars of the concerto. To Maria her voice sounded very funny, very shy and strange. Laughter broke the tension in the room, first hers and Starker's, and then joining in were all the other cellists in the room. They were just imagining themselves in her position and were all secretly relieved that it was Maria and not them.

Then he said, "You see, the way you were singing is the way you were also playing. It was so shy. You were not projecting. You were not doing anything with the music, just moving from the right side to the left with your bow. There was no articulation, no dynamics, no nothing!" And then he started teaching, explaining things. He was so convincing and so very logical.

Maria was wide-eyed, thinking, "Oh my! This is fantastic! This is exactly what I have been looking for! He just tore me apart completely. But then he started to explain things, making cello playing no longer a mystery. I recognized that I had no idea how things worked. I was very ashamed, actually, because I have won competitions. From that moment on, I knew that working with Starker was exactly what I needed to fill the gaps in my playing and thinking. With new motivation, I really got into my practice, more excited that ever before. Then after a few days, he invited me to study with him in Bloomington. With that, my whole life changed. I didn't go back to Germany after that master class but started my studies with him instead. Once I got to Bloomington, I worked like hell. I was learning so much and was so motivated and having so much fun! It was the best thing that ever happened to me.

"After a couple of semesters of study in Bloomington, I played in a lesson the second movement of the *Concerto in D Major* by Haydn. I knew that he always concentrated in each lesson on some point, either intonation or shifting, or whatever. He never said anything twice to me for I immediately tried to apply what I learned. For about two minutes he did not say a word. He was looking at me, lighting up a cigarette, and the smoke was going up to the ceiling. I was just sitting there, and I thought, 'That wasn't so bad. I am curious to know what he is going to say.' I thought it was pretty okay.

"Then he looked deeply into my eyes, looking very serious while I was getting smaller and smaller in my chair. Very quietly he said, 'If you ever play so much out of tune like you have just done, I will deny that you ever have been my student.' That was it. I had no idea what to say. I didn't dare to play any more. I was so shocked at what he said because I was so proud to be his student. In fact, I wanted to tell the whole world that I was studying with Starker. This was such a frightening thing he said to me! His enormously strong personality completely swept over me. My own individual self was pretty small then. I was so young and proud and impressionable. But in retrospect, it was fantastic to get this 'hint,' and it still sticks in my mind to this day. It still has a wonderful effect.

"Now I understand after being a teacher myself for twenty-one years that you have to give short-cuts to your students, things that will stick in their minds and never be forgotten. Don't talk too long and say too much. You have to give them big hints, even shock them at times. It makes people wake up and think!

"During my two years of study with him, and even later when I was his assistant in Essen, Germany, he told me many more things, much of which I have more or less forgotten. But that one sentence was so impressed into my thinking and still is strong to this day, twenty-five years later. He meant, always watch your intonation. Open your ears. Intonation is one of the most serious things in the life of a string player. You have to care for quality in your work and for intonation. It is never there. It is never 'in the bag.' You always have to work for it.

"Sometimes people say that Starker is a 'cold fish,' he is not projecting, or whatever. Not only is this absolutely untrue, but it shows the one saying so to be opinionated, and frankly ignorant! But I have known him as a teacher and the private person that he is. In the depths of my heart. I know that he is one of the warmest, most caring persons ever to have walked this earth! In Bloomington I was a good friend of his daughter, Gwen, and have been in his home many times. He really has been helpful to me in many tricky situations. He proves himself even now as a genuine and rare friend.

"When I was his student, I felt many times like I was in a plaster cast. But underneath the plaster cast I knew that there was something very healing. I knew my playing was getting better. He likes to 'put people into very strong frames' for quite a while concerning not making scratching sounds, or playing out of tune, or whatever they need to hear. He wants people to play on the highest level of excellence and discipline. I knew that if I followed his instructions, learned the rules of good musicianship, if I could trust him and dive into what he was telling me to do, feeling this straight jacket for a while, that later I would experience immense freedom. I knew that I would have a good base from which to go and find my own individual way of playing and teaching. To this day I still learn from what I gained from him twenty-five years ago. I still draw many of my ideas from that source and feel the roots of my musicianship there. This gives me a great store of inner richness and peace.

"I always felt from listening to him teaching others in the master classes that he really cared very deeply for each individual on the level of their own talent. Sometimes he was brutally honest, very hard on people, sometimes hurting them in the process. But he always made people wake up early on and think! He wanted people to face their own talent, their own responsibility in life, and what they should do with the cello in their lives. He always told young cellists to find their own path. He did not want young cellists to become copies of himself. He said, 'Recognize who you are. Are you an extrovert or an introvert? What are your talents? Where do your strengths lie? What are the areas in which you have less talent? Work on developing the best in yourself, and work on improving your weaknesses. With honesty in your heart, find the truth within yourself, regardless of what other people think. Learn to care for yourself. Become a positive egotist.' The way he said this, you know that he really wanted you to improve, and he sincerely wanted to help, not just with the fingerboard and the bow. He cared very deeply about his students, wanting everyone to develop their best. For young persons, for grown-up persons, for older persons he really has a feeling for every stage of life. I am so grateful to him and so glad that he was my teacher. My deep admiration for him is still increasing to this day."

Conversations with Gary Hoffman

Gary Hoffman, prominent solo cellist who lives both in France and New York, had a relationship with Starker over many years, beginning when he was a ten-year-old. Long before he ever dreamed that he would be Starker's student, Gary heard Starker perform a couple of times in Chicago, once with the Chicago Symphony. Following the concert, Gary's dad introduced him to the great cellist. When Gary asked for Starker's autograph, he wrote, "to Gary, my cellist friend, Janos Starker." At the time Gary's dad, associate conductor of the Chicago Symphony, was also conducting the orchestra in a summer concert series in Grant Park. The park is located alongside Lake Michigan at the foot of the nearby towering buildings of Chicago. Starker was soloist from time to time with the orchestra. Again Gary was in the audience.

A few years later, Gary's family moved to Florida where his dad was conducting an orchestra in the Gulf Coast area. They had a hard time finding a cello teacher for Gary in that area, and for several years he had no teacher. One time when Starker was performing on the East Coast of Florida, Gary and his mother went to hear the concert. After the concert, she asked if Gary could study with him. So as a high school student Gary had infrequent lessons with Starker in Bloomington. Every couple of months or so he flew to Indiana where he was hosted by the Starkers in their home. Mr. Starker would not accept a penny for the lessons, knowing that it cost the Hoffmans quite a lot for the plane fares. Says Gary, "Mr. Starker is a very generous, magnanimous person. He is known for not being very demonstrative, musically or otherwise, and because of that, he is often misjudged by people who do not know him." Gary always knew a part of him that was most human and kind. It was always clear to Gary that Starker liked him, and whenever he made criticisms, which was quite frequent, Gary always took them as constructive. He knew that was his teacher's job.

One time at one of Starker's Saturday master classes Gary performed, and, as usual, Starker made his comments to Gary about what he needed to do to improve his playing. Afterward he was approached by other students in the class who said that he must have been devastated by Starker's comments. Gary asked, "By what?" "The things that he said to you," was the reply "What did he say that was so bad?" asked Gary. He was never devastated by what Starker said because he knew that the criticisms were made in order to continue to help him grow and develop. Gary said, "I know that he is not attacking me personally." He knew that he was included in Starker's class because he was accepted and well liked by his teacher. Starker believed in him. Perhaps others in the class were not as secure personally. Gary knew that his austere, severe exterior was only that, just an exterior. Inside there was a warm and wonderful man. "I did not go to study with him seeking compliments. But deep down I knew that I would not be there if he didn't think that I should be there."

Starker has strong ideas of what a student-teacher relationship should be. In the lessons he never allowed a student to cross the line and become too familiar with him. When students went to his home, they saw another side of him. And when one is no longer his student, he is treated by Starker as a colleague.

Uri Vardi, a former Starker student teaching in Madison, Wisconsin, performed once with Starker. Vardi said to Gary, "Recently I played a two-cello concert with him. Naturally I was nervous and told Mr. Starker so." Starker's reply was, "Why should you be nervous? You are no longer my student." After the concert, Starker said to Uri, "You should be very proud of yourself!" Like his playing, his comment was not effusive. Starker says what he has to say with economy of means, always clear and to the point.

During Gary's years as a commuter student, he experienced several memorable evenings in the Starker home. One of these was an event when Joseph Gingold came to Starker's for an evening of chamber music. Gary was introduced to Mr. Gingold as a talented kid, and he listened attentively to their performance. It was a joy for Gary to hear the two playing together. He especially enjoyed their warm, brotherly relationship. Although they were very different personalities, they were complimentary to one another, both musically and personally. Gary recalled one moment when Mr. Gingold played a particularly beautiful phrase. Mr. Starker got up from his chair, put down his cello and planted a big kiss on Gingold's cheek, a sign of the great affection they shared for each other. That was indeed a very special moment.

Eventually, Gary was enrolled in the university as a freshman. He studied with Starker for five years and became Starker's assistant for the last couple of years. Starker obviously had enough trust in Gary as a cellist to assign him to teach in his absence when he was away concertizing. As a twenty-one-year-old Gary was teaching a number of cellists, many of whom were older than he. Starker felt that this experience of teaching was invaluable not only for the other cellists but also for Gary and his development. Of course it was for Gary a high honor, and he took it with great seriousness and responsibility. He understood very well how important his position was and treasured an inner pride.

One of the most valuable aspects of Starker's work with his students is that he teaches one to teach himself and in so doing to be able to teach others. He wanted to instill this in his students who shared his interest and passion for the cello. As much as he is renowned as a performer, Starker feels that his real legacy is as a teacher.

Upon graduation in 1979 with his music degree and artist's diploma, Gary was appointed to the faculty at Indiana University. For seven or eight years he had his own class of budding young cellists. Of course he and Starker worked closely together because there were students at I.U. who wanted to study with Starker but could not yet get into his class. In the School of Music there was a frequent exchange of students in lessons as well as master classes between all of the cello teachers on the faculty. Gary soon found that as he gained more experience, there were actually students who came to I.U. expressly to study with him. He was very pleased about this. That was something Starker wanted for Gary as well, knowing that it is not easy to work in the shadow of such an imposing figure in the music world. Gary was teaching top level cellists and making his own mark at the same time.

Starker always made it clear that he did not want his students to play like him. In fact, he wanted his students to develop their own style. In spite of the fact that his view of music and the cello are so clear, with its analytical aspects in particular, it was his intention never to make puppets of his students. His teaching was never systematized so that students had to play a piece a certain way. He had his stylistic and interpretive ways. His interpretations are fairly fixed in terms of the greater design, but within that he always gave himself a great deal of freedom. In addition, never did a student bring a piece in to him more than once. Hence there was little time for Starker to mold an interpretation. It was up to the student to come to that on his own. Because Starker was such an imposing person, he knew that if a student could make it in his class, he could make it in the music world. Like Gary's father, Starker is very demanding of himself and others, very disciplined. So Gary's studies with Starker were quite in line with the standards he had been brought up with in striving for excellence. What a fine father figure Starker was for Gary!

One memorable event for Gary was the first ceremony for the Eva Janzer Memorial Foundation, Chevalier du Violoncelle, where each year a revered cellist is honored who has made a significant contribution to the world of cello teaching during his or her lifetime. It is designed to honor those who are teachers, not necessarily performers. The thinking is that performers already have received enough accolades from the public. The first person to be honored in this way was Pierre Fournier. This was in 1979. There was a dinner followed by a party in the Starker's home. An amazing collection of luminaries were in the home for the party including Fournier and his wife, Aldo Parisot, William Primrose, and Raya Garbousova to name a few.

At the party one of Starker's students went to him and said, "Gary does imitations of you." She came and told Gary this. "You didn't!" he replied. "Yes, I did, and he wants to see it," was her comment. "Now!" "In front of all these people?" he wondered. Gary had no idea how Starker would take this. When Starker approached him demanding that he do the imitation of him for everyone, Gary said, "I can't!" He thought, "But I am going to look like a real idiot if I don't. I have to go through with this." He immediately switched gears and went into the performing mode. "Okay, here goes," he thought. "Either I am going to withdraw and regret it the rest of my life, or I am going to do it and take the consequences! I might as well go for broke." With all the people sitting around waiting for his performance, he immediately requested a bottle of Scotch. Then William Primrose yelled out, "He is going to play the Scotch Fantasy," as in Max Bruch's *Scottish Fantasy*.

"As I took Starker's cello I thought to myself, I cannot believe I am really going to do this." He swigged a couple of belts to strengthen his resolve, then played a couple of Bach *Suite* movements. Gary imitated Starker's sound, his vibrato, the bow strokes, shifting the weight of his body, putting his leg out to one side, etc., exaggerating everything for maximum effect.

Starker, who was sitting just a few feet away, was laughing so hard that he literally fell off his chair onto the floor, demonstrating his own great sense of humor about himself, especially considering this was going on in front of a room full of people. He obviously did not feel ridiculed and took it in the spirit of affection and good humor that it was intended. Gary has seen others in a similar situation look very embarrassed and unhappy, not Starker. He said to Gary, "I wish I played so well in tune as that!" After that Gary felt that he been initiated and accepted into the club.

In the fall of 1997 Gary attended the Cello Festival in Kronberg, Germany. It is quite a big event in the city, well attended, well publicized. Gary spoke with the organizer of the festival to recommend doing something at the next event to honor Starker for his seventy-fifth birthday. When Gary brought this up to Starker, he was quite reluctant, not wanting the attention to be brought upon himself but rather on the music. It took some "arm-twisting" on Gary's part to convince him to participate. As a result on October 21-24, 1999 the Kronberg Cello Festival was a celebration of Starker's seventy-fifth birthday.

Conversations with Rafael Figueroa

Rafael Figueroa is principal cellist in the Metropolitan Opera Orchestra which gives two hundred twenty-two opera performances each year. Rafi shares the principal cello chair with another cellist, and the job is divided between them. In addition to the operas, the orchestra has a chamber music series and a series of orchestral concerts at Carnegie Hall. Rafael is originally from Puerto Rico. He grew up in a musical family where at an early age he was exposed to the playing of the legendary cellist, Pablo Casals. At the Casals Festival he heard performances each year from the time he was three years old. In Puerto Rico Rafael studied with a Russian-Argentinian named Adolfo Odnoposoff, a former student of Emmanuel Feuermann. Later he studied with Joaquin Vidaechea who was a student of Gaspar Cassadó and Casals.

As a fifteen-year-old Rafael attended an early morning dress rehearsal at the Casals Festival with his teacher. That is where he first heard Janos Starker perform. Rafael noticed that Starker looked very serious as he came on stage. The look on his face appeared almost angry with intensity. It was not anger, Rafael later learned. Starker was just very focused. When Rafael heard Starker perform the *D Major Concerto* by Haydn, he was truly captivated. Near the end of the third movement, Starker was playing a complicated passage high in the cello register when he heard a sneeze come from the viola section. Without missing a note, he turned around and said, "Gesundheit," and continued playing.

Rafael was amazed with Starker's impeccable intonation and complete control of all the aspects of execution. Over the years Rafael heard many cellists perform at the Casals Festival, and they were all fantastic, but never quite like this. Starker played with an excellence that set himself apart from all the others. Rafael's father is a violinist and a long-time fan of Jascha Heifetz. In Starker's playing, Rafael could clearly hear the kind of focus and perfection on the instrument that one hears in the recordings of Heifetz. He identified with Starker's sound immediately.

After his years of study with Vidaechea, very productive years in developing mainly a very good left hand, Rafael went to study with Starker. "Once I had decided to go to Indiana University to study with Starker," he says, "I sent him a recording of my performance of Tchaikovsky's *Rococo Variations*. I was accepted into Starker's class, not knowing that he was about to take a sabbatical leave. When I arrived in Bloomington I asked, 'Where is Mr. Starker?' only to learn that he was away for a year. I had heard of Gary Hoffman, a young hotshot cellist, only twenty-two years old and already teaching at I.U., so I studied for three years with Gary. Although he was only four years older than I, he helped me a great deal. As a boy in Puerto Rico I was playing out of sheer talent and raw ability, not knowing what I was doing. At the time I was somewhat lacking in bow technique. Gary helped to prepare me for my work with Starker, particularly in the area of sound production. Although Gary's approach to teaching was rather free, he helped to develop my own concept of sound. Starker, however, was very specific in how

I should do things. He would tell me exactly what to do, and when I did, I saw the results. In my work with Mr. Starker I learned many great concepts of string playing. Then I began to understand the concepts and how to apply them.

Rafael continues, "Starker sanitized my playing, especially helping me with bow technique, bow distribution and control of the bow speed. Previously I always played portato, pulsing the bow with each note. As I developed my own sound I became more aware of the sounds of other players, their pushing and pulling of the bow, swells in the sound because of lack of bow speed control, changes of the bow speed in the middle of a note, all of which are mannerisms.

"Starker always maintained a strict teacher-student relationship, no small talk, no chitchat, just down to business. For me, a lesson with Starker was always a performance, like being on stage in Carnegie Hall, serious business. As a matter of cordiality, I always greeted him at each lesson saying, 'Good morning. How are you?' His response, silence, not a word, just a gesture to take my cello out and play. Each lesson I said the same greeting with no response from Mr. Starker until finally one time, face to face, I said to him cheerily, 'Good morning. How are you?' He said to me, 'You'll find out in a minute! Play.' I learned very quickly not to try to be too friendly.

"I always had a great deal of respect for him and came to the lessons wearing a shirt and tie, ready for business. As a matter of course I practiced eight to ten hours a day. It became clear to me that when I was in Puerto Rico I was very unfocused. My energies were not wasted but perhaps misdirected. Lessons with Starker were very intense. He pushed me to my limit, giving me, one after another, Popper and Gruetzmacher *Etudes*, Piatti *Caprices*, sonata and concerto movements to be learned in just one week. At one lesson he gave me the Schumann *Concerto* to learn and memorize in just five days. He wanted to see how much I could handle.

"Then one day he stopped giving me such volumes of music to learn and focused instead on some very basic aspects of playing technique such as bow placement, use of the arms, circular motions, breathing, looking for the balance when sitting, how to sit with the instrument, etc. Many teachers just give the students a formula: do as I tell you, take this, and learn it. But Starker never asked me to blindly follow and imitate him. Rather he always asked my opinion about things and respected my ideas if they were valid. After all, I was twenty years old when I went to study with him. He helped me a great deal in developing my own thinking and my own style.

"In the Saturday seminars I often heard students copy him like parrots, playing exactly with his fingerings and bowings, the same mannerisms and all. Some of them were very successful. They sounded just like him, but they sounded just like a 'bad copy' of Mr. Starker. He became very frustrated with students who did not show their own personalities.

"Once I had moved to New York, people heard me perform on many occasions. I often received comments about my playing such as, 'You don't sound anything like Starker, but when I watch you play, it is all there: The mechanics and the understanding of the instrument, the Starker influence.' The sound and the phrasing, I like to think that these are my own.

"Starker's Saturday seminars were incredible marathons. I wondered how he did it all, with his concertizing and travelling, coming to town and having to make up all of those lessons. He taught all day long, day after day. Then Saturday performance seminars went from 10:00 a.m. until 4:00 p.m., one student performing after another. It was required that each student perform at each class. Starker is such an imposing musical figure, bringing a great deal of intensity to the seminars. Once I performed Schubert's *Arpeggione Sonata* for the class, feeling rather proud of myself. Then Starker took out his cello, and with no warm-up played the piece flawlessly. The beautiful thing was that he could explain everything he does on the cello and why. He could find solutions for each person's playing to suit their physical type: If one is tall or short, has big hands or small, is slim or fat. In addition he encouraged the students to play for each other and critique one another. For example, if when walking down the hall I overheard one of my fellow students practicing, I might stop and make a suggestion or comment. This brought about a dialogue about cello playing, encouraging cooperation rather than competition between students.

"One incident has remained embossed in my memory. It involved a fellow student who came to study with Starker after working in France with Andre Navarra. He came up to me one day saying, 'Rafi, could you help me? I am very confused. Navarra told me to hold the bow like this, and then Starker told me to hold the bow like that. Could you come to my lesson?'

"So I said, 'Sure I'll come to your lesson.' There was always somebody listening in the lessons, and Starker did not mind that I was sitting in on the lesson. Besides, this fellow was also having lessons with me. He started playing, and I do not know exactly what it was that he did, but he made Starker very angry. Starker lit up a cigarette. When he finished playing, Starker just looked at him and was silent for a while. Then he said, 'Every time I hear you play like that, you give me the impression you don't know what the hell you are doing!' I thought to myself, now is when I make my exit and said, 'Bye, everybody.' Later I saw the poor guy come out of Starker's studio in tears. This was obviously an intense session. Not everybody could handle Starker's criticism. He is extremely honest and direct, never beating around the bush. He doesn't pat you on the back and tell you how great you do this or that. Instead he goes straight to the point, to exactly what needs to be fixed. That is what he wants his students to do later as professionals, not to wallow in self-congratulation, first letting little flaws go by the way, then bigger flaws. He wants people to listen to themselves and think clearly about all aspects of their playing.

"One time Starker asked me what I wanted to do with the cello. I gave him a rather shy, noncommittal response. He said, 'What's the matter? Are you embarrassed to say it?' It was clear to him that I had potential and was wasting time. He knew that I needed to take things more seriously. There were so many sensational lessons, times when from sheer excitement I could almost 'jump out of the window!' Sometimes I left his studio with a headache from the intense concentration. Apart from the cello, he gave me valuable life lessons, lessons in coping with different stages of life and career. Starker was most helpful in opening many doors in my mind.

"Starker teaches in such a way that you learn to teach yourself. Eventually you reach a point when working with Starker when you don't need him any more. He uses a very simple formula: You isolate the problem, and find the solution. In so doing you don't waste time. When I started with Starker, he said to me, 'What we are going to do here is like putting money in the bank. You are going to take out of that bank account what you need, not only for your own playing but also for your teaching when you are helping others to find their solutions. You will have all this information in your head. You learn how to think for yourself.' Every day of my life, with my cello in hands, I have him sitting in front of me, telling me what I need to hear. Not a day passes that I don't hear his words. It all comes back. He was very successful in putting all this information into my head. One thing he tells his students when they graduate, 'Now you are part of my family whether you like it or not!' He is always keeping in touch with his former students all over the world. It is like a network. He has a way of keeping his hand over you.

"I was very fortunate that Mr. Gingold was at I.U. when I was a student there. He was like another teacher to me. Often I would go to his studio and play chamber music for him. I could knock on Mr. Gingold's studio door any time. He would say in his gravelly voice, 'My friend, come in.' Sometimes I would catch him eating his lunch, and he would talk with me. He was an open encyclopedia of knowledge and experience. On occasion Yuval Yaron invited Mr. Gingold and others to his home for chamber music. Mr. Gingold knew the quartet repertoire so well that most of the time he played from memory. Those sessions were such a pleasure. We had access to great teachers like Gingold, Starker, Pressler and so many others. For us students they were a bridge to the *Golden Era* of music making. The I.U. School of Music was like a big cocoon, and we were all growing inside and being exposed to all these great schools of music making in piano, voice, violin, cello, etc. It must have been something like Starker's experience growing up in Budapest before World War II. The Indiana University School of Music was a rarefied atmosphere within a large university where students were required to study, math, history and everything else. Understandably, this created a bit of conflict for serious music performance students. It was a challenge to make a performance career and yet fulfill the university requirements.

"I was twenty-five when I started teaching at I.U. and playing competitions. One day in 1985 Starker told me about the Casals Competition in Budapest. Although he generally does not believe in competitions for his students, this was one that he wanted me to prepare for. He had recently gone to Budapest for concerts and a television interview. This was the second time he had been in Hungary since the end of the war. I had the feeling that he really wanted me to represent his school in Budapest. With his encouragement I had everything ready in a couple of months. It was a very tough competition, very much Soviet and Communist controlled. Because of this I felt very pleased to have won the bronze medal, the third prize. I was the only American finalist there and learned later that the last American who had won a prize in the Casals Competition was Ron Leonard. These events are very political. Often the results have nothing to do with one's playing. Each person on the jury has his own students competing, and the judges want their students to win. Everything is done by manipulation. Competitions, as a result, have lost a great deal of credibility.

"At the time I was performing lots of cello repertoire, everything from Bach to the Dvořák *Concerto*. With the Casals Competition I started doing the competition circuit. There are a small number of competitions that are by invitation only, and one day Mr. Gingold said to me, 'By the way, I got you this opportunity. You could receive a call from the New England Conservatory to audition.' I did get a call inviting me to audition and prepared myself for the Piatigorsky Competition. For the competition, I was required to perform the repertoire for three recitals over a couple of days' time, a lot of music to prepare. On the last concert I performed the *B Flat Major Trio* of Schubert with members of the faculty at the New England Conservatory. Then before a jury I gave a master class with several students from the Conservatory performing all manner of repertoire. I had no way of knowing the repertoire in advance. In this way the judges could see how I would handle a master class situation. It was quite an experience from beginning to end! That was in 1986, and I won first prize in the Piatigorsky Competition.

"One of the great moments in my career was when I made a phone call to Starker from Aspen. I had just received a call from the manager at the Met informing me that I was being offered the job as principal cellist of the Metropolitan Opera Orchestra. It was 10:30 a.m. in Bloomington. When Starker picked up the phone, I told him, 'I just got your old job!' 'What do you mean?' he asked. 'I just got your old job at the Met!'" At Raphael's words, Starker was ecstatic! Although they were separated by many miles, his exuberance travelled over the phone wires in full technicolor! Then Starker looked at his watch and said, "It is too early now, but at five o'clock today I will have a drink in your name!"

Rafael was warned by Starker that playing in the Met orchestra was an exhausting job. Some of the old timers in the orchestra remember hearing Starker say, "Playing in the Met orchestra is the best method of contraception there is. You're seldom at home, and when you are home, you have nothing left. It is a job that requires the stamina of a horse." When Starker was the principal cellist, he had to play seven performances each week plus rehearsals. Sometimes the orchestra played a matinee on Sundays as well, an unbelievable schedule. On top of that, many a night he was recording well into the wee hours of the morning. During his years with the Met, Starker recorded the complete Beethoven *Sonatas*, the Bach *Suites*, Brahms' *Sonatas*, and more. Then he played an unbelievable opera schedule! Raphael's contract is somewhat easier. There are two principal cellists who alternate operas. That allows him to practice and stay in top shape, ready to perform Dvořák's *Concerto* with a day's notice. What was Starker's solution? Sleep less.

Says Rafi, "There is a player in the Met Orchestra who I enjoy chatting with, an English horn player. Just after the war ended, he joined the Met orchestra. That was fifty-two years ago. He remembers that Starker would come to the Met rehearsals and performances, do his job and immediately leave. Orchestra members knew that Starker was doing his recordings well into the middle of the night. It was obvious to many that Starker would not be with the Met for long. During those years there was a great amount of flux in the personnel of the orchestra. On the other hand, however, there were some who came to the orchestra and stayed until they died.

"When Starker was the president of the Third American Cello Congress in 1986, there was a competition as one of the events. The winner got to perform the *Rococo Variations* with orchestra. I was one of two first place winners, and we both played *Rococo Variations* back to back in the gala concert. In the audience were six hundred cellists including Zara Nelsova, Bernard Greenhouse, and others. With such an audience, I felt that if I could keep my bow on the string I was a success. Starker threw a great party afterward. It was a very pleasant competition.

"As a result of that competition I performed a recital at the Kennedy Center in Washington, D.C. When I reached the entrance of the building, the security guard asked, 'Are you Figueroa? There is a telegram for you.' I had not seen Starker for a year. I opened the telegram and read, 'Keep up the flag. Starker'

"With those words I remembered something he had said to me in Bloomington. When I shared with him my fears and concerns about leaving Bloomington and moving to New York, I said, 'Maestro, going to New York is kind of scary.' I was expecting him to tell me to call so and so, do this or that. Instead, he said, 'Just think you are going to a war. You may lose a few battles. You may win a few battles. The important thing is that in the end, you win the war.' Years later, now I understand.

"This winter he will be performing the entire works of Beethoven with Shigeo Neriki here in New York at the 92nd Street YMCA. I look forward to hearing him. I am always amazed at how much music he is prepared to perform at any time. He has a genius capacity for music. If he had not been a cellist, he certainly would have been a great scientist, mathematician, or trail blazer in some other field. I expect Starker will be playing well into his nineties and will always play well. He keeps himself in remarkable shape, slim and strong and so disciplined. He has complete control of what he is doing and uses his body economically and effectively.

"When I think about Jacqueline DuPre, I believe her multiple sclerosis may have resulted from the way she played the cello. When she performed, she played with brutal force, with unbelievable intensity. There is only so much abuse one can take.

"Because I was in Bloomington for so long, seven years, Starker and I became quite good friends. In fact, I asked him to be the best man at our wedding. He said that he would be delighted. At the wedding he was 'all teary-eyed.' That experience brought our relationship into a completely different dimension.

"As a result of my work with Starker, I have learned to hold at all times a high standard, requiring a high level of musical integrity. One thing he made very clear to me, he expected no less of me than he expected of himself. One time I went into his office unprepared for a lesson. He could see it in my face and said, 'What's the matter?' My reply was, 'I haven't been able to practice. I have papers to write for my classes and have had no time to practice.' 'That's your problem,' he said, 'not mine.' As a result, I have on my mind every day when I come to the Met a certain level of expectation. I see so many problems in orchestras in general, people who haven't practiced for years. Some come unprepared or perhaps do not care. If they think that the conductor is not so good, they may use that as an excuse for anarchy. That to me is like bringing your home life to your job. I believe there is no excuse for less than professional behavior. Because of my work with Starker, I am compelled to maintain my integrity. When I sit down to play, I must play the very best that I can, no excuses. Starker really pounded that into me. I cannot and must not compromise my professional standard."

Conversations with David Shamban

While Israeli cellist David Shamban was a student of Starker's at Indiana University 1975-1980, he remembers attending the master classes on Saturdays from 12:00-4:00 p.m. Says Shamban, "Starker was in town only a few months every year, and these were valued learning sessions for his students. Not only cellists performed but singers and other instrumentalists as well. During the week there was a sign up sheet on the door to Starker's teaching studio. Students would write down on the sheet the music they wanted to perform."

"Whenever a cellist performed in the class, Starker would always play the music back for them with extreme accuracy and musical know-how. At times when he would play for the student, he would sit like a sphinx and look them straight in the eye while playing. He would not move his eyes." It was as though he wanted to communicate his thoughts without having to verbalize them.

"The way he teaches," according to Shamban, "he is like a scientist who has figured out things. He knows how to word his explanations, using the same way to explain things now as he did twenty years ago. One example of this is how he explains the difference between anticipated and delayed shifts. Sometimes in master classes he would tell some of the same jokes, just to break the tension after someone has performed. He would also give the same explanation of a fingering, for example, or when the music starts being detaché and when it is spiccato."

According to Shamban, "his explanations though quite intricate were made to sound simple. For example, he would say, If you just touch these fingers, they will move. But if you increasingly go toward the tip of the bow, then something entirely different happens." This is exactly the minimum energy, maximum sensitivity principle. He would not exactly explain how to do things, but he would help the student to understand in nonverbal ways, perhaps a small demonstration. Sometimes he would simply play it back showing what to do, leaving the student open-mouthed with amazement. On other occasions he would show by pressing the right muscles on the player's body and explain how the body works.

"A lot of people thought he taught technique, but he never did. He taught music making. Technique is only used as a tool in making music. There was no technique for technique's sake. Sometimes he would use vowel and consonant combinations to indicate the kind of sound one should make.

"Starker's own playing is so beautifully in tune. He felt that a person is born with good intonation. If he heard a student play out of tune, he would sometimes just go on with no comment. He would only talk about intonation with a student who had good ears."

As a student, Shamban always waited anxiously for the next lesson. He brought not only his repertoire to his lessons, but also all kinds of exercises and etudes by such cellists as Grützmacher, Popper, or Piatti. And he says, "Starker loved it. I think it was a chance for him to show off a little. He would grab his cello and play it back for me, just immaculately." At the end of his first semester with Starker, Shamban was completely in awe of him. Such a difference Starker had made in his own playing! "Starker had a plan with each student according to his or her talent, knowledge and ability. He kept a mental file on each person and maintained that path."

"Sometimes during a lesson there would be a knock on the door and he would go on and on in Hungarian with Sebök or Eva Janzer or her husband. I loved to listen to them rattle on in Hungarian."

While he was in Indiana, Shamban often attended the chamber music classes as well as piano classes given by pianist György Sebök. "Like Starker, he also exercised the principles of the Hungarian School, namely minimum energy and maximum sensitivity. Only the energy which is needed to play the instrument should be manifested, nothing in excess. All of one's resources go into the music making, into the mental activity. Sebök and Starker both talked about using the larger or smaller muscles of the body, the power flow from the back muscles towards the hands. For the cellist, the bow would be an extension of the right arm and the cello would be an extension of the left arm." Occasionally Sebök and Starker would perform together at the university. "When they performed," says Shamban, "there was nothing like it. It was as though they were one person. They felt and breathed the music together."

"Regarding his career, perhaps Starker felt that he did not get the respect and recognition from the musical world which he deserved." On occasion he mentioned to Shamban that Gregor Piatigorsky or Leonard Rose were to play with the New York Philharmonic, and he was not. "Unfortunately it is not how well you play in absolute terms," says Shamban, "but a lot of politics go into the making of one's career."

(In response Starker says that Shamban misunderstood him. He relayed to Shamban a story, saying that one time Starker and Leonard Rose were in a recording session together. Rose was complaining that no one else plays concerts other than Casals and Piatigorsky. These two cellists were controlling the cello soloist market. Says Starker's press secretary, Mary Johnson, "It was just Rose's nature to complain and feel slighted. He was often depressed, and he would attribute his problems to somebody else." Starker knew exactly why he was not playing with the New York Philharmonic. He did not cater to any musicians in order to get a job. "In 1951," said Starker, "I played a concert in the home of Madame Fornaroff. Before entering I was warned not to mention the name Heifetz. Branislaw Gimpel, a Russian violinist, was livid, thinking he was unable to make a career as a violinist because of Heifetz." A few months later Ruggiero

Ricci was told the very same thing. Ricci said, "He's worried about Heifetz? I am worried about Gimpel! He plays my concerts! Heifetz does not play my concerts.")

Says Shamban, "Sometimes Starker has been criticized for lack of warmth. He is a man of few words, very direct. Sometimes people interpret that to mean that he considers himself superior. I believe he carries within himself a lot of pain. Another factor is that he does not care to have much to do with mediocrity. At a cocktail party following a concert, for example, perhaps someone there does not care for his sense of humor. Or maybe his intelligence is too much for them."

Shamban believes that in Starker's move, coming from Hungary, perhaps his words came out very curt in the mental translation process. That was before he was thinking in English. "Although Starker is a very private person, those who know him will attest that he is a very warm, caring, giving person. But he is very protective of his time, his talent, and what he has to give to the musical world. And he will not compromise in his standards when it comes to teaching and performing."

Conversations with Rowena Hammill

Rowena Hammill, cellist from Australia, studied with Starker for two years. During the first twenty minutes of her first lesson, she reportedly learned more about playing the cello than she had in all of her previous years of music lessons. She remembers being just "blown away" by that first lesson.

He merely pointed out to her later what seemed obvious, mainly the principle of anticipation. Every shift is prepared first in the back, then in the upper arm and then into the forearm and fingers. The same is true with the use of the bow arm. It all comes from the upper arm. You don't try to do things with just the fingers. If you anticipate the movement first in the upper arm, the motion will work. These things seem to make so much sense. Until he pointed them out, she never understood them or thought of them. She would not have figured them out on her own. These concepts go along with very natural processes, such as a swimming motion with the arms or letting the arms fall from the shoulder. That is how one arrives at Starker's kind of bow stroke. Other teachers don't refer to the natural use of the arms or perhaps have other strange ways of using their arms, ways that, according to Rowena, are perhaps unnatural or ineffectual.

Another powerful concept for Rowena was the idea of bow distribution. Use only the amount of bow that you need instead of using all of the bow all of the time. Another concept for Rowena was the production of vibrato. At the time she was using a rotation vibrato, the most common type of motion. Instead of a rolling motion, she learned to move the forearm, letting the knuckle give. That way the hand maintains a consistent angle. He said, "Go home and work on that." In ten minutes he had changed her vibrato. She remembers spending a week working on the new vibrato concept. When she came back the next week, he did not say a word about her vibrato.

She pretty much thought she had changed it, but she was not sure. She said, "I worked on the vibrato." To that he abruptly replied, "That's fine." He never said another word about it. It was not necessary. He explained things so well. He said so much so economically. In a very few minutes, he planted "bombshells" to be worked on for a lifetime. He said what is relevant so quickly. He never patted himself on the back for being such a great teacher. It was like, okay, you got that just fine. So let's move on.

To her, Starker is fully dedicated to really being a teacher. Since then Rowena has met many teachers who live vicariously through their students. Of course, he does not need to do that. But nevertheless he does not get a big ego trip out of being a master teacher. He loves what he does and does truly want to help people.

While she was an Indiana University student, Rowena won a concerto competition for which she performed the Elgar *Concerto* with orchestra. Starker was unable to be there for her performance. But when he returned to town, he said to her, "I heard that you played well. But I heard that you came out on stage and tuned for five minutes, and I hate that! She asked, "Who told you that?" To this he replied, "One of your friends." She said, "Some friend!" He had never said a word to her about not tuning on stage. She had come out as usual, the oboist gave the A, and she tuned. That is what most performers do before a concerto performance. Not Starker. He hates to disrupt the drama of the experience with something as mundane as tuning.

It is hard for him to rave. Then when he gives someone a compliment, it really means something. Compliments from Starker are hard won, even backhanded ones such as, "I heard you played well, BUT...."

In her second year at Indiana University, Rowena was appointed Starker's assistant. This was largely due to her valuable accompanying skills. It was always a struggle for him to find a pianist who could come in and do a decent job of accompanying during lessons. Starker deserved to have a good pianist. Since she knew the cello repertoire, she was an even better accompanist for his students. Instead of spending only one hour in a lesson with Starker each week, Rowena was in his studio several hours. Sometimes she found herself accompanying Starker when he would demonstrate a piece. She could not play the really difficult music but was at ease with concerto accompaniments, Baroque sonatas and such. One time after playing a Baroque piece with him, he turned to Rowena and said, "I want to take you on tour with me." That made her feel great!

Rowena discovered later that it is during the lessons that he practices. He has little time because he is so busy. One time she brought Brahms' *F Major Sonata* to the lesson, and he said, "I am so glad you brought that today because I have to play it in a couple of weeks." She said, "He is the kind of person who can do a tremendous amount very quickly. He does not have to practice a lot like most ordinary humans."

She found that he was a completely different person, a different teacher with each student. It was as though he was a therapist who would have a different way of dealing with each person's needs. People are all so different. Some people he would be really hard on. Rowena wondered why but knew there was always a reason. "Perhaps that person needed the cockiness knocked out of him," she said. "He had a reputation for being hard on people. There must have been some psychological reason for doing that."

He was never hard on Rowena. Perhaps he knew that she could not handle too much harsh criticism. He was always extremely nice to her. There were such stories and rumors about him. Perhaps he used to be much gruffer, meaner. People thought that once he had a grandchild, he was different. Perhaps he is just different to women. But, on the other hand, Rowena found that occasionally he would be harder on a female student also. She knew he had his reasons.

"Because he is such an incredible person," said Rowena, "some people wanted too much from him. Perhaps they wanted to be friends, or wanted to make him like a father figure or a counselor. Some students went into a lesson wanting to tell him all of their problems, putting him in the role of a counselor. That put the wrong kind of pressure on him. They wanted more than a student-teacher relationship." Rowena never expected that. She expected a distance because of the great respect that she felt for him. Growing up in Australia, one keeps a certain distance with people who are not family, especially someone who is so highly esteemed. She had complete and utter respect for him. Perhaps that is why he never came down hard on her.

Rowena recalls his sixtieth birthday. At that time he was gone probably half of the semester concertizing. That made the lesson times in Indiana all the more precious. He had seventeen or eighteen cellists in his class. That was a lot of students. It amazes her that after many years if she sees him, he always remembers her. He is always interested in her life. Over the years he has had many students. That he cares about and remembers each one means a lot to his former students. Said Rowena, "He has the kind of mind where no time seems to have passed at all."

In her own teaching she has found that Starker's method seems to work with students who catch on. She hesitates to call it a method which would connote any type of rigidity. She says, "His principles are so right. They work." She feels that studying with Starker has prepared her so much better to be a teacher herself. It is a good feeling to pass on something of value to the next generation. Hopefully, they will pass it on too. That is what Starker wants. She says, "He seems to be one of the last of the *Old World European Masters of the Cello*. It is a shame to think of that generation passing. I do hope he goes on strong for many years to come."

Conversations with Sebastian Toettcher

Sebastian Toettcher, cellist from Germany, studied with Starker for four years at Indiana University. He said, "I was very amazed that Starker took me on as a student. I auditioned for him in Europe twice, one time in Berlin and later in Munich. My playing then was very mediocre, even though I knew a lot of repertoire. I was scared to play for him. My nervousness when playing for him would always take over. But he must have seen something of value in me, some kind of musical expression. Otherwise he would not have taken me on as a student."

"I went through a very difficult first two years with him. I did not improve. In fact, my playing got worse at first. Starker predicted that. He always said, 'Don't worry about that. If you keep at it, you will come out of this all right. And your playing will be much better because of the rethinking process.'"

Says Sebastian, "Starker has the ability like no one else to help one understand how to play the cello. But for me, it was a brain overload. There were so many new things that I had to remember such as a different bow hold, different left hand approach, different sound, watching the curve of the bow change, etc. These are things that I could not learn in just a week. I had to experiment with them over and over until they finally came out satisfactorily. He would say, 'Watch the bow change. Watch this or that.' His whole approach of being in the most relaxed state possible, using physical preparation, these concepts were not easy to achieve. He would always tell me, 'You are tense here. Loosen up. Relax, and put more weight into the bow.' All of these commands are so vivid in my memory. For my mind at the time, it was a tremendous amount to think about. I was constantly thinking about these problems and not enough about the actual music. Maybe it just did not sound like I was. But then later on, once the technical stuff was on automatic pilot, it all came together.

"After a couple of years I was able to concentrate more on music making. That to me was a great relief. I started getting better and better. The only two times I felt good playing in the master class were toward the end of my four years. I think Starker decided then that I wasn't such a bad cellist after all. He finally gave me a compliment and did not criticize anything I had done. In one performance I played the Chopin *Sonata*, second movement, and he was really very complimentary. He just did not have very much to say. That in itself was a very big compliment. After the class other cellists told me how well I played. The other time I played an encore piece, *Figaro* by Mario Castelnuovo-Tedesco. It is technically a very difficult piece, and the left hand is all over the place. I experienced a great deal of relief when he said, 'That is a very fine performance.' Other than that, I can count the compliments on the fingers of one hand."

"It was very hard to please him. That was good because the highest standards were used at all times. There was nothing that was left undiscussed. When I came out from a lesson or master class, I knew what the highest standards were. It is these standards that eventually got his cellists the good jobs. So when I auditioned for the assistant principal position with Berlin Radio Orchestra, I was prepared. That was my first big orchestra job. I was very fortunate to be able to play with a fine orchestra for five years. I moved on to a teaching position at the University in Florida in Jacksonville, then Wichita State University in Kansas. Then I came to Los Angeles to do a doctorate degree at U.S.C. I stayed on to work as a studio recording musician, to play a lot of chamber music and teach.

"In the lessons I was very attentive to everything he said. I took notes after the lessons and tried to apply what he had verbalized so well to me about cello technique. I have always felt that his teaching was just the right thing for me, and I paid utmost attention to his directions. If he said something, I would not dismiss it. I would put the utmost importance on it and really try to accomplish it.

"I wanted to try to please him as well. He was such a difficult man at the time that I studied with him. Perhaps he was going through a difficult time himself. That was in the early seventies. Students sometimes felt that he would take out his frustrations on them. At that time in his career, he was very hard on his students and would tell them right to their faces how boring or unimaginative their playing was. In fact, that was the time in Starker's life when things were going very well. He was immensely busy and successful. Perhaps these factors led to his seeming impatience. His humor back then was rather sarcastic and, in Sebastian's opinion, not always supportive.

"He told one woman that she should take all of her clothes off and practice naked in front of a mirror. Of course, she was very embarrassed. Sometimes he made sexual comments in the master classes. Perhaps his favorite was about two porcupines who make love very carefully, describing those who play very gingerly. When you are playing for the class, you feel very naked and exposed anyway, totally defenseless.

"His playing was just brilliant. His master classes were always so exciting. You could hear him at his best in the master classes. He really loosened up. But in the master classes I was very nervous and did not play my best. What I felt was always very humble, very intimidated as well. That hung together with my own shortcomings. I was a young guy, nineteen when I came to this country from Germany. I really wanted to please him in the lessons. Sometimes we would have such a good time together. I felt that in every lesson I was gaining so much more in terms of my progress that I was very excited about it. With regard to repertoire, I was very glad because I was able to learn about many pieces that I had never heard about.

"In the lessons and seminars, he is able to verbalize so well. I have always had the feeling that no other teacher could do it as well as he. I remember word for word many things he told me, and it stuck somehow. Toward the end of my studies, we became quite good friends. Now, whenever I see him, he is incredibly nice to me."

Sebastian first met his wife, Norma, at Indiana University where she was studying piano. Norma tells, "At the end of every semester, each student had to play for a jury. There in the studio were Mr. Starker, Mr. Gingold and various other people. Students were waiting their turn in the hall. I came in and accompanied a violinist in her jury. We played a movement from a Brahms *Violin Sonata*. The violinist was a sophomore at the university. For a moment there was some murmuring among the judges about hearing an unaccompanied violin piece. That meant that I could leave. Then Starker said in a cynical voice, 'Unless the pianist would like to stay and decorate the room with her red face.' With that, I was thoroughly embarrassed and slunk out of the room. I was very happy to get out of there."

Then Sebastian and Norma met again at Starker's fifty-sixth birthday celebration in Germany in 1980. Said Norma, "He had invited twelve of his former students living in Europe at the time to come to a villa near Essen to his party. My sister was one of the twelve cellists, so I went along. The villa was a beautiful place up on a hill with a big park. The students were staying in pensions nearby. They got together to play the Jean Francaix *Aubade* for twelve celli. That was the birthday present for Starker. Then Maria Kriegel had a gathering at her house." Said Sebastian, "The second day I met Norma, I was madly in love with her. I had one weekend to convince her to come with me to Berlin. We were married two months later."

The second day of the party, Starker was always asking, "Where are they? What are they doing? Are they upstairs?" He was checking up on Sebastian and Norma. For Sebastian and Norma, that was a birthday party to remember!

Conversations with Daniel Rothmuller

"Fritz Magg was my *cello father* and Starker was my *cello uncle*," reminisced Danny Rothmuller as he talked about his years "growing up in Bloomington as a faculty brat." Danny was a typical second generation American whose immigrant parents had moved from Zagreb, Croatia. Once situated in Indiana, his father joined the voice faculty in the School of Music at Indiana University in Bloomington. He was well-known as an opera singer with an impressive career that included concert stages from Zurich to London. For thirteen years he sang with Zurich Opera, and he was famous in England where he sang in Covent Garden and Glyneborne Opera. "I was a young teenager when faculty members would come to our house for dinner. My mother would prepare beautiful parties. She was a great hostess," he said. It was no mystery then that Danny grew up surrounded by vocal repertoire which later became a major influence on his playing style.

More than anything else, Danny really loved playing the contrabass and chose a "vocal approach" to playing. He particularly enjoyed playing when his family had dinner guests and played cello repertoire on the bass with his father accompanying him at the piano. He even achieved celebrity-like status in high school when he was invited to play with the contrabass section in the Indiana University Philharmonic.

Once they had moved to Bloomington and they had their own home, Danny's dad took up carpentry in the most enthusiastic way. He discovered woodworking, making furniture, doing repairs, etc. In Zagreb that kind of activity was rare. Before moving to Indiana, he was a typical European and was lost around tools. Europeans usually hired out carpentry jobs in their homes.

One night Starker was in the Rothmuller home for dinner. Starker, knowing that Danny's father was an avid carpenter, said to him, "You should really take a hatchet to that bass." Danny was putting his bass away when he overheard this remark. He was truly devastated! He ran up to his room and cried for about twenty minutes. He could not believe it! He thought, "I didn't think I played that badly. In fact, I thought I played the bass really well. But then I hear one of the most famous cellists in the world say to take a hatchet to my bass."

The next day his parents sensed that something was wrong. It was then that they explained to Danny that what he did not hear was that Starker said he should "take a hatchet to the bass and make a cello out of it." Danny played the bass so beautifully and in such a cellistic way that Starker felt that the cello would suit him better than the bass. Starker thought that Danny would be happier in his life as a cellist. "Thank God," thought Danny. "That trauma lasted only twenty-four hours."

But he was saddened to hear this news because he did not want to play the cello. Playing the bass was second nature to him. He could hear well in the lower register, had good intonation, his vibrato and tone were well blended, and he could read anything. Moreover, he never got nervous. He "had it all" as a contrabass player. But his dad said, "If Starker says you should try the cello, then you will try the cello."

Danny was very resistant. He felt comfortable with the bass and was very happy and successful doing it. Doing something new, he knew he would have to "work his buns off," especially starting as a beginner to get to the level he had achieved on the bass. But he did his best and entered the university as a freshman cello major the following year.

In his audition for the string faculty, which included conductor Tibor Kozma, Danny said, "I probably lost ten pounds before the audition from worry and five pounds in sweat alone during the fifteen minute audition. The cello was a very difficult instrument compared to the bass." But soon Danny was completely immersed in playing the cello and was loving it. Starker was responsible for that.

Due to Starker's long absences on concert tours, they chose Fritz Magg for his teacher whom he saw for a weekly lesson. Magg was for Danny the perfect choice, and a wonderful teacher he was! Under Magg's watchful eye, Danny went through Klengel and Romburg's music, two Dotzauer books in a month, scales etc. When Magg was on sabbatical or not available, Danny studied with Starker and attended his weekly seminars during all of his student years. Starker and Magg were always very good friends and cooperative colleagues.

In 1961 Danny asked Starker and Magg to help him choose a new cello—other than one of those "factory jobs." The choices were narrowed down to two cellos. One was a very old cello with a gargoyle for the scroll. This was valued at $350. The other was valued at $700. It was an old Italian cello that today would be worth about $50,000. Both Starker and Magg came to the Rothmuller home to try out the cellos. The price to them, of course, was dinner. So after dinner they took the cellos out. "At one point they started playing the *Prelude* to the *C Major Suite* of Bach. As they started out, they were playing in unison. Then one would lay out for a measure, and the other would play the next measure. They were alternating measures with each other. Then they alternated half measures. Then they alternated beats. I don't know too many cellists who could do this. It took more than just concentration but rather a total mastery of the music.

They could have done this with probably any of the six Bach *Suites*. They were both such masters! It was a remarkable phenomenon. It was frightening for me to think about how much I *didn't* know and how much they *did* know."

When Danny studied with Starker, he had already been playing the cello four years. During that time he worked on Popper *Etudes*, the Prokofiev *Sonata*, Brahms' *E Minor Sonata* and the Kodály *Solo Sonata*. One day he was waiting outside Starker's studio before a lesson on the Kodály *Solo Sonata*. To this day, there are still sweat marks on the music! Danny says, "I had no idea how difficult the piece would be." He was not particularly industrious at practicing and was resting on the honeymoon of his first day of working on the first movement, thinking, "Wow, this is great!" The scordatura tuning did not bother him one bit since he did not have perfect pitch. He just used the right fingerings and everything was just fine, not having to transpose a thing. He also had Starker's fingerings which required the transposition of only a few notes while Kodály's fingerings are predicated on the cellist knowing what pitches Kodály wanted. One could finger passages in different ways.

"During the lesson I was really nervous," says Danny. "The first movement went better than I expected. Starker was sitting in his desk chair listening. He would very often not use his own cello but would borrow mine. He grabbed my cello, quickly accommodated his body to the instrument, not adjusting the end pin or anything, and just started playing. In the lesson he gave me something of a survey of the piece. Starker knew me inside and out and realized from the moment I walked in the room that I did not have this piece prepared for him. But, for some reason, he was never impatient with me. Usually the closer you are to someone the more impatient you become. But this was not true with him. Among all of the sarcasms he is famous for, I never experienced any of them. Some people just got under his skin and inspired all kinds of sarcastic remarks. But with me he was as patient as a saint. Even though I waited for the ax to fall, it never did."

"This particular day he rattled off something about, 'Just don't look at my second finger.' Then he started playing some of the runs in the last movement of the piece just to show me the elbow action, anticipating shifts, and such. After a while I was not listening to anything, just watching him in amazement, thinking, 'How can anybody do that? I don't care how well he knows the piece, how can he do that?' He had apparently injured his second finger, and simply played the last movement, a movement of amazing speed and flying fingers, with the other three fingers while simultaneously refingering major passages. And of all fingers, that one! In attempting the same feat, I have concluded that I do not have the mental capacity. My fingers would get tangled up even trying to do the most familiar runs. To me it seemed like a miracle. I just could not stop telling people about it. He is one of the few who is so intellectually in control, that he has that potential. To this day I am still astounded.

"One time I was attending one of Starker's Saturday seminars up on the fourth floor in the music building. He was sitting in a cloud of smoke, listening to a graduate student trio, a threesome who were about to perform Tchaikovsky's *Piano Trio* for a doctoral recital. They finished the first movement. After a long silence they heard, 'So when are you performing this piece?' The pianist hesitantly said, 'Next Tuesday.' There is an even longer silence. By this time everyone in the room is ice cold. No one wants to be there. No one wants to hear what is going to happen next. In his inimitable way, as the smoke cleared, Starker said with a smile on his face, 'You know, this is like going into a bachelor's apartment and trying to clean up the entire place by taking one sock out of the sink.' It was an inoffensive way to let them know that it was too little and too late. These were three not particularly stellar players, although doctoral students. They were not the seat-of-the-pants kind of people. In Bloomington there were some, even undergraduates, who were capable of putting together a program like this in a few days. These three, however, would require a month to prepare this trio. They did not have the technique nor the musical instinct. They would have had to learn it from scratch. You could see the pain in Starker's face. He seldom shows emotion outwardly. You don't know what he is thinking. But this situation was beyond help.

"So he did a few general things. He said to the pianist, 'Why is your wallet on the piano?' To this the poor pianist replied, 'It just does not feel comfortable when I play with the wallet in my pocket.' Starker said, 'Just put the wallet in your pocket, and try it again.' It really had nothing to do with the wallet at all. He would just do anything to just create a different world for them. He was very clever in how he could get your mind off of yourself or away from what you thought you were doing or what you thought was important and focused in another direction, into a more objective state. He would disturb people this way and direct their minds. I was surprised at how gently he did this. But after a while they played a hell of a lot better. In retrospect, I think he recommended they play only the first movement for the recital, either that or postpone it.

"Speaking of pointing one's mind in another direction, I was about to perform the Saint Saëns *Cello Concerto in A Minor* with the University Philharmonic. Starker was standing back stage with me. It was one of the few times he was going to conduct an orchestra. I was the soloist. I was nervous beyond belief, sweating buckets! Just as we were about to go on stage, Starker grabbed me by the back of my pants at the waist, gave a tug, and shoved my shirt back in. That completely took my mind off of myself and my nervousness. We walked on stage and did a job on that piece!

"As a student I was jobbing along with many other students in the Evansville Philharmonic. We would go there for a couple of days, staying overnight in some rat-infested hotel. But we didn't care. Starker had just arrived for the rehearsal after driving himself, alone, from Bloomington. He got out of the car, took the cello out of the case, walked on stage, and played flawlessly the entire Schumann *Concerto*. He explained to me later that you can prepare to play when you do not have a cello in your hands. You can prepare your fingers, doing little exercises in getting ready to play. You don't have to sit there for twenty minutes with cello in hand and warm up, as long as you are already generally warmed up. Maybe warming up on the instrument is more for your reflexes than for your muscles. Use your fingers, not doing strenuous things, just get the blood flowing. Do some Cossmann Exercises in a narrow position. Whenever you see Starker play, you can see that his hand is not extended. It looks constantly very compact, no matter what he is doing. In discussing this with his teacher, Fritz Magg replied, "It is very good that you observe. This way you learn what to do and what not to do. With Starker, observing is such a learning experience because he exhibits so well how to use your body. No effort is wasted."

Says Danny, "All of my good cellistic habits come from my three teachers including Magg, Starker, and Piatigorsky. They each approach the instrument completely differently from a physical standpoint. But they all have had this in common, economy of motion and getting unbelievable results. They each had very efficient ways of producing their own personal result, each with his own style, perhaps one more flamboyant than another. All of the great virtuoso players who lived into their seventies were performing into their seventies. They all looked different, but they were all doing it correctly. I just heard Starker perform in Japan, and I can attest to the fact that he plays as well now at seventy-three years old as he ever has."

Danny is associate principal cellist with the Los Angeles Philharmonic and has played with the orchestra since 1970.

Conversations with Tsuyoshi Tsutsumi

Tsuyoshi Tsutsumi is Professor of Music at Indiana University and former first prize winner in the Rostropovich Competition. This is the story of his first encounter with Professor Starker:

"The first time I met him was in December of 1960 in Tokyo, Japan. Starker was on his first concert tour to Japan with Professor Sebök, pianist. His fame preceded him in Japan because of his numerous recordings. I was told later that it was Professor and Mrs. Starker's honeymoon trip as well.

"At that time I had already won a Fullbright Grant to do college level study in the United States. I did not know much about music schools in the United States, so I was undecided. At one of his recitals in Tokyo, Starker played as an encore the third movement of the Kodály *Solo Sonata*. Hearing it was a shock to me. It was so impressive and unusual! My teacher, Professor H. Saito was also greatly impressed with Professor Starker's playing. After the concert he went to talk with Professor Starker about me. He discovered in their conversation that they both had the same idea about Saito's former teacher in Berlin, Emmanuel Feuermann. They believed that Feuermann had been the greatest cellist ever and that they had a responsibility to preserve and promote what Feuermann had accomplished and taught.

"So the next day my mother and I visited Professor Starker in his hotel room in Tokyo so that I could play for him. I vividly remember how extremely nervous and tense I was as I played the Dvorák *Concerto* for him. I neither spoke nor understood English very well. Perhaps I was able to comprehend only half of what he said to me. As far as I could understand, he said, 'I will be happy to have you in my class next fall. Please get in touch with Dean Bain at Indiana University School of Music and make arrangements to be enrolled in the fall. As far as your cello playing is concerned, I shall try to add to what you already know.' I had the feeling that at that moment, he was developing in his mind his teaching plan for me.

"Arriving at the Bloomington airport was a real shock for me! From the airplane, for many miles in all directions all I could see were cornfields! I came from the biggest city in the world. In Tokyo I attended a specialized high school with special emphasis on music training, Toho Gukuen High School of Music. I just could not imagine Professor Starker teaching in the middle of the cornfields.

"It was quite a change of environment coming to a big university with different schools and departments and with students in all different fields, not just music. The only person on this huge campus I knew was Professor Starker. In addition I had the added difficulty with the language. It took easily a year before I was somewhat comfortable with English. I always brought a pencil and note pad to my lessons, not wanting to miss anything he told me. Also, there were many words I needed to look up in the dictionary after the lessons. I think he was rather bemused seeing me always writing things down. One day with his usual serious face he said, 'I must point out to you three important things in order to become a really fine cellist.' Naturally, I was ready to write them down. He continued, 'First, one should be able to drink a lot; Second, one should be able to smoke a lot; Third, one should be a good ping-pong player!' Of course I took all of this very seriously. I thought I must have heard him wrong. It took me several years to figure out this was a joke!!

"At my lessons I played the cello for about a quarter of an hour. The rest of the hour was spent talking. He insisted that I should be able to explain clearly what I was doing so that I had a clear understanding of everything he was teaching me. It was very painful for me, especially at first. However, I realize now how valuable that was for me. He was a very strict teacher, particularly with respect to aspects of technical control and true professionalism. He repeatedly emphasized that one should be able to handle the cello with perfect control and absolute ease in order to truly express oneself. I learned so much from him. Things that I learned from him are so valuable pedagogically and artistically that I apply them daily in my performing and teaching."

50. Starker, Janos, *Roll Call of the Blessed Ones*, illustrations by Jorge Sicre, Dorrance Pub. Co., Inc., Pittsburgh, PA, 15222

Closing

Starker's personal attitudes toward music, musicians, and the people around musical life derive in part from his wartime experiences. "Nothing worse could possibly happen to me than what has already happened in my life," he says. As a result, he is not afraid of anyone. And if he believes in something, due to his personal experiences as a young man, he will not let anyone influence him.

But his wartime experiences have nothing to do with his musicianship. His experiences being bombed as a youth have nothing to do with the way he plays Bach. Rather, his musicianship is due to his learning experiences with Leo Weiner and Adolph Schiffer, the influences of Bartók, Dohnanyi, Kodály, and indirectly David Popper, hearing performances by Casals, Feuermann, and Heifetz, and, lastly, the nine years he spent with Fritz Reiner. Credit must also be given to his mother, how she helped him to develop good practice habits early on.

Starker never went out of his way to write to, speak with, or call other musicians. He was always a very private person and placed great value on his own privacy. Perhaps this was the result of his Hungarian upbringing. He assumed that other musicians were as protective of their privacy. Because of this he offended some who believed that he did not contact them because he considers himself so much better. That had nothing to do with reality. He simply respected their privacy. As a result, he missed out on performing with many people whom he greatly admired. They may have figured that Starker did not "give a damn about them." He avoided making associations because he wanted no one to believe that he was friendly in order to get an engagement. Perhaps he did everything wrong socially; he did not associate with people for business reasons just because they happen to be famous or successful, and he did not live in New York City where many of the rich and famous congregate. He never asked anyone for an engagement, and he never allowed anyone to do something for him unless it was hiring his services. Perhaps it is because of this aspect of his personality that in his lifetime his name did not "become a household word."

JANOS STARKER, VICTOR AITAY, GYÖRGY SEBÖK

Starker has been very outspoken, sometimes in ways that were harmful to his career. His first wife, Eva, has said that some people cannot handle his kind of criticism. Being openly critical of major orchestras and conductors did not endear himself to them, even though he felt that he was only stating the truth. In fact, at times his friends have told him, "You made a career in spite of yourself."

Otherwise he achieved everything that he could dream of including wife, children, grand-children, wealth, comfort, and a fabulously successful career. He worked very hard during his life, but he never had to "work for a living." He never asked for anyone's help. Says Starker, "I know who I am and what I have done, not because of having played better than anyone else or played more concerts, but rather because of the cumulative effect of my work. I know of no one else who has led the kind of life I have had. This was not the result of being someone special but rather because of the conditions, the circumstances under which I grew up, which I survived. Because of these things, I have had the dedication and the determination to do the things I have accomplished. Everything I have gained and achieved in my life has been done with my head and my hands."

In the realm of cello playing, Starker has been the greatest influence of any cellist in history. From a very early age, he knew what he wanted to do with his life, to play the cello as well as it can be played and to help others toward the same end. For seven decades he steadily pursued his goals and was seemingly never sidetracked. Although the war delayed the start of his career, he was still very young when he became principal cellist of the Budapest Opera, his first official job in a long career. It is fortunate for the world of cello playing that during the war neither the Nazi exterminators, the Russian military men, the American bombers, or the starvation condi-tions prevailed against him. When so many died, he lived. Perhaps the war experience, followed by his "playing like a sleepwalker," was just the right catalyst to bring him to become very analytical in his approach to cello playing and subsequently teaching.

As a seventeen-year-old, a Hungarian countess, Baroness Wenckheim, approached Starker's parents offering to take him to London for the sake of his musical education. She suggested that she adopt Starker and take him to England where some of her extended family lived. Had that happened, his life would have undoubtedly unfolded in different ways. One would wonder what would have been the course of his life had he grown up in London with ample means. Perhaps living in Budapest and having to make his way in the world early on through most difficult circumstances, he became significantly more independent and strong-willed in the direction of his life.

At any rate, he has profoundly in-fluenced thousands of young cellists, not to mention millions of listeners with his peerless recordings, perform-ances, and cello seminars. His aesthetic is on the highest level with zero toler-ance for himself and others for any-thing less than excellence. Janos Starker has set the standard, a tireless master demanding only the best, to which the rest of us aspire. For him there are no excuses. By his own exam-ple he is an inspiration to us all.

JANOS STARKER, VICTOR AITAY, GYÖRGY SEBÖK

Coda

My countryman George Mikes wrote of his discovery that the whole world was Siklos: the little town, district, city, country, and continent that one comes from. As he discovered each of these ever enlarging domains, he became a "foreigner," a white man as opposed to other colors, until it dawned on him eventually that he was ultimately a Human Being.

What then of me, told at age twelve that I was stateless—a foreigner in the country of my birth? At age seventeen I had to flee from home in order to escape deportation from the country of my birth? And was reminded, after four years of relentless persecution as a Jew, as a foreigner, as an enemy, that my duty was to help restore the culture of the country of my birth?

After two years of fighting for permits to stay in more civilized countries to the West, I reached the Land of Promise, and yet remained blacklisted in the country of my birth, at a cost to my parents still too vivid to share. And then, slowly, I was claimed to be a "son" to be proud of by countries and religions whose bonds caused nothing but suffering.

No, for me the order was different than for Mikes. First came the discovery that I am a Human Being, then the realization that I am from somewhere I have never been. Just let me be the musician who tries to do the job for which I am qualified. Do not expect me to be like others who belong, and always belonged. Let the record decide if I fulfilled my destiny. From wherever.

Janos Starker, Bloomington, 1980

Appendix

Starker's Recordings, Bibliography, Chronology of Events, About the Author, Index

STARKER'S RECORDINGS (available on amazon.com)

Listeners' favorites among Starker's Recordings:

Janos Starker Concerto Collection
  C.P.E. Bach, Boccherini, Vivaldi

Romantic Cello Favorites
  David Popper; recorded with Shigeo Neriki, piano

The Road to Cello Playing
  Etudes by Sebastian Lee, Karl Schroeder, Dotzauer, Duport, Piatti, Popper,
  Gruetzmacher and Paganini

Starker's Encore Album
  Bach, Haydn-Piatigorsky, Saint Saëns, Schubert, Bloch. Popper, Frescobaldi,
  Schumann, Weber-Piatigorsky, Bartók

Janos Starker, Virtuoso Music for Cello
  Händel, Paganini, Fauré

Janos Starker, Bach Suites for Solo Cello

Janos Starker, Bach Six Suites and Sonatas

Starker Plays Kodály
  op. 4 cello-piano, op. 7 violin-cello, op. 8 solo cello

Romantic Cello
  Tchaikovsky, Elgar, Delius

Italian Cello Sonatas
  Boccherini, Vivaldi, Corelli

Janos Starker
  Chopin, Mendelssohn, Martinu

Peter Menin, Symphony 5 and 6, Cello Concerto
  with Janos Starker

Janos Starker
  Brahms and Mendelssohn Sonatas; György Sebök, piano

David Diamond, Symphony no. 3, Psalm, Kaddish
    Gerard Schwarz, cond; Janos Starker, cellist

Alan Hovaness, Symphony 22 (City of Light), Cello Concerto
    Dennis Russell Davies, cond., Seattle Symphony; Janos Starker, cello

Janos Starker, Dvorák Cello Concerto, Tchaikovsky Rococo Variations

Complete Chamber Music of Brahms

Great Moments in Cello Playing
    Emmanuel Moor, Haydn & Popper

Brazil '88, "A Brazilian Music Extravaganza"
    Prokofiev, Bartók, Tchaikovsky

Engineer's Choice
    Shostakovich, David Schiff, Deems Taylor

Essential Bach
    Seiji Ozawa, Neville Mariner, Janos Starker

Cello for Relaxation
    Saint Saëns, Bruch, Fauré

Haydn Symphony 21 & 96, Cello Concerto in C Major
    Gerard Schwarz, cond., Seattle Symphony; Janos Starker, cellist

Haydn Symphony 61 & 103, Cello Concerto in D Major
    Gerard Schwarz, cond., Seattle Symphony; Janos Starker, cellist

Romance Classics
    Schumann, Rachmaninoff & Grieg

Janos Starker, Cello
    Shostakovich, Haydn & Bach

Leo Weiner Album

Janos Starker
    Boccherini, Fauré, Dvorák

Walton and Elgar Cello Concertos

STARKER'S RECORDINGS (available on iTunes)

Goyescas: Intermezzo, Janos Starker: Virtuoso Music for Cello, Janos Starker

The Barber of Seville: Figaro, Janos Starker: Virtuoso Music for Cello, Janos Starker

Abendlied, Starker Encore Album, Janos Starker

Adagio and Rondo, Starker Encore Album, Janos Starker

Amor Brujo: Ritual Fire Dance, The Romantic Music of Spain, Janos Starker

Andaluza: The Romantic Music of Spain, Janos Starker

Apres un Reve, Janos Starker: Virtuoso Music for Cello, Janos Starker

Apres un Reve, Op. 7 No. 1, Cello Essentials, Janos Starker

Arioso, Cello Essentials, Janos Starker

Arioso, More Bedtime Serenades, Janos Starker

Arioso, Starker Encore Album, Janos Starker

Cantata No. 156, "Ich Steh Mit Einem Fuss Im Grabe," BWV 156: II. Aria Con Choral, More Classics for Yoga, Janos Starker & Shuku Iwasaki

Cello Concerto in E-Flat, K. 285: I. Allegro, The Legendary Period LP's (The music of Mozart, Boccherini, Kodaly and Bartok), Janos Starker & Maximilian Pilzer

Cello Concerto in E-Flat, K. 285: II. Romance (Larghetto), The Legendary Period LP's (The music of Mozart, Boccherini, Kodaly and Bartok), Janos Starker & Maximilian Pilzer

Cello Concerto in E-Flat, K. 285: III. Allegro, The Legendary Period LP's (The music of Mozart, Boccherini, Kodaly and Bartok), Janos Starker & Maximilian Pilzer

Cello Concerto in A Minor, Op.129: 1. Nicht Zu Schnell, Schumann, Lalo & Saint-Saëns: Cello Concertos, Janos Starker, London Symphony Orchestra & Stanislaw Skrowaczewski

Cello Concerto in A Minor, Op.129: 2. Langsam, Schumann, Lalo & Saint-Saëns: Cello Concertos, Janos Starker, London Symphony Orchestra & Stanislaw Skrowaczewski

Cello Concerto in A Minor, Op.129: 3. Sehr Lebhaft, Schumann, Lalo & Saint-Saëns: Cello Concertos, Janos Starker, London Symphony Orchestra & Stanislaw Skrowaczewski

Cello Concerto in B-Flat, G. 483: I. Allegro moderato, The Legendary Period LP's (The music of Mozart, Boccherini, Kodaly and Bartok), Janos Starker

Cello Concerto in B-Flat, G. 483: II. Andantino grazioso, The Legendary Period LP's (The music of Mozart, Boccherini, Kodaly and Bartok), Janos Starker

Cello Concerto in B-Flat, G. 483: III. Rondo:Allegro, The Legendary Period LP's (The music of Mozart, Boccherini, Kodaly and Bartok), Janos Starker

Cello Concerto in B Minor, Op.104: 1. Allegro, Dvorak: Cello Concerto, Bruch: Kol Nidrei & Tchaikovsky: Variations On a Rococo Theme, Antal Dorati, Janos Starker & London Symphony Orchestra

Cello Concerto in B minor, Op.104: 2. Adagio ma non troppo, Cello Adagios (2 CDs), Antal Dorati, Janos Starker & London Symphony Orchestra

Cello Concerto in B Minor, Op.104: 2. Adagio Ma Non Troppo, Dvorak: Cello Concerto, Bruch: Kol Nidrei & Tchaikovsky: Variations On a Rococo Theme, Antal Dorati, Janos Starker & London Symphony Orchestra

Cello Concerto in B Minor, Op.104: 3. Finale (Allegro Moderato), Dvorak: Cello Concerto, Bruch: Kol Nidrei & Tchaikovsky: Variations On a Rococo Theme, Antal Dorati, Janos Starker & London Symphony Orchestra

Cello Concerto in D Minor: 1. Prélude: Lento - Allegro Maestoso, Schumann, Lalo & Saint-Saëns: Cello Concertos, Janos Starker, London Symphony Orchestra & Stanislaw Skrowaczewski

Cello Concerto in D Minor: 2. Intermezzo: Andantino Con Moto - Allegro Presto, Schumann, Lalo & Saint-Saëns: Cello Concertos, Janos Starker, London Symphony Orchestra & Stanislaw Skrowaczewski

Cello Concerto in D Minor: 3. Andante - Allegro Vivace, Schumann, Lalo & Saint-Saëns: Cello Concertos, Janos Starker, London Symphony Orchestra & Stanislaw Skrowaczewski

Cello Concerto No. 1 in A Minor, Op. 33: I. Allegro non troppo, Janos Starker: Perspectives, Antal Dorati, Janos Starker & London Symphony Orchestra

Cello Concerto No. 1 in A Minor, Op. 33: II. Allegretto con moto, Janos Starker: Perspectives, Antal Dorati, Janos Starker & London Symphony Orchestra

Cello Concerto No. 1 in A Minor, Op. 33: III. Un peu moins vite, Janos Starker: Perspectives, Antal Dorati, Janos Starker & London Symphony Orchestra

Cello Concerto No.1 in A Minor, Op.33: 1. Allegro Non Troppo, Schumann, Lalo & Saint-Saëns: Cello Concertos, Antal Dorati, Janos Starker & London Symphony Orchestra

Cello Concerto No.1 in A Minor, Op.33: 2. Allegretto Con Moto, Schumann, Lalo & Saint-Saëns: Cello Concertos, Antal Dorati, Janos Starker & London Symphony Orchestra

Cello Concerto No.1 in A Minor, Op.33: 3. Un Peu Moins Vite, Schumann, Lalo & Saint-Saëns: Cello Concertos, Antal Dorati, Janos Starker & London Symphony Orchestra

Christmas Oratorio: Part I: Grosser Herr Und Starker Konig, J.S. Bach: Christmas Oratorio (Highlights), J.S. Bach

Concerto for Piano, Violin, and Cello in C, Op. 56: II. Largo, Beethoven Adagios, Claudio Arrau, Eliahu Inbal, Henryk Szeryng, Janos Starker & New Philharmonia Orchestra

Dance of the Green Devil: The Romantic Music of Spain, Janos Starker

Danse Rituelle Du Feu, Janos Starker: Virtuoso Music for Cello, Janos Starker

Divertiment in D Major, Starker Encore Album, Janos Starker

Dreaming, The Ultimate Most Relaxing Classics for Kids In the Universe, Janos Starker

El Amor Brujo: Ritual Fire Dance, Cello Essentials, Janos Starker

Elfentanz, Op. 39, Popper: Romantic Cello Favorites, Janos Starker & Shigeo Neriki

Fandanguillo: The Romantic Music of Spain, Janos Starker

Gavotte No. 2 in D Major, Op. 23, Popper: Romantic Cello Favorites, Janos Starker & Shigeo Neriki

Gnomentanz (Dance of the Gnomes), Popper: Romantic Cello Favorites, Janos Starker & Shigeo Neriki

Goyescas: Intermezzo, The Romantic Music of Spain, Janos Starker

Grave, from the Style of W.F. Bach, Starker Encore Album, Janos Starker

Hungarian Rhapsodie, Op. 68, Janos Starker: Virtuoso Music for Cello, Janos Starker

Hungarian Rhapsody, Op. 68, Cello Essentials, Janos Starker

Hungarian Wedding Dance (Lakodalmas) - version for Cello and Piano, Janos Starker: Perspectives, György Sebök & Janos Starker

Kinderszenen Op. 15, No 7: Trumerei, Cello Essentials, Janos Starker

Kol Nidrei, Op.47 - Adagio On Hebrew Melodies for Cello and Orchestra (Adagio Ma Non Troppo), Dvorak: Cello Concerto, Bruch: Kol Nidrei & Tchaikovsky: Variations On a Rococo Theme, Antal Dorati, Janos Starker & London Symphony Orchestra

La Fille Aux Cheveux De Lin, Janos Starker: Virtuoso Music for Cello, Janos Starker

Malaguena: The Romantic Music of Spain, Janos Starker

Moment Musical No. 3, Starker Encore Album, Janos Starker

Piano Trio No. 1 in B, Op. 8: I. Allegro con brio, Brahms: Piano Trios Nos. 1 & 2, Josef Suk, Julius Katchen & Janos Starker

Piano Trio No. 1 in B, Op. 8: II. Scherzo (Allegro molto), Brahms: Piano Trios Nos. 1 & 2, Josef Suk, Julius Katchen & Janos Starker

Piano Trio No. 1 in B, Op. 8: III. Adagio, Brahms: Piano Trios Nos. 1 & 2, Josef Suk, Julius Katchen & Janos Starker

Piano Trio No. 1 in B, Op. 8: IV. Allegro, Brahms: Piano Trios Nos. 1 & 2, Josef Suk, Julius Katchen & Janos Starker

Piece En Forme De Habanera, Janos Starker: Virtuoso Music for Cello, Janos Starker

Prayer, Starker Encore Album, Janos Starker

Prayer, The Ultimate Most Relaxing Sacred Music in the Universe, Janos Starker

Requiebros: The Romantic Music of Spain, Janos Starker

Rumanian Folk Dances, Cello Essentials, Janos Starker

Rumanian Folk Dances, Starker Encore Album, Janos Starker

Sicilienne, Janos Starker: Virtuoso Music for Cello, Janos Starker

Sonata for Cello and Continuo No. 3 in G minor, BWV 1029: 2., Cello Adagios (2 CDs), György Sebök & Janos Starker

Sonata for Cello and Continuo No.3 In G Minor, BWV 1029: 2. Adagio, Baroque Adagios, György Sebök & Janos Starker

Sonata for Cello and Continuo No.3 In G Minor, BWV 1029: 2. Adagio, Essential Bach, György Sebök & Janos Starker

Sonata for Cello and Continuo No.3 In G Minor, BWV 1029: 2. Adagio, Movie Adagios, György Sebök & Janos Starker

Sonata for Cello and Piano in D Minor: I. Prologue (lent), Janos Starker: Perspectives, György Sebök & Janos Starker

Sonata for Cello and Piano in D Minor: II. Sérénade (Modérément animé), Janos Starker: Perspectives, György Sebök & Janos Starker

Sonata for Cello and Piano in D Minor: III. Finale (Animé), Janos Starker: Perspectives, György Sebök & Janos Starker

Sonata for Cello and Piano No. 2 in F, Op. 99: I. Allegro vivace, Janos Starker: Perspectives, György Sebök & Janos Starker

Sonata for Cello and Piano No. 2 in F, Op. 99: II. Adagio affettuoso, Janos Starker: Perspectives, György Sebök & Janos Starker

Sonata for Cello and Piano No. 2 in F, Op. 99: III. Allegro appassionata, Janos Starker: Perspectives, György Sebök & Janos Starker

Sonata for Cello and Piano No. 2 in F, Op. 99: IV. Allegro molto, Janos Starker: Perspectives, György Sebök & Janos Starker

Sonata for Cello and Piano, Op. 4 - "Fantasie": I. Adagio di molto, The Legendary Period LP's (The music of Mozart, Boccherini, Kodaly and Bartok), Janos Starker & Otto Herz

Sonata for Cello and Piano, Op. 4 - "Fantasie": II. Allegro con spirito, The Legendary Period LP's (The music of Mozart, Boccherini, Kodaly and Bartok), Janos Starker & Otto Herz

Sonata for Unaccompanied Cello, Op. 8: I. Allegro maestoso ma appassionato, The Legendary Period LP's (The music of Mozart, Boccherini, Kodaly and Bartok), Janos Starker

Sonata for Unaccompanied Cello, Op. 8: II. Adagio (con gran espressione), The Legendary Period LP's (The music of Mozart, Boccherini, Kodaly and Bartok), Janos Starker

Sonata for Unaccompanied Cello, Op. 8: III. Allegro molto vivace, The Legendary Period LP's (The music of Mozart, Boccherini, Kodaly and Bartok), Janos Starker

Sonata for Viola Da Gamba and Harpsichord No. 1 in G, BWV 1027: I. Adagio, Bach, J.S.: Suites for Solo Cello & 2 Cello Sonatas, György Sebök & Janos Starker

Sonata for Viola Da Gamba and Harpsichord No. 1 in G, BWV 1027: II. Allegro Ma Non Tanto, Bach, J.S.: Suites for Solo Cello & 2 Cello Sonatas, György Sebök & Janos Starker

Sonata for Viola Da Gamba and Harpsichord No. 1 in G, BWV 1027: III. Andante, Bach, J.S.: Suites for Solo Cello & 2 Cello Sonatas, György Sebök & Janos Starker

Sonata for Viola Da Gamba and Harpsichord No. 1 in G, BWV 1027: IV. Allegro Moderato, Bach, J.S.: Suites for Solo Cello & 2 Cello Sonatas, György Sebök & Janos Starker

Sonata for Viola Da Gamba and Harpsichord No. 2 in D, BWV 1028: I. Adagio, Bach, J.S.: Suites for Solo Cello & 2 Cello Sonatas, György Sebök & Janos Starker

Sonata for Viola Da Gamba and Harpsichord No. 2 in D, BWV 1028: II. Allegro, Bach, J.S.: Suites for Solo Cello & 2 Cello Sonatas, György Sebök & Janos Starker

Sonata for Viola Da Gamba and Harpsichord No. 2 in D, BWV 1028: III. Andante, Bach, J.S.: Suites for Solo Cello & 2 Cello Sonatas, György Sebök & Janos Starker

Sonata for Viola Da Gamba and Harpsichord No. 2 in D, BWV 1028: IV. Allegro, Bach, J.S.: Suites for Solo Cello & 2 Cello Sonatas, György Sebök & Janos Starker

Sonata in D: I. Allegro, Janos Starker: Perspectives, Janos Starker & Stephen Swedish

Sonata in D: II. Adagio, Janos Starker: Perspectives, Janos Starker & Stephen Swedish

Sonata in D: III. Minuetto, Janos Starker: Perspectives, Janos Starker & Stephen Swedish

Sonata, Op. 19 in G Minor: Andante, The Rachmaninoff Collection, Janos Starker & Shigeo Neriki

Suite for Cello Solo No. 1 in G, BWV 1007: 1. Prélude, Essential Bach, Janos Starker

Suite for Cello Solo No. 1 in G, BWV 1007: I. Prélude, Bach, J.S.: Suites for Solo Cello & 2 Cello Sonatas, Janos Starke

Suite for Cello Solo No. 1 in G, BWV 1007: II. Allemande, Bach, J.S.: Suites for Solo Cello & 2 Cello Sonatas, Janos Starker

Suite for Cello Solo No. 1 in G, BWV 1007: III. Courante, Bach, J.S.: Suites for Solo Cello & 2 Cello Sonatas, Janos Starker

Suite for Cello Solo No. 1 in G, BWV 1007: IV. Sarabande, Bach, J.S.: Suites for Solo Cello & 2 Cello Sonatas, Janos Starker

Suite for Cello Solo No. 1 in G, BWV 1007: V. Menuet I-II, Bach, J.S.: Suites for Solo Cello & 2 Cello Sonatas, Janos Starker

Suite for Cello Solo No. 1 In G, BWV 1007: VI. Gigue, Bach, J.S.: Suites for Solo Cello & 2 Cello Sonatas, Janos Starker

Suite for Cello Solo No. 2 In D Minor, BWV 1008: I. Prélude, Bach, J.S.: Suites for Solo Cello & 2 Cello Sonatas, Janos Starker

Suite for Cello Solo No. 2 in D Minor, BWV 1008: II. Allemande, Bach, J.S.: Suites for Solo Cello & 2 Cello Sonatas, Janos Starker

Suite for Cello Solo No. 2 in D Minor, BWV 1008: III. Courante, Bach, J.S.: Suites for Solo Cello & 2 Cello Sonatas, Janos Starker

Suite for Cello Solo No. 2 in D Minor, BWV 1008: IV. Sarabande, Bach, J.S.: Suites for Solo Cello & 2 Cello Sonatas, Janos Starker

Suite for Cello Solo No. 2 in D Minor, BWV 1008: V. Menuet I-II, Bach, J.S.: Suites for Solo Cello & 2 Cello Sonatas, Janos Starker

Suite for Cello Solo No. 2 in D Minor, BWV 1008: VI. Gigue, Bach, J.S.: Suites for Solo Cello & 2 Cello Sonatas, Janos Starker

Suite for Cello Solo No. 3 in C, BWV 1009: I. Prélude, Bach, J.S.: Suites for Solo Cello & 2 Cello Sonatas, Janos Starker

Suite for Cello Solo No. 3 in C, BWV 1009: II. Allemande, Bach, J.S.: Suites for Solo Cello & 2 Cello Sonatas, Janos Starker

Suite for Cello Solo No. 3 in C, BWV 1009: III. Courante, Bach, J.S.: Suites for Solo Cello & 2 Cello Sonatas, Janos Starker

Suite for Cello Solo No. 3 in C, BWV 1009: IV. Sarabande, Bach, J.S.: Suites for Solo Cello & 2 Cello Sonatas, Janos Starker

Suite for Cello Solo No. 3 in C, BWV 1009: V. Bourrée I-II, Bach, J.S.: Suites for Solo Cello & 2 Cello Sonatas, Janos Starker

Suite for Cello Solo No. 3 in C, BWV 1009: VI. Gigue, Bach, J.S.: Suites for Solo Cello & 2 Cello Sonatas, Janos Starker

Suite for Cello Solo No. 4 in E-Flat, BWV 1010: I. Prélude, Bach, J.S.: Suites for Solo Cello & 2 Cello Sonatas, Janos Starker

Suite for Cello Solo No. 4 in E-Flat, BWV 1010: II. Allemande, Bach, J.S.: Suites for Solo Cello & 2 Cello Sonatas, Janos Starker

Suite for Cello Solo No. 4 in E-Flat, BWV 1010: III. Courante, Bach, J.S.: Suites for Solo Cello & 2 Cello Sonatas, Janos Starker

Suite for Cello Solo No. 4 in E-Flat, BWV 1010: IV. Sarabande, Bach, J.S.: Suites for Solo Cello & 2 Cello Sonatas, Janos Starker

Suite for Cello Solo No. 4 in E-Flat, BWV 1010: V. Bourrée I-II, Bach, J.S.: Suites for Solo Cello & 2 Cello Sonatas, Janos Starker

Suite for Cello Solo No. 4 in E-Flat, BWV 1010: VI. Gigue, Bach, J.S.: Suites for Solo Cello & 2 Cello Sonatas, Janos Starker

Suite for Cello Solo No. 5 in C Minor, BWV 1011: I. Prélude, Bach, J.S.: Suites for Solo Cello & 2 Cello Sonatas, Janos Starker

Suite for Cello Solo No. 5 in C Minor, BWV 1011: I. Prélude, Janos Starker: Perspectives, Janos Starker

Suite for Cello Solo No. 5 in C Minor, BWV 1011: II. Allemande, Bach, J.S.: Suites for Solo Cello & 2 Cello Sonatas, Janos Starker

Suite for Cello Solo No. 5 in C Minor, BWV 1011: II. Allemande, Janos Starker: Perspectives, Janos Starker

Suite for Cello Solo No. 5 in C Minor, BWV 1011: III. Courante, Bach, J.S.: Suites for Solo Cello & 2 Cello Sonatas, Janos Starker

Suite for Cello Solo No. 5 in C Minor, BWV 1011: III. Courante, Janos Starker: Perspectives, Janos Starker

Suite for Cello Solo No. 5 in C Minor, BWV 1011: IV. Sarabande, Bach, J.S.: Suites for Solo Cello & 2 Cello Sonatas, Janos Starker

Suite for Cello Solo No. 5 in C Minor, BWV 1011: IV. Sarabande, Janos Starker: Perspectives, Janos Starker

Suite for Cello Solo No. 5 in C Minor, BWV 1011: V. Gavotte I-II, Bach, J.S.: Suites for Solo Cello & 2 Cello Sonatas, Janos Starker

Suite for Cello Solo No. 5 in C Minor, BWV 1011: V. Gavotte I-II, Janos Starker: Perspectives, Janos Starker

Suite for Cello Solo No. 5 in C Minor, BWV 1011: VI. Gigue, Bach, J.S.: Suites for Solo Cello & 2 Cello Sonatas, Janos Starker

Suite for Cello Solo No. 5 in C Minor, BWV 1011: VI. Gigue, Janos Starker: Perspectives, Janos Starker

Suite for Cello Solo No. 6 in D, BWV 1012: I. Prélude, Bach, J.S.: Suites for Solo Cello & 2 Cello Sonatas, Janos Starker

Suite for Cello Solo No. 6 in D, BWV 1012: II. Allemande, Bach, J.S.: Suites for Solo Cello & 2 Cello Sonatas, Janos Starker

Suite for Cello Solo No. 6 in D, BWV 1012: III. Courante, Bach, J.S.: Suites for Solo Cello & 2 Cello Sonatas, Janos Starker

Suite for Cello Solo No. 6 in D, BWV 1012: IV. Sarabande, Bach, J.S.: Suites for Solo Cello & 2 Cello Sonatas, Janos Starker

Suite for Cello Solo No. 6 in D, BWV 1012: V. Gavotte I-II, Bach, J.S.: Suites for Solo Cello & 2 Cello Sonatas, Janos Starker

Suite for Cello Solo No. 6 in D, BWV 1012: VI. Gigue, Bach, J.S.: Suites for Solo Cello & 2 Cello Sonatas, Janos Starker

Suite No. 6 in D, BWV 1012 \ Allemande, Cello for Relaxation, Various Artists & Janos Starker

Tarantella, Op. 33, Cello Essentials, Janos Starker

Tarantella, Op. 33, Popper: Romantic Cello Favorites, Janos Starker & Shigeo Neriki

Tarantelle, Starker Encore Album, Janos Starker

The Barber of Seville: "Figaro", Cello Essentials, Janos Starker

The Girl With the Flaxen Hair, Soundtrack for Your Lifestyle, Janos Starker & Shigeo Neriki

The Swan, Starker Encore Album, Janos Starker

Toccata, Starker Encore Album, Janos Starker

Trumerei, Starker Encore Album, Janos Starker

Variations On "Preghiera" from Rossini's "Mosè," for Violin and Guitar, MS. 23, Cello Essentials, Janos Starker

Variations On a Rococo Theme, Op.33, Dvorak: Cello Concerto, Bruch: Kol Nidrei & Tchaikovsky: Variations On a Rococo Theme, Antal Dorati, Janos Starker & London Symphony Orchestra

Variations On One String On a Theme By Rossini: Moses Fantasie, Janos Starker: Virtuoso Music for Cello, Janos Starker

Vito (Spanish Dances), Op. 54, No. 5, Popper: Romantic Cello Favorites, Janos Starker & Shigeo Neriki

BIBLIOGRAPHY

Aitay, Victor, interview, summer, 1996

Bing, Rudolph, *Five Thousand Nights at the Opera*, Doubleday & Co., New York, 1972

Bodnar, Zoltan and Piri, interview, January, 1998

Fenyo, Mario, *Hitler, Horthy, and Hungary*, Yale University Press, New Haven, 1972

Figueroa, Rafael, interview, January, 1999

Gingold, Joseph, interview, summer, 1996

Kliegel, Maria, interview, June, 1998

Hammill, Rowena, interview, January, 1998

Gary Hoffman, interview, January, 1999

Kliegel, Maria, interview, summer, 1998

Lang, George, *Nobody Knows the Truffles I've Seen*, Alfred Knopf, New York, 1998

Los Angeles Times, "Violinist and Visionary Yehudi Menuhin Dies at 82,"
    Saturday, March 13, 1999, p. 1 and p. 16

Mantel, Gerhard, *Cello Technique and Forms of Movement,* 1975, Indiana University Press

Marton, Kati, Wallenberg, *Missing Hero*, Arcade Publishing, New York, 1995

Mullens, Shirley Stroh, "The Intriguing World of Janos Starker," *The Instrumentalist,*
    November 1986, volume 41, Number 4, pp. 16-19

Neriki, Shigeo, interview, January, 2004

Norris, Jane Dunlop, "Starker bridges composers, voices, audiences," *Daily Progress*, p. 3,
    Charlottesville, Virginia, March 28, 1997

Parisot, Aldo, interview, fall, 1997

Rothmuller, Daniel, interview, April, 1997

Shamban, David, interview, fall, 1997

Starker, Janos, assisted by George Bekefi, *An Organized Method of String Playing, Violoncello* Exercises for the Left Hand, Peerless, Int., New York, Hamburg

Starker, Janos, *The Roll Call of the Blessed*, illustrations by Jorge Sicre, Dorrance Publishing Co., Inc. Pittsburgh, PA 15222

Starker, Janos, *The World of Music According to Janos Starkeer*, Indiana University Press, 2004

Sulzberger, C.L., *A Long Row of Candles,* Macmillan, New York, 1969

Toettcher, Sebastian, interview, summer, 1997

Tsutsumi, Tsuyoshi, interview, summer, 1998

Vago, Bela, *Jewish Assimilation in Modern Times*, Westview Press, Inc., 1981

Wilder, Thornton, *The Bridge of San Luis Rey,* Grosset & Dunlap, 1927

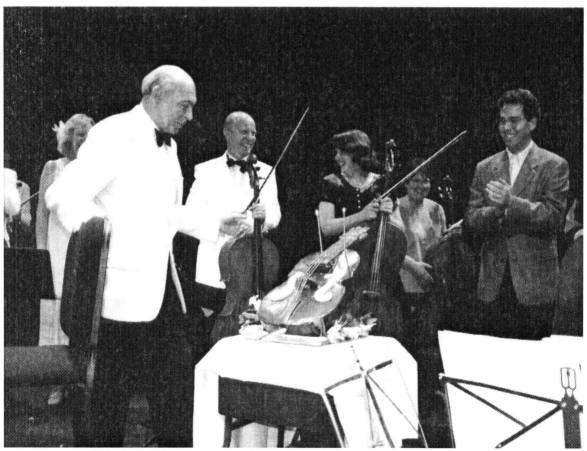

STARKER'S 75th BIRTHDAY CELEBRATION, COMPLETE WITH CHOCOLATE CELLO CAKE,
FOR WHICH 300 FORMER STUDENTS PERFORMED TOGETHER ON STAGE AT INDIANA UNIVERSITY

CHRONOLOGY OF EVENTS

1939 - 1942	— Cultural life in Budapest was flourishing, influx of some Jews from Germany and Austria to Budapest. The effect was not significant.
1941	— Starker family spent six weeks in the mountains in hiding.
1943 (early)	— Labor camps.
1944	— Nazi takeover of Hungarian government.
April, 1944	— German takeover of Hungary.
July 31, 1944	— American bombs - Csepel Island, Budapest.
Nov. 11, 1944	— Janos and Eva married.
Dec, 1944, before Christmas	— Siege of Budapest; Starker and Breuer, medics.
Jan., 1945	— Russian occupation of Budapest; atrocities, isolation from the rest of the world.
July, 1945	— Return to Budapest for hernia operation, first passport, job offer from Budapest Opera, return to Rumania to get cello, encounter with Enescu.
1945	— Starker and Eva in Rumania; concert by Enesco around March, 1945.
Sept., 1945 - Feb., 1946	— Principal cellist with Budapest Opera fall, '45, Starker took a leave of absence for concerts in Rumania where he met Enesco and Sebök.
March - Sept. 1946	— Vienna, April - sleepwalker recital in Vienna.
July - Sept., 1946	— Badgastein.
Oct., 1946	— Geneva Competition, Belgian visa, Paris, Cannes, Indig Quartet.
Jan., 1947	— Limoges, France - fog lifted, return to Cannes to get belongings, Tortelier concert.
Summer, 1947 (two months)	— Return to Hungary to visit parents, concerts canceled because of reference to Dohnanyi, return to Paris, day after Communist takeover.

March, 1948	— Job offer from Dorati.
1948 - 1949	— Concert season, Dallas Symphony.
Summer, 1949	— Spent in New York.
1950 - 1952	— Roth Quartet in the summers, also recordings.
Fall, 1949 - 1953	— Metropolitan Opera Orchestra.
Fall, 1953 - 1958	— Chicago Symphony.
1956	— Hungarian Revolution.
1957	— Starker and Sebök meet in Paris, record cello-piano repertoire.
1958	— Starker and Sebök begin to concertize in Europe, performing concert tours for ten years.
1958	— Indiana University, concertizing.

DINNER IN THE GEETING HOME, 2003. STARKER WITH FRIENDS AND FORMER STUDENTS:
JENNIFER LANGHAM, JOYCE GEETING, DANIEL ROTHMULLER, MARGARET MOORES

ABOUT THE AUTHOR

As soloist and chamber musician, Joyce Geeting, cellist, has performed many concerts throughout the United States and in European countries including England, Norway, Germany, Austria and Italy. Her credits include many televised solo performances in Europe and the United States; live radio broadcasts as soloist and with the chamber ensembles, Descanso Players and California Chamber Artists; solo cellist and faculty member for the American Institute of Musical Studies in Graz, Austria; touring in Western Europe with Vienese pianist, Norman Shetler and the Collegium String Quartet; principal cellist with the Eisenstadt Music Festival in Austria, soloist with the Rome Festival in Italy, and guest artist with symphony orchestras throughout the United States. Her concerto repertoire includes the Beethoven *Triple Concerto*, *Elegy* by Carol Worthey (commissioned by Geeting), the Elgar *Concerto*, the Dvorák *Concerto*, Tchaikovsky's *Rococo Variations*, Bloch's *Schelomo*, Brahms' *Double Concerto*, Haydn's *C Major* and *D Major Concertos*, and J.C. Bach *Concerto*.

In addition to her performances, she aids young cellists in their musical development. She has numerous award winning students as well as former students who are now professionals throughout this country and in Europe. Mrs. Geeting has served on the faculties of the University of Wisconsin at Oshkosh, Cornell College and the University of Redlands. She currently teaches at California Lutheran University and is the director of the CLU Conservatory of Music. Although she is a protegé of Janos Starker, she holds a Doctorate of Musical Arts degree in cello pedagogy and performance from the University of Oregon. As a freelance cellist she has performed in hundreds of symphony orchestra concerts and recordings in the Los Angeles area. She has performed on several tours with the San Francisco Opera Company, has performed also with Los Angeles Opera, the West Coast Opera, Riverside Opera, Redlands Bowl Opera and Zachary Opera Companies. As a member of Descanso Players and California Chamber Artists, Dr. Geeting has performed in hundreds of chamber concerts throughout California.

She plays a two-hundred-thirty-year-old cello made by John Edward Betts, Royal London Exchange, with "an extraordinarily exquisite tone." (*Oregon Statesman*)

Web Site: www.joycegeeting.com, e-mail: joyce@joycegeeting.com

INDEX

Goldsmith, Harold 108
Goodwin, Noel, Daily Express 79
Göteborg Symphony 25, 27, 31
Grammophone 106
Grand Prix du Disque, Sebok 88
Grand Prix du Disque, Starker 54, 63, 131
Grant Park Symphony, Chicago 79
Greehouse, Bernhard 162
Gruetzmacher, Friederich 158
Guarneri del Gesu (cello maker) 131
Guarnerius, Andreas (cello maker) 129, 131
Gulli, Franco 116
Gyömrö 5-6, 119

Hammill, Rowena 165-167
Harris, Alan (Cleveland Inst.) 150
Harsanyi, Nicolas 70
Hartke, Thomas, Senator 88
Harvard-Radcliffe Orchestra 96
Haskins, John, Kansas City Star 83
Hausmann, Robert 105
Haviland 49
Haydn, Franz Joseph 10, 18, 27, 42, 82
Heiden, Bernhard 70, 80, 104
Heifetz, Jascha 9, 12, 98, 110, 125, 136, 157, 164
Henahan, Don, Chicago Daily News 79, 80
Henkel, Kristoph 150
Hermann, Paul 4
Hermann, Emil 3, 129-130
Herz, Otto 57
HIAS, Jewish Refugee Organization 44
Hill, W.E. & Sons (instrument dealer, London, England) 130
Hindemith, Paul 23, 54, 63, 82, 83, 88, 103, 106
Hochner, Leo 30, 34, 35
Hochstrasser, cello teacher 7
Hoffman, Gary 150, 153-156, 157
Horrenstein, Jasha 67

Horthy, Miklos 27
Horzowski, Mieczyslaw 80
Hubay, Jeno 12
Hubermann, Branislaw 9, 127
Hudebni Rozhledy, periodical (Prague) 82
Hungarian Revolution of 1965 65, 87, 144

Indiana University 65, 116
Indig, Alfred 46, 47
Interlochen 70

Janigro, Antonio 42, 49, 73
Janzer, Eva 9, 30, 42, 116, 118
Janzer, Eva Foundation 89, 156
Jenkins, Florence Foster 61, 94

Karajan, Herbert von, Berlin Philharmonic 68, 143, 144
Kaston, Henryk (instrument maker) 58
Katims, Milton 79
Kerpely, Eugene 4, 13
Kindler, Hans 73
Klemperer, Otto 66
Kliegel, Maria 117, 150-153, 170
Knapik, Eugene (instrument maker) 131
Kodály, Zoltan 2-4, 12, 13, 36, 37, 50, 54, 56, 57, 82, 85, 88, 99, 124, 127, 129, 174, 176
Kolodin, Irving, Hi-Fi Stereo Review 106
Kozma, Tibor 69, 171
Kreisler, Fritz 106
Kronberg Cello Festival 156
Kun, Bela 23

L.A. Chamber Orchestra 71
Lalo, Edward 10, 49, 75
Lang, George 13, 38, 43-46
Lang, Paul Henry, Herald Tribune 79
Langlet, Waldemar 27
Laport, Lucien 59